MW00931696

GIFTS FROM A CHALLENGING CHILDHOOD

CREATING A PRACTICE FOR BECOMING YOUR HEALTHIEST SELF

Foreword by Pia Mellody

JAN BERGSTROM, LMHC

Copyright ©2019 by Jan Bergstrom, LMHC
ISBN: 978-1686015281
All rights reserved. This book may not be duplicated in any way without the express written consent of the publisher, except in the form of brief excerpts or quotations for the purposes of review. The information contained herein is for the personal use of the reader and may not be incorporated in any commercial programs or other books, databases, or any kind of software without written consent of the publisher or author. Making copies of this book or any portion of it, for any purpose is a violation of United States copyright laws. This is a work of fiction. Names, characters, places, and incidents either are the product of the author's imagination or are used fictitiously. Any resemblance to actual persons, living or dead, events, or locales is entirely coincidental.

Published by Mountain Stream Publishing Company
Contact info@MountainStreamPublishingCompany.com for more information
Book Design by Teresa Lauer
Cover by Zack Trapper Fey
Copy Editor: Sarah Goodman
Substantive Editor: Janice Harper

GIFTS FROM A CHALLENGING CHILDHOOD

Creating a Practice for Becoming Your Healthiest Self

Jan Bergstrom, LMHC

Foreword by Pia Mellody,
bestselling author of
Facing Co-dependence and founder of The Meadows

©2019, all rights reserved

This book is
dedicated to my precious sons,
Luke and Zack.
Parenting you, I learned to reparent myself.

All the cases in this book are composites. They have been deliberately changed in order to protect my clients' rights, privacy, and confidentiality.

This book is meant to be a self-help guide for healing. If at any time you find yourself dysregulated and feeling out of control, please seek professional assistance.

Jan Bergstrom, LMHC has been 25 years in practice as a counselor and trainer in the field of codependency, developmental and relational trauma. She studied extensively with Pia Mellody, a pioneer in treating childhood trauma. Jan also practices Susan Johnson's Emotionally Focused Therapy, an attachment model for communication as well as Terrence Real's Relational Life Therapy model for couples. She is a Somatic Experiencing Practitioner, a technique that uses a body-oriented approach for healing, a method developed by Peter Levine.

In 2008, Jan created the Healing Trauma Network, a directory of therapists who offer the techniques of Pia Mellody. In 2013, with Dr. Rick Butts, she created the Healing Our Core Issues Institute (HOCII), dedicated to teaching therapists an integrated methodology for healing childhood trauma and which trains practitioners in a developmental and relational trauma model.

Jan currently resides in the Boston area, with her husband of 30 years. She is the mother of two adult sons. As a therapist and guide to others, Jan lives a restorative practice and reaps its many gifts.

Contents

FOREWORD

I first met Jan about 18 years ago, while I was facilitating one of my intensive workshops called "Survivors." Survivors is a workshop I developed that deals with developmental immaturity, formerly known as codependence. Jan wanted to investigate and learn to heal some of her own childhood trauma. I respect therapists who want to clean up their side of the street before they start using my techniques on others, and I came to respect Jan. Months later I met Jan again, in my Post Induction Therapy training workshops for therapists in Phoenix, Arizona. She was eager to learn and deepen her understanding of my model, so she could use the model on her clients that were struggling with developmental trauma.

For the past 18 years, Jan has intensely studied with me, learning and deepening her techniques for, not only an individual's trauma work, but also, how to use my methodology for working with couples. She was determined to use some of my techniques in her own clients' intensives in her private practice. Throughout her 18 years of doing these workshops, she has understood what I have been trying to pass on as a path for recovery and healing trauma.

During these last ten years, Jan has created and managed a directory for therapists who have learned my Post Induction Therapy work and who actively use it in their own practices.

This directory, HealingTraumaNetwork.net, is a listing of each therapist and any groups or workshops that they offer. I know this directory has been a resource for many individuals seeking help with addiction, mental illness, and trauma.

Jan has also combined my work with new pioneering methods, such as mindfulness, somatic body-based work, and attachment theory, to create a compilation practice/ method. Along with her dedication for making available childhood development trauma work, she teaches classes, with her colleague Dr. Rick Butts.

It's clear to me that Jan writes this book to continue her passion for the work that was given to me through a source I call my "higher power." I fully support her as she fills these pages with her truth and the wisdom gained from her experience.

Pia Mellody

AUTHOR'S NOTE

In 2003, I had the good fortune of studying the effects of childhood trauma under the remarkable leader in the field of codependece, Pia Mellody. In the years that followed, I took many of her workshops at The Meadows, and, as those years passed, she became not just my mentor, but my colleague. Under her mentorship, I became a seasoned therapist, putting her concepts into practice and discovering just how insightful and effective her teachings are for those who have been wounded or traumatized as children.

As I applied her theories into my practice, I found that, like every therapist, I began integrating my own techniques into those I'd been taught. Over time, I developed a clear and easy-to-follow series of guidelines for my clients that helped them understand and apply Pia Mellody's work into their own recovery process. Many of those colleagues asked me to write a book that would help them to see how Pia Mellody's work could be applied to their own practice.

Gifts from a Challenging Childhood is the answer to those requests. The first five chapters will show you what Mellody's work has meant to me, and how I've used it in my practice. I include my own adaptations of her work, and I explain how—

and why—I've found these adaptations useful. Most importantly, in Chapters 7 through 12, I provide clear instructions for readers who are struggling with their own healing, so that they can recover from their own traumas by implementing the theories of Pia Mellody into their therapeutic process.

I want to be clear, however, that this book is not intended as a replacement for understanding the work of Pia Mellody. Quite the contrary, it is my hope that this book will serve as a workbook to accompany her brilliant books, and encourage the reader to seek out Mellody's work. For anyone who can immerse themselves in Mellody's fascinating and ground-breaking theories, the rewards are deep and lasting. I have written *Gifts from a Challenging Childhood* as a direct result of that immersion. Every chapter in this book is an expression of my gratitude to my mentor. It is also my way of giving Mellody's work new applications and expanded relevance, and bestowing on my readers the healing gift of her ideas as I have put them into practice.

INTRODUCTION

If you suffered serious neglect or trauma as a child, you probably know that the damage didn't just go away once you grew up. Whether you've struggled with having and maintaining healthy relationships, succeeding in your career, setting and reaching goals, substance abuse and addictions, or just having confidence in yourself, you know that resolving the pain and confusion arising from your past is not easy. But here's the good news: it is possible—even probable—that you can and will learn to lead a healthier, more fulfilling life, if you read the pages that follow, and put into practice the techniques I discuss. How do I know this? I know because for the last 15 years, I have been working closely with adult survivors of childhood trauma and abuse, and I have seen for myself the remarkable progress my clients have made on their healing journeys. This work is based on my training with Pia Mellody, and in this book I introduce her ideas and show how they can help you to heal from family of origin trauma.

Since studying under Pia Mellody, I have discovered just how effective her techniques are. I have been able to adopt them in my own practice, as I've integrated my own ap-proaches with her work. It is exciting to contribute to the field of trauma treatment, a field which has transformed from obscure academic musings to cutting-edge therapies based on scientific insights into how trauma impacts the brain and development.

The last few decades have brought us a steady stream of books about child abuse and neglect and its devastating impact on children. Attention to the problem has drifted from the relative obscurity of academic journals to the realm of mainstream audiences. As a society, we have gained new understandings into how the ways we were raised and the kind of parenting we received have affected our physical and mental health as adults. Research is now showing that adults who were exposed to chronic interpersonal traumas as children are predisposed to alcoholism and alcohol abuse, depression, illicit drug use, a diminished quality of life, physical health problems, reduced work performance, and financial stress. They are also at a higher risk for intimate partner violence, sexually transmitted diseases, suicide attempts, adolescent pregnancy, smoking, sexual violence, and poor academic achievement. In other words, a traumatic childhood doesn't end with adulthood! It lingers on.

One of the most significant investigations of child abuse and neglect—and their relationship to these later-life health and wellbeing issues—is the Center for Disease Control's (CDC) Adverse Childhood Experiences (ACE) Study. The original ACE Study was conducted by Kaiser Permanente from 1995 to 1997, with two waves of data collection. Over 17,000 patients, receiving physical exams at Health Maintenance Organizations (HMOs) in Southern California, completed a confidential survey regarding their childhood experiences and current health status and behaviors.[1] The results showed a strong relationship between the length of exposure to abuse or household dysfunction during childhood and multiple risk factors for several of the leading causes of dysfunction and death in adults.

These and similar studies and research have paved the way for a real understanding of how early childhood and family systems can have a significant impact on later life. From such understandings, we are now able to reverse many of these impacts—by helping people to identify the behavioral patterns that once served them as children, but now limit their potential as adults. If this sounds like you—because you grew up with chronic or extreme adverse childhood experiences yourself and now struggle with life challenges as an adult—then this book is for you.

But you might be wondering: "What does she know of trauma, aside from what she's read in textbooks, and learned as a graduate student studying counseling, or as a student of Pia Mellody?" Well, let me tell you my story.

I had my first taste of childhood trauma at the age of four. My mother suffered from a deep depression that began years before I was born, when a physician's error led to the preventable death of her healthy newborn baby boy. My and my brother's births, a few years later, were not enough to ease her grief. When I was four, I found my mother collapsed from an

---

[1] Take this ACE survey yourself (https://www.npr.org/sections/health-shots/2015/03/02/387007941/take-the-ace-quiz-and-learn-what-it-does-and-doesnt-mean), and learn more about what the results may mean for you and its impact on your health and well-being (https://www.cdc.gov/violenceprevention/aces/about.html).

overdose on her bedroom floor, having tried to take her own life. She was rushed to the emergency room, and she then spent six months in a psychiatric hospital.

During my mother's hospital stay, as my father drove me and my older brother to the store for groceries, he collided head-on with another car. My father was thrown through the windshield and severely wounded, while the other driver died. With both my mother and father in hospitals, I became parentless for several months—formative months that felt like years.

This background set the stage for a lifelong interest in the impact of childhood trauma, and it sparked my passion for healing. More importantly, my research on trauma has led me to discover a fascinating and effective way to turn the legacies of childhood trauma into a creative journey toward renewal and growth. In the pages that follow, I am going to share that journey with you.

In the last 15 years, I have run nearly 100 "Family of Origin Intensive Workshops," where I take my clients through a 3-day process of Post-Induction Therapy, a tech-nique based on the work of Pia Mellody. With over 2,800 experiential direct client hours from these workshops, I have gained an expertise in helping people to identify and recover from their childhood traumas and to live their lives in a more rewarding, enriching, and holistic manner.

As I've done so, I've come to realize that not everyone who is traumatized will seek out trauma therapists to help them, but they will still struggle to recover from their wounded childhoods. That is why I've written this book. I want to help those I have not worked with and help those I have worked with on their healing journeys—to ease their pain and give them hope in achieving healthier, happier lives.

For many of my readers, I am confident that this book will introduce you to the benefits that come from being in a relationship *with your trauma*. That's right—I want you to embrace your trauma, rather than reject it, and to enter into a relationship with that trauma, rather than to continue to live as if it isn't there. Your trauma lives inside of you every hour of every day and night, and there is only one way to be free of it—and that is to invite it to join you on your healing journey.

The journey will be difficult at times, but as it progresses, it will feel like a spiritual homecoming, delivering you to a dimension of experience far beyond your current perception of life. It will not be easy at first. Indeed, while there may be moments of joy and excitement, the journey will include some painful first steps. But you will find that, after six months or so of committing to the concepts and practices in this book, you will see that there is a higher purpose in the life you have been given. I have found in my own life that sharing my insights, clinical experiences, and expertise with others has been my deeper purpose, and I feel this truth so profoundly that I can only explain it as a divine direction to help others—including you, the reader.

As I've indicated, this methodology is based on the groundbreaking work of Pia Mellody, who is noted for her work in codependency, following publication of her groundbreaking book, *Facing Codependence* (Harper and Row 2003). Mellody has since published several best-selling books on addiction, relationships, and intimacy. What is less known to the public, however, is the valuable work she has done in training therapists like me in how to help our clients heal.

As I've indicated, the pages that follow are based on this training and on Mellody's teachings, as well as my own clinical experience, and a compilation of experiential and body-based techniques, along with a synergistic blend of mindfulness, Gestalt, psychodrama, and somatic interven-tions. The methods that you will learn in this book will include, not only self-reflection, but role playing, meditation, breathing techniques, and cognitive restructuring. It won't be a sit-back experience by any means!

This is not a book about taking an inventory of your family of origin history and giving you a score. Nor is it about figuring out why you are the way you are. Most importantly, it is not about blaming your parents or caregivers for the misfortunes in your life. Instead, this book is about *examining the emotional and behavioral patterns you learned—or adapted to—when you were growing up in your family.*

These adaptations you learned as a child are still in use in your life today—because, as maladaptive as they might be, in many ways, they *have* helped you survive. At a certain point, however, the very habits and practices that help us survive in one context can hinder our growth in another. If you have picked up this book, I'm guessing you are at that point in life—a point where you're ready to change. You are ready to discard the maladaptive habits you've learned and perfected, and ready to replace them with practices and routines that are empowering and life-affirming.

By identifying some dysfunctional patterns, and by start-ing a journey toward healing, you will learn a remarkable strategy for implementing restorative practices in your life.

The truth is, many of these dysfunctional patterns were not just adaptive ways to cope with the dysfunctional parenting you may have received but are behaviors you learned—through role-modeling—from your parents. I know it is frightening sometimes to think that you are reproducing many of the behaviors your parents engaged in, behaviors which you may have resented while growing up in your family system. There is no need to fear looking inward to discern those habits that have been carved into our lives. It's perfectly natural and normal to replicate our family patterns, even while we rant and rave against them. We are all drawn to what is familiar from the past, and we will seek it out in our lives today because, however imperfect, when we are familiar with something, we feel we can control it. Unfamiliarity means uncertainty, and uncertainty leaves us feeling anxious.

Now I know what some of you are thinking. Some of you are thinking that you are nothing like your parents; that you have gone out of your way to discern the dangers in what they taught you; and that you have developed none of their bad habits. Well, if that's the case, you've beaten the nature and nurture game.

Instead, my guess is that you have indeed learned a number of habits and practices that have left you wounded by your family, and not always in ways that you—or they—ever wanted. For example, if your parents had an unhealthy marriage, or they failed to establish loving and protective relationships with you, a great question to ask yourself is, "Where did I get a good, practical education on healthy parenting or having and maintaining good relationships?"

In school? Not a chance. On the streets? I doubt it. How about television or the movies? Did you learn about love from watching happy couples on sitcoms or romantic comedies? What we learn from TV or movie dramas, rather than actual interactions with people, is far more likely to have shaped our *ideals* of relationships, but not to have shaped actual relationships.

No, chances are you learned *how to interact in* relationships from your parents and from other family members. The Family creates the template for relational interactions, which, due to our humanity, can be wounding. Your internal template was shaped by how your parents loved and fought, and how you were parented. These wounds set up your template for when you engage with other people in love and life, in your adulthood. That's a sobering thought and one to investigate as you turn these pages.

According to Pia Mellody the Five Core Areas below are the major areas where childhood developmental trauma manifest as "woundings":

- Being valued
- Being protected
- Being validated emotionally for the person that you are
- Having basic needs and some wants met
- Being free to moderately express yourself

I will discuss these Five Core Areas in detail, and how they correspond to the wounds you carry today. By recognizing and embracing your wounds in one or more of these areas, you will be better able to actively work through your pain, and, as you do so, you will establish daily practices that—over time—create new healthy life experiences. These areas then also categorize the gifts that are possible to receive after you know the truth about your own unique life experience. Knowing that truth is a remarkable journey, one that this book will guide you toward.

This book is organized into two parts. The first part presents an overview of the many ways in which families can traumatize a child, intentionally or not; how trauma is experienced; and how it shapes a child's developing sense of Self, as well as their behaviors and perceptions into adulthood. I've included many stories of clients and others to illustrate my points and to help you recognize your own experiences and history. (Their names and places have been changed.) While no two histories are identical, you will recognize your own childhood in many of these stories.

Part Two shifts to the actual techniques that I use in my practice to help people recover from family of origin trauma, including techniques from Pia Mellody and techniques I developed in my own work. While it may be tempting to jump directly to Part Two, I urge you to wait. It's important to understand the complexity of childhood trauma and the various ways different types of traumas manifest, as well as to familiarize yourself with the concepts and terms.

As you read the chapters that follow, you may start to perceive your experiences in a new light. You may have felt your whole life as if the entire world is normal, except for you. My bet is that the entire world is as troubled as you are, in one way or another. Over the last few generations, there has been a rise in mental illness and addictions among adults, and these conditions derive in many ways from coping mechanisms— attempts to manage the pain, sadness, or loneliness that have come from our traumatic experiences. The only way out, however, is through this journey of self-discovery—because pain and unresolved trauma will not go away until we finally commit to facing and taking on our past.

Drawing on Pia Mellody's trauma work, I've developed a paradigm for making this quest to self-discovery. which uses the following components:

- Cultivating a more functional adult Self
- Getting our story straight
- Knowing and reparenting our historical Selves
- Standing in our own truth
- Practicing affirmation, abundance, and gratitude in our daily life

Each of these components to the process of healing constitutes an important technique that I will explain, so that you may get started on your recovery. Practicing these techniques will help you to see your childhood in a different light and to feel differently about it, which is the first step in transforming the traumas of that childhood into something uniquely wondrous and empowering. But I must warn you— this journey will not always feel comfortable, for no worthy adventure ever is. By taking this journey and making this investment in yourself, you will gain the world, that is you will gain an experience of yourself that is life-affirming and life-enhancing.

Before we begin, however, let's be clear that when we speak about trauma, we aren't just talking about adversity. In Chapter 1, I'll discuss the definition of trauma in more detail, but for now, I want you thinking about how trauma differs from adversity. Everyone suffers challenges growing up. For some children, though, childhood was a period of lasting trauma— whether through abuse, neglect, or emotional manipulation. That is the kind of trauma I'm talking about. And if you've picked up this book, my guess is that you didn't do it because you faced ordinary childhood adversities, but that you have more than your fair share of egregious stories to tell.

It is possible that, though you've grown up, the consequences of one or more devastating experiences continue to color your life in ways that keep you from living it fully. Perhaps you are experiencing personal relationship failures, or you feel depressed, struggle with addiction, or find yourself acting or responding in the same damaging ways your parents acted toward you. Perhaps you are just angry or depressed about life in general. If that is the case, you are not alone—and you are not doomed to continue living in pain. Just by opening these pages, you have taken the first step in your healing journey.

The most important concept to understand, as you read this book, is that not only is this journey *not* about blaming anyone, it is also *not* about your relationships with your parents or siblings or anyone else in your past. We will explore those relationships because they are important, but your journey forward is—first and foremost—about your relationship and commitment to your Self. When I talk about your *Self,* capital *S,* I'm talking about the core of who you are in all its complexity and entirety. All too often we think of our core identity in terms of how we have been taught to view our Selves—in relation to others, as a wife, a husband, a mother, a father, a son, or a daughter. We measure our worth in terms of what we have been taught we are supposed to be—valuing ourselves in terms of our professional identities and success, our income and assets, the homes in which we live.

But that is not who you are. You could be stripped of all those things overnight—or obtain all those things overnight, and it would not change the core of who you are. Your Self is not something that exists only in terms of your relationships to others or to things. *Self* is something that exists in relation to your own perceptions, your own thoughts, your own experiences, and your own soul. By having a great relation-ship with your Self, you will discover that you can and will change the relationships you have with others.

Finally, to get you started thinking about the journey ahead, let me share a memory with you, a memory you may have had as well, but one that, for me as a young child, left a profound impact. That memory is of watching (and re-watching) *The Wizard of Oz.*

Back then, we couldn't just stream *The Wizard of Oz* any-time we wanted. Instead, watching the classic 1939 film was an annual event. Once a year, families gathered around the TV to watch the adventures of Dorothy and her friends, as they battled the Wicked Witch of the West. And, every year, we loved it as if we'd never before seen such an adventure.

One of my favorite characters from childhood was Dorothy. She was unlike any other female character I saw on TV or read about in books. Dorothy was unhappy with her life in Kansas and wanted to flee to a better life. Determined to find that better life, and convinced that no one cared about her feelings, her concerns, or her life circumstances, she set out with her dog, Toto, to find her destiny.

Right from the start, Dorothy's journey was a terrifying one—beginning with a fierce tornado that tore through the sky and swept her and Toto away in a funnel cloud of images and words from her childhood past. She landed with such a crash, she blacked out, and she awoke to find herself in a strange world, where she was told that if she wanted to go home, she would have to follow the Yellow Brick Road to find the Wizard who could help her get there. Convinced that finding this mysterious wizard was her only hope, Dorothy traveled across the unfamiliar land of Oz, facing many trials and tribulations along the way. She was tormented, tricked, exhausted, and set back, again and again, yet she persevered.

Finally, after enduring more brutalities than anyone should ever have to face, and after reaching the point where she thought all was lost and she was doomed, Dorothy learned that the way to reach home had been in her control the whole time. All that talk about needing the Wizard to help her reach her goals and find her place in the world was yet another trick. The truth was, Dorothy had more power than she realized. She could set herself free.

I just loved that story. Dorothy was, like so many of us, a

child who didn't know her own heroics. She didn't know her own strength, and she sure didn't know the secrets that resided inside her Self, a Self she never knew—not until she'd faced a great deal of pain and fear and uncertainty.

This book may feel a bit like landing in an unfamiliar and frightening land and following the Yellow Brick Road toward the place where you belong, the place you truly want to be. I will present you with unfamiliar concepts, unexpected encounters, and, yes, at times, some discomfort. But by the time you reach the end, you will realize that you had the power within you all along for your own healing and transformation. More importantly, you will discover that you have had the power to create your own internal "home" at any given moment.

The truth is, you have, within your Self, the power to create a place in your soul that feels comfortable, grounded, and available to the infinite gifts of life. All the guidance, experience, and techniques I share with you will be critical to the healing journey of coming home. But this book represents a road that will take you to your own homecoming by embracing your truth, establishing a practice of commitment and self-care, and receiving the precious—and often un-expected—gifts that will come to you from your own unique and deeply personal history, however painful it may have been. Once you open your arms—and your heart—to receiving these gifts, you will discover that, like Dorothy, for all the pain and weariness you've suffered, you've grown in wondrous ways you never could have imagined. Are you ready? Well, ready or not, welcome to your recovery! Now let's get started.

Part I

Understanding Family of Origin Trauma

JAN BERGSTROM, LMHC

Part I

Understanding Family of
Origin Trauma

CHAPTER 1

THE PAIN OF A CHALLENGING CHILDHOOD

B efore beginning your healing journey, I want to take you back in time, to your earliest years when you were just beginning to discover the world. Think back to your childhood, whether joyful or painful, easy or difficult. By exploring those early years, you will find the roots of obstacles that hold you back today. Whether there was a great deal of abuse or trauma, a singular but profoundly disturbing incident, or whether your childhood was full of pervasive neglect or intrusive involvement, by understanding and facing these childhood challenges, you can discover the gifts they offer you. Further, you can transform the challenges they once presented: from barriers that have held you back, into launch pads that will enable you to soar.

To begin, let's give a name to your childhood challenges, the challenges that have become roadblocks to your current quest for a healthy and productive adult life. The challenges you faced as a child are called "complex trauma."

Complex trauma encompasses the range of psychological and somatic legacies of a traumatic childhood that may or may not include Post Traumatic Stress Disorder (PTSD).

PTSD is a psychiatric disorder that can occur after witnessing or experiencing a life-threatening or violent event, such as military combat, natural disasters, terrorist incidents, serious accidents, or physical or sexual assault. PTSD can also occur following persistent stress during a period when you were too young to be able to cope with that stress effectively. The symptoms of PTSD include recurring thoughts of the trauma, hyper-startling, hyper-vigilance, insomnia, nightmares, mood swings, and a number of other cognitive and neurological symptoms.

Not everyone who is traumatized suffers from PTSD; in fact, most don't. But that doesn't mean trauma doesn't leave a trail of wounds that, years later, remain unhealed. A traumatic childhood can lead to an inability to form healthy and lasting relationships, poor job performance, a lack of joy and pleasure in life, a number of somatic disorders from headaches to gastrointestinal disorders to chronic pain, as well as a variety of impulsive and self-destructive behaviors.

I am focusing here on the traumatic childhood ex-periences that have had a profound impact on many different areas of adult functioning. These traumas may include being sexually abused, witnessing a violent assault, losing one or both parents or siblings, becoming homeless, or some other unexpected disaster that has shaken your life. Trauma may also be ongoing, such as being exposed to alcoholic parents or domestic violence, and, as a result, not feeling secure in childhood. Other ongoing traumatic events are chronic neglect or overly-controlling parenting behaviors that limit a child's ability to form an independent sense of their own (capital S) Self.

Just how is the *Self* formed? The creation of Self comes from our sensory organs—our ears, noses, eyes, tongues, and skin—as they bring information to the brain. We then form thoughts based on how we have assigned meaning to the information our brain has absorbed. These thoughts—or meanings—combine to form stories in the mind about why something was said or done and what it means about us, and about the world around us.

These thoughts and stories produce emotions and physi-cal sensations in the body, and our actions and behaviors follow. Through these actions, we create our reality.

Some of our life stories are painful and filled with fear, anger, shame, and guilt. Other stories are filled with joy and love. Regardless of the nature of these stories, they form our life's narrative arc, and they shape how we perceive the world around us, our relationships, and our Selves.

Unfortunately, for far too many, that narrative arc is a painful one, and is comprised of such sad and horrific stories that it is a wonder any of us made it to adulthood. For those who did, despite a childhood of chronic or extreme trauma, adulthood is often marked by mental health disorders and struggles to get through even the most mundane of life's demands.

Think of this process as the workings of a computer. Our metaphorical circuit board and microprocessor are interpreting information all the time, even when we sleep. From birth, throughout our lives, our brains are recording all that is happening to us, storing everything on one big hard drive, so to speak. From birth to about the age of 20, this information is primarily focused on programming the brain. After that, through the rest of our lives, our brains tend to follow repetitious patterns based on this programming. The task of healing is therefore to reset the computer—to understand and to own a Self, independent of the early programming.

The mystery is that by observing the programming you've received, you are better able to begin recreating your own reality and Self, free of the damaging codes that have been implanted over many years through neglect, abuse, and other corrupting influences.

It may sound bleak, I know. But the good news is that many of my clients grow tired and fed up with the dys-functional patterns they've adopted based on the faulty programming they received as children. They want change. And that's when change can happen—when you most want it.

DEFINING DEVELOPMENTAL TRAUMA

Trauma is a complex experience and comes in many forms. *Covert* trauma, like neglect, refers to what a child or teen *did not* get, and it can be hard to detect. *Overt* trauma, on the other hand, is what a child *did* get—intrusively—physically, verbally, or falsely. Addressing both polarities of a person's trauma history is essential when trying to heal them. Some of my clients received pervasive neglect throughout their childhoods, whereas others received intrusion or *enmeshment* (which I discuss in Chapter 2). Still other clients received a mixture of both. In exploring and addressing these traumatic experiences, as they relate to the type of parenting a person received as a child, it is important to identify which parent they experienced it with. Understanding that dynamic helps you to understand how the wounded child, once grown, will relate to partners and others in the future.

When looking at any form of complex or developmental trauma from childhood, it is important to understand your own unique woundings. Some people suffer more wounds than others, and yet we all suffer. According to my colleague and business partner, Dr. Rick Butts, "Trauma, as defined in the Greek, is a wound to the soul. In childhood, the 'wounding' is exposure to multiple chronic experiences that would be described as abusive including neglect and enmeshment. It is usually of an interpersonal nature."

In later pages, this book addresses both neglect and Pia Mellody's concept of *enmeshment,* which is an intrusive shaming, or over-involvement, in a child's life. The impor-tant thing to understand right now is that trauma wounds the soul. It is a form of abuse. And it is interpersonal in nature—it affects our relationships and how we communicate with others.

In his book, *Waking the Tiger*, somatic therapist Peter Levine adds to this concept. "Traumatic symptoms are not caused by the event itself. They arise when residual energy from the experience is not discharged from the body. This energy remains trapped in the nervous system where it can wreak havoc on our bodies and minds."

Finally, in her book, *Facing Codependence*, Pia Mellody defines *abuse* as, "Any experience in childhood (birth to age seventeen) that is less than nurturing." Although her definition is a broad one, and not accepted by everyone, it strikes to the core of my own thinking—that children need to be nurtured in order to become healthy, thriving adults.

Thus, I've modified Pia Mellody's definition slightly to suggest that *all family-of-origin trauma, from birth to adulthood, is relational, meaning it has to do with a parent or caregiver being either too far away, neglectful, and absent, or—conversely—being too close, intrusive, and involving a child in intrusive enmeshment.*

Family-of-origin trauma can be covert—defined by an absence of action, such as not providing for the child's physical or emotional needs, or it can be overt—defined by abusive actions, whether physical, sexual, or verbal. Either way, the impact of such trauma is devastating.

PSYCHOTHERAPY AND TREATMENT OF CHILDHOOD TRAUMA

These are exciting times in the therapeutic field when it comes to understanding and recovering from childhood trauma. In the last quarter-century we have seen a vast increase in our knowledge about the fundamental processes that underlie human trauma. This knowledge has opened new possibilities for treatment. New experiential methodologies have been developed which utilize the full mind-body connection, in turn helping people to heal, not just emotionally, but physically as well.

Emotional wounds often express themselves through the body, a process known as somatization, and may take the form of chronic pain, cardiovascular disorders, respiratory disorders, gastrointestinal disorders, rashes on the skin, headaches, and even serious chronic illness, such as cancer—because stress affects the immune system just as readily as any toxin. Thus, healing the mind can and does help heal the body. So how do we do that?

In psychiatrist Bessel Van der Kolk's book, *The Body Keeps the Score*, the noted expert on PTSD discusses the three primary ways for working with trauma, which include talk therapy, medication management, and experiential trauma treatments.

Through talk therapy, the patient gains a cognitive understanding of the trauma they experienced and its impacts on their lives. They connect with others via individual or group therapy, while uncovering and under-standing memories and ways they have processed their trauma.

Medication management helps change the way the brain organizes and handles information, and it makes it easier to control and deter extreme reactions in the brain, so that the patient can handle stress with greater moderation.

Experiential trauma treatments work from the bottom up by allowing the body to have experiences that deeply counter the powerlessness, rage, and emotional or physical collapse that result from trauma. These experiential techniques are observed and felt factually in the body, and they are unique and functional, thus rewriting the helplessness of the trauma so that the patient gains mastery over their thoughts and emotions related to the traumatic experience. Perhaps most amazing of all, experiential trauma treatments can actually create new neuropathways in the brain.

From their inception, most of these therapies have been cognitive-based and have included educational components. Importantly, they have provided patients with new insights into their experiences and emotions, which have proven effective for mental health treatment. Furthermore, over the last two decades, medication management has improved exponentially, and we now have more effective drugs to target a wide variety of specific symptoms. However, we can no longer keep the mind and body separate as medicine once did.

Just as treating the mind helps heal the body, in order to treat the mind, we must also treat the body that absorbs our traumatic wounds in multiple ways.

According to psychiatrist Bessel van der Kolk, the conventional cognitive therapies for treating trauma are effective for approximately half the symptoms. The other half of the symptoms are effectively treated with experiential, body-based therapies such as yoga, mindfulness practices, and other somatic therapies.

These experiential and somatic techniques work with awareness of the present moment, by focusing on the body while the patient re-experiences the past. These treatments have been found to help regulate the nervous system and can reduce the reactivity symptoms of complex trauma and PTSD—symptoms such as the autonomic nervous system becoming aroused following exposure to a triggering event, including heart palpitations, elevated blood pressure, and other physical anxiety reactions and panic attacks.

Another promising treatment for trauma was created by Pia Mellody and is called Post Induction Therapy. The premise of Post-Induction Therapy is that childhood trauma is the origin of developmental immaturity (formerly known as codependence).

Based on her model of Developmental Immaturity, which she articulated in the early 1980s as the Five Core Areas of childhood wounds" (discussed in this book's Introduction), Mellody identifies Five Core Areas for healing these wounds of our childhood traumas.

THE FIVE CORE AREAS FOR HEALING

- Loving ourselves
- Protecting ourselves through external and internal boundaries
- Knowing ourselves by creating a sense of Self
- Taking care of our needs and wants; and establishing interdependence with others
- Moderating or containing ourselves, especially in relationships with others

In my experience in learning this model, these areas get to the very foundation of our essential Self and what we need to grow and cultivate that Self. In this book, we'll explore Pia Mellody's Five Core Areas closely, as I guide you through your healing journey, and I'll show you how I've adapted it to my practice working with patients and my own recovery.

Healing from these woundings in the Five Core Areas involve experiential techniques that create and cultivate a wiser more functional adult Self, one that can help to energetically release the toxic emotions that have persisted from painful childhood experiences, and help the adapted childhood parts to be reparented and experience healing.

These healing techniques, which you are about to learn, in the chapters that follow, are something I have adapted from Mellody's teachings and have come to know intimately, working for decades with adult survivors of childhood trauma.

When exploring childhood trauma, I work with my clients to create a timeline of major life events, so that we are better able to understand, not only what these traumatic experiences were, but at what stage they occurred in child development. and we look at the broader context of family history.

As you work through your own childhood trauma, while reading this book, you will create your own timeline, which will help you to see your past woundings more clearly. The significant life events you will record will include such unexpected and painful family experiences as divorce, death, a chronic illness or disability in a sibling or parent, one parent or caregiver absent for a long time, or serially moving from place to place. Each of these factors leaves a child with a constant sense of insecurity, making it difficult for them to form trusting and long-lasting friendships.

Depending on the age of the child and how developed their nervous system is, such significant adverse events can manifest later in life as a decreased capacity to deal with normal human emotions. For some people, emotions become so frightening that they shut emotions down altogether, finding it difficult to experience deep feelings or respond to the emotions of other people. For others, emotions may be felt so intensely that reactions are inevitably extreme, particularly during stressful times when emotional control is needed.

Tracking these significant events in a timeline is therefore essential for uncovering the roots of our emotional responses and our reactions to the stressors and surprises that life brings us. Yet the timeline is just the first step. Before you take that first step, let's consider how these life events intersect with the developing child's brain, a key to understanding family of origin trauma.

TRAUMA AND BRAIN DEVELOPMENT

All children can only act their age. A dysfunctional family system can cause a child to act older than they are—or much younger. Either the parents demand that their child act older, and the child learns to suppress his or her innate mercurial emotions, joy, and spontaneity, or the parents may indulge or ignore the child when they are chaotic and out of control, treating them as if they are younger than their years and incapable of making choices or controlling behaviors. These patterns lead children to present themselves as super immature or super mature.

Unfortunately, as they grow older, these children fail to mature in a healthy manner—they remain stuck in this stage of exaggerated immaturity or maturity.

All people, children and parents alike, are imperfect, human and fallible, but children are more imperfect than adults. When children are born, their brains are not fully developed. Not only is the brain itself growing, but the neurological process that enables information to be processed for decision making, a process known as myelination, is also developing.

Myelination is a process where a protective sheath develops around nerves, which in turn helps nerve impulses to fire more quickly. This process continues from birth into young adulthood, allowing neurons in the brain to fire more rapidly the older the child becomes.

The brain myelination process isn't completed until about the age of 23 or 24. At that point, the prefrontal cortex has excellent capacity for executive functioning. Executive functioning includes decision making, social interactions, cognitive skills, and pretty much everything involved in making sense of the world around us and interacting effectively. But until the myelination process of the prefrontal cortex has fully developed, this executive functioning—this ability to think clearly, make decisions and interact appropriately with others—is not fully functional. As you think of a child growing up with so many changes to their brains and bodies, it's no wonder that their capacity for thinking, emotions, and body sensations is as limited as it is amazing.

There is another important role that myelination plays in child development, and that is in regard to how trauma is processed. During the adolescent years, myelination becomes particularly active in the frontal lobe of the brain, enabling adolescents to have better executive functioning than they had previously. This executive functioning includes planning, reasoning, and decision-making skills. Executive function also aids in inhibiting impulses more efficiently and demonstrating greater self-discipline.

What this means is that how old you were when you were traumatized will impact how you gave meaning to the event— in other words, how you understood it. The more developed the myelination process when your trauma occurred, the better able you were to understand and respond to it. Conversely, the younger you were when you were traumatized, the more difficult it will be for you to recall, interpret, and work through that trauma because of how that information is stored in the brain.

When a child is older, their brain is more developed and has a higher cognitive functioning, or ability to interpret what is happening. They will be able to take it less personally and they will have a greater cognitive capacity for dealing with it. A younger child, say at the age of six, would internalize the trauma as their fault.

I have had clients who recall being small children when they suffered a trauma, and even though they were grown and cognitively functioning at a higher level when they sought treatment, they continued to believe they *caused* the trauma— because their trauma struck at a time when their brains were undeveloped. Their thinking persisted along the belief that they were not good enough, or doing enough, and it was their fault, even if intellectually they knew otherwise. Emotionally, they had lived their trauma their whole lives as if they were still small children.

How we interpret the traumatic events of our lives therefore requires understanding the multiple layers of our mind's experience, which begin with the early years of our brain's formation. In turn, our interpretation of trauma shapes how we will come to construct a sense of Self. As you seek explanations for your suffering, and the ways that you have been treated by the people you love, you will gradually shape your whole adult Self anew.

On the following page, please see my chart entitled *Brain Development Timeline and Incoming Trauma*. This chart, as well as the others in this book, may also be downloaded at: forms.MountainStreamPublishingCompany.com.

Brain Development Timeline and Incoming Trauma

Birth — 4 — 5	5 — 10	10 — 18
Wounded	**Adaptive Responses**	
Too vulnerable	Brain not fully developed and myelinated – can take in information as they are the problem	Brain really starts to develop, and myelination is connecting the nerves to the pre–frontal cortex
Overwhelmed, flooded, and dissociative	Porous; no protective boundary - takes everything personally	Usually finishes myelination process around ages of 22–24
Agitated, highly sympathetic response, dysregulated	Can feel Less in value	More executive functioning and complex reasoning due to pre–frontal cortex engagement
Mostly limbic system sensations	Can Identify as bad or defective	
Minimal cognitive functioning	Can feel powerless and overwhelmed or angry	Can compare more viewpoints
	Too vulnerable	Ability to use more sophisticated defenses
	Latency development	Puberty – hormonal influx
		More protection vs. less vulnerability

Adapted by Jan Bergstrom, LMHC from the work of Pia Mellody

FAMILY RESPONSES TO THE DEVELOPING CHILD

Given their maturing and changing brains and bodies, children will make mistakes. In a functional family system, these mistakes are expected and accepted for what they are— reflections of their developmental stage.

If you grew up in a dysfunctional family system, however, when you made mistakes you may have been attacked for simple errors consistent with your age. The parents in such dysfunctional systems do not understand that children are biologically unable to process information the same way adults can—no matter what input they receive. As a result, in the eyes of parents who expect perfection from their children, there exist only two polarities: good and perfect, or bad and a problem.

Functional parenting recognizes that children are, by nature, imperfect and still maturing. The functional parent helps the child by providing direction or guidance on what constitutes age-appropriate behavior. Functional parents confront their children about their behavior in a constructive and loving manner, rather than shaming or blaming. Functional parenting regards children as precious, and in such a system, a child's sense of Self is not in question or debate.

When parents try to make their children perfect, the child will start having issues with who they are, internalizing the idea that they are either good or bad. How a parent affirms and nurtures their child's reality, determines how authentic or real a child will become.

If you had parents who were unable to appreciate your developmental abilities, either by viewing you as good and perfect, or bad and constantly-a-problem, you are likely to have grown up believing those messages about your innate Self.

For you to have developed a healthy sense of Self, you would have needed to be recognized as perfectly imperfect and in need of guidance, as you developed your self-esteem apart from your parents' needs and identities. Without attentive guidance and acceptance, your only option was to become what your parents wanted or needed—not who you truly were or might be.

Functional families provide a set of rules, and parents follow and apply them as consistently as possible. The family supports the child's thinking, and also lets the child know that he or she is okay, that the child has a right to his or her—or their—own thoughts and feelings, *independent of their parents*. The child's Self is accepted as whole and intact, complete with needs and limitations. If a child is different from their parents, that difference is supported and respected. *Who* the child is, is never attacked in a healthy system.

At the same time, in a functional family, when a child does make a mistake, faces a challenge or difficulty, or does something wrong, a system of problem-solving is given to them. They are taught that to have problems is normal, and that problems are opportunities for learning. If a child lives in a family where they are taught to do as their parents say, regardless of the child's needs, values, or perceptions, where rules are not clear or followed, the child cannot do or say anything without risking making a mistake—and being abused for that mistake.

If your parent did not give you rules and limits, or the rules and limits you were given were maladaptive or anti-social, you were traumatized—whether that was your parent's intent or not. Children need rules and limits, and they need to be able to make mistakes as they learn to negotiate these rules and limits, if they are to grow up healthy, whole, and willing to take the risks necessary in life to succeed.

In a functional family system, parents respond to their child's mistakes and their needs constructively. Over time, they teach the child how to take care of his or her own needs. The parents know what to expect at each age of their child's development, and they help the child work through new situations, with patience and guidance. The child is neither punished for their mistakes nor ignored, but, instead, is helped to do for themselves what is appropriate for their age. If there is a problem, the functional parent will try to understand what is happening and help the child resolve it, rather than shaming and blaming the child. The child is free to act their age, so they get to experience their childhood, rather than roleplay being miniature adults.

Unfortunately, many children don't get to act their age, and, as a result, later in life they may act out, never having genuinely matured because their maturity was arrested.

Finally, in a functional system, the parents know that they, too, are imperfect. They know that they are accountable for their actions, that they will make mistakes, and that when they do, they will make amends to anyone harmed by those mistakes, including their children. By modeling mature behavior, they teach their children that it is okay to be fallible, but that it is also important to make amends to people when mistakes affect others. Children who have parents who modeled making amends are able to know that they are not perfect but are perfectly—acceptably—human.

In the dysfunctional system, however, a child never learns that mistakes are acceptable. Being wholly unable to avoid making mistakes, they may become so afraid to do anything that they rely on others to do everything for them—becoming overly dependent in adulthood. Or they may attempt to achieve perfection in everything they do, viewing any mistake as a failure.

At this point, you have probably recognized yourself and your family in more than one respect. Whether the trauma you experienced in your childhood was related to neglect or abuse, that neglect, or abuse was the outcome of how the parent projected their needs onto you. In so doing, they failed to provide for your needs in one or more critical ways. In the next chapter, we'll take a closer look at two primary ways in which a child's needs are not met—either through outright neglect, or through such intrusive negative abuse or inappropriate idealized attention that the child's need for a separate identity is obscured. Either way, the child is trauma-tized.

CHAPTER 2

THE MANY FACES OF TRAUMA

D o you feel you were you traumatized as a child? If you've come to this book for help, chances are, even if you were smothered with attention, you were profoundly neglected emotionally, if not physically.

People who have suffered from family of origin trauma almost always suffer from neglect. Neglect is a failure to attend to a child's basic needs. Neglect can be hard to recognize because it isn't something that happened to you—it's something that did *not* happen to you. It's an inaction, a non-event. Neglect is the hardest form of trauma to detect and treat because it is a non-event—defined by what did *not* happen, what you did *not* receive, what was sorely needed but *not* given. Neglect is a form of covert child abuse. It includes failing to provide adequate healthcare, supervision, clothing, nutrition, and housing, as well as failure to attend to the critical areas of a child's physical, emotional, social, educational, and safety needs.

Neglect may result from problems one or both parents suffer, such as mental illness, substance abuse, domestic violence, cognitive impairment, and poverty. In therapeutic practice, neglect is often called "covert shaming" because it leads a child to feel as if they don't matter. Like in the presence of carbon monoxide, which is invisible, those inside the home suffer the effects of something they cannot see or notice.

Neglect can be deadly because it can lead to our needs not being met, and our needs are basic to survival. Basic needs keep our body and soul intact. Any threat to body or soul constitutes a trauma.

Among our needs are the three major ones of food, shelter, and clothing. A child can receive all three of these needs in abundance, and still be neglected, however. There are other needs that all children have that are essential to a healthy life. These needs include medical and dental care, education, protection and guidance, money management, physical and emotional nurturing, and some form of spiritual or moral direction. Having these needs met requires interacting with other people. Because other people can themselves be a threat, however, children must be protected and taught to recognize appropriate and safe people who can help them. Otherwise, children will inevitably seek out others to meet their needs, unprepared for the harmful damage some might cause them— whether through sexual abuse, physical harm, theft, duplicity, or other manipulative acts that traumatize children.

Although taking care of a child's needs is a parent's responsibility, parents are equally responsible for teaching their children how to take care of their own needs. Unfortunately, that does not always happen. When children are not taught to take care of their own needs, either through neglect or by having everything done for them, they become overly dependent on others, which can cause lasting damage. Such neglect can make forming healthy relationships especially difficult. In some cases, gender stereotypes can lead to over-dependence. For example, girls who are never taught how to change a tire, mow a lawn, or manage money will grow up to depend on men to do those things. Similarly, boys who are never taught to cook a meal, wash laundry, or clean their rooms will grow up to depend on women to do those things. Gender stereotypes are one of the most common forms of learned dependence, yet depending on your family of origin, the dependence you have developed may extend far beyond common gender stereotypes. It can affect some or all of the most fundamental responsibilities of adulthood, from managing personal finances to choosing your own spouse or career.

While children clearly shouldn't be expected to handle responsibilities on their own—beyond what their brain development is capable of, it is important to remember that after reaching adulthood, regardless of the programming you received as a child, part of taking care of yourself includes taking care of your own needs. By taking care of your needs, you will avoid being too dependent on others. Fulfilling your needs will also help you in your relationships because you won't ask for too much or become overly needy, dependent, or clinging. Similarly, children must be able to ask for help when they need it. If they are expected to provide for their own needs at too early an age, they will grow up not knowing how to ask for help when they need it. To be mindful of each of your essential needs, and to assess your relationship with each need, will prepare you for healthy relationships. Just how you do that is something this book will help you explore further. For now, let's distinguish between our needs and our wants.

Caring for the Self (the true or essential Self), means not only addressing our needs, but satisfying our wants in a healthy manner. Wants are very different than needs. Whereas needs are necessary for our basic survival, our wants are not. We can survive without any of our desires being fulfilled. But our desires are an important part of our sense of Self, and our sense of abundance. Our wants are unique to each of us and bring us a sense of hope, purpose, and a sense that we can experience something meaningful in life. This sense of hope may bring us joy. While having our wants constantly fulfilled can lead to a sense that we never have enough, having our wants fulfilled within reason and moderation will have just the opposite effect.Wants fulfilled provides us with a feeling of abundance, a sense of having enough.

Many adults who have had severe developmental trauma have difficulty meeting their own needs or fulfilling their own wants appropriately. Either they know what to do but lack the will and spirit to do so. Or they don't know, and hence experience repeated frustration. Or they may lack any clear awareness of what it is they need or want at all. The child who is attacked, ignored or neglected, will start ignoring their needs and desires. Eventually, this child may not even recognize that they have desires.

To get a better sense of what happens when a child's needs are not met, let's consider the stories of Ned and Martha—one child who grew up in a family where few of his needs were met, and the other who grew up in a family where her every need was seemingly met.

A STORY OF CHRONIC PHYSICAL NEGLECT

Ned grew up the oldest child in an Irish Catholic family. With four younger siblings and a father who was rarely sober, he did not get much parental attention. Financially struggling, his parents never bought him new clothes. Instead, Ned wore his father's hand-me-downs. During his early to teenage years, Ned's parents never took him to a doctor, unless it was absolutely necessary, never took him to a dentist, and never taught him how to shower, groom, or take care of his body.

It wasn't until he was a teen and working, when his employer told him he had to shower, cut his hair, and be presentable with customers, that Ned realized there was something wrong with how he took care of himself. He had always wondered why his peers laughed at him. Because his parents were so unavailable, Ned had never learned the basics of self-care that most people take for granted. As he grew older, Ned had internalized his sense of shame and inferiority, or "less than" self-perception.

Although he made a good living, he was unable to spend money on nice things for himself, nor to enjoy a nice meal out, nor to go on a vacation. He struggled to care for himself—

because no one had ever taught him how to do so.

Ned's childhood was a classic case of neglect. While he was fed and provided with housing, his basic hygeine needs were ignored, as were his medical and dental needs. His emotional needs were barely met. As for wants, they were so out of reach that they weren't even on his radar. When Ned came to me for help, we identified the areas of pervasive neglect that he had received in his childhood. We created a practice of self-care, and I taught him techniques to reparent the parts of him that were so emotionally neglected. While Ned still sometimes struggles with "having his own back," by failing to care for himself emotionally when he is stressed, he is now able to enjoy the abundant life he has created because he has discovered new ways to care for himself and to repair the damage so many years of neglect had caused. In Chapter 11, I'll introduce you to these same reparenting techniques, which proved to be so powerful in helping Ned heal.

A STORY OF CHRONIC EMOTIONAL NEGLECT

In contrast to Ned, whose neglect was tied in part to the severe and chronic financial stress his parents suffered, Martha's childhood was seemingly idyllic.

She was raised in an upper-class neighborhood in New York City, the second daughter in a family of two girls. Her mother was a former teacher who became a stay-at-home mom, and her father was a successful marketing executive. While growing up, Martha had everything that Ned did not—a great school, clothes from the most expensive stores, access to the best libraries, and resources for studying and advancing academically. She appeared to have it all—except the emotional and physical nurturing she so badly needed from her parents.

Martha was active as a child in sports, schools, and had many friends. But what she was missing were the critical elements of a physical and emotional connection to the people she interacted with. Simple physical touch, emotional validation, and nurturing, which are essential for creating a sense of Self and bringing a child to life, were all absent in her life.

Her father was preoccupied with his demanding career, and rarely home, and, when he was home, he was emotionally distant. Her mother rarely hugged her daughters or told them she loved them. Busy with her own social life, she relegated the care of her daughters to teachers and tutors, just as she relegated the care of the home to housekeepers. Love and pride were expressed through gifts and financial rewards, while the emotional concerns of the girls were regarded as messy—conflicts to be avoided, rather than problems to be solved.

Unsurprisingly, by the time Martha came to me, she was both self-involved, and self-neglectful. She had difficulty extending nurturance and support to others and put her own needs before anyone else's. At the same time, she pushed people away, keeping anyone from knowing or getting close to her true Self, leading to problems in her relationships in all phases of her life.

Through our work together, however, Martha was able to recognize the ways in which her emotional needs were neglected as a child, and how that neglect led her to erect walls, keeping others out. She is now better able to practice self-care, and to express her thoughts, emotions, and needs, and to interact more effectively with those she loves.

TRAUMA THROUGH PARENTAL ENMESHMENT

The opposite pole of neglect is enmeshment. Argentinian family therapist Salvador Minuchin coined this concept in 1962 to describe families where personal boundaries are not clear and the emotions of one become the emotions of another.

Such over-concern for the other family member leads to a loss of autonomous development for both. Enmeshed parenting represents a style of parenting that can cause problems in a child's successful development of their person-ality, ethics, and values. In a family with enmeshed parenting, a child's good or challenging behavior—or the child's successful or unsuccessful achievements—define, not the child's worth, but the *parent's* worth. Thus, the parent's identity is so inextricably bound with the child's that the child feels constant pressure to conform to their parent's ideals and dreams.

In his classic book, *Healing the Shame Within,* theologian and counselor John Bradshaw, an expert in codependency, also used enmeshment to describe a form of bonding within a family, where a child (usually of the opposite sex) becomes a surrogate spouse for their mother or father. Such a relation-ship may, but often does not, include sexual abuse. What defines the enmeshment is the role the child plays as *a partner* to the parent, rather than as a subordinate whose dependence on the parent declines with age. Enmeshed parents typically resent the child's attentions toward others and become increasingly controlling as the child matures and strives toward independence.

NEGATIVE ENMESHMENT

Any form of enmeshment is damaging to a child. However, the term *negative enmeshment* is used to describe the worst features of enmeshment, when the relationship is characterized by a parent who uses yelling, screaming, shaming, criticizing and other manipulative tactics to manipulate their child into compliance with the parent's emotional needs. The child experiences that closeness as abuse and intrusion. Negative enmeshment occurs when the parent views the child as a reflection of their worst, or most feared, qualities, and thus reacts with anger and sometimes violence to force the child to extinguish those qualities. For example, parents who fear homosexuality may become abusive to children who display qualities typically attributed to the other gender, or parents from strict religious backgrounds may react forcefully to any sign their child is questioning or straying from religious doctrine. Negative enmeshment can be less obvious as a form of abuse to the child suffering from it. In most cases, the child perceives the abuse as a reflection of their own faults, and desperately tries to change to please the unhappy parent.

To better understand a relationship of negative enmeshment, let's take a look at Paul.

Paul was the eldest and only son in a family of three children. His father was a plumber by day and an alcoholic by night. His mother was a stay-at-home mother who focused most of her attentions on her younger daughters. From the age of five, Paul's father bullied him and belittled him with cruel names. Paul, a sensitive, soft-spoken boy, was slapped, punched, and laughed at by his father, and called a sissy. His mother never intervened when her husband abused Paul, no matter how extreme the abuse became. Instead, she was cold and emotionally shut down.

When Paul was seventeen, and no longer timid and weak, he and his father had a knock-down-drag-out fight in the kitchen. This violent brawl left them both bloody. Paul left home and slept in his car for three months until he saved the money to find an apartment. He graduated from high school and enrolled in trade school—to become a plumber, like his father.

As he matured, Paul had learned to mask his innate sensitivity and emotions by adopting a hyper-masculinity. Paul now emulates his father in many ways. At the same time, Paul struggles with authoritarian men. He either withdraws out of fear, or he becomes aggressive and tries to fight them. His impulse toward aggressive behavior is like a hair trigger. He struggles with keeping close relationships. And, just as his father had turned to alcohol to ease his own pain, Paul has used alcohol, drugs, and pornography to try to soothe the pain that continues to haunt him.

During our therapy, Paul realized that his father used physical abuse against Paul. He also realized his father projected his unhappiness onto Paul, as his son. Further, Paul began to see that the abuse was not due to Paul's failures, but to his father's inability to parent him appropriately. Paul now understands that his father's anger was never Paul's fault, and that he can heal his life and not be like his father. Paul still struggles with the "carried shame" that came from his father, yet Paul is now able to hold himself in warm regard, and with compassion. He has learned to control his anger, and he has regained his enthusiasm for life.

Paul's father displayed negative enmeshment. He was too enmeshed in his son's life and viewed his son as a reflection of himself. Thus, when Paul displayed any weakness or vulnerability, his father became enraged—because he had never dealt with his own insecurities and vulnerabilities. The weakness he perceived in his son triggered his own anxieties about failing to live up to a masculine ideal of strength. Rather than explore his own fears, weaknesses and vulnerabilities, Paul's father presented a hyper-masculine mask to the world— a mask that he feared his son's vulnerability might expose.

IDEALIZED ENMESHMENT

In contrast to negative enmeshment, idealized enmeshment takes place when a parent is using the child for their own purposes, by idealizing the child so much that the parent essentially gives the child an adult role or position in the family.

Sometimes, a child in this relationship is called a "parentified child." The parent does not overtly abuse the child; in fact, the parent may become overly protective and defensive of the child, often failing to discipline the child, regardless of the child's behavior. The parent may also be overly involved in the child's life, becoming too personal. Such a parent may not respect the child's privacy, acting as if every facet of the child's life is of interest to the parent. They either respect no boundaries at all, prying into everything, or they may yield to the child's demands for privacy to the point that they ask no questions, idealize the child, ignore signs of mental illness or disturbance, and interpret a child's secrecy as no cause for worry, because the child, as a reflection of the parent, is "perfect" and can do no wrong. An example of idealized enmeshment would be what are called, "helicopter parents" who hover over their child into their adulthood, making decisions about their college education, closely monitoring their friendships, activities and classes, and sometimes even calling their professors to ask about grading and assignments.

Children and teens in these idealized enmeshment relationships may feel special about the attention they receive from their parents. They may even receive some form of performance-based self-esteem. But their self-esteem is fragile because it is not really about who the child is; rather, it is about what the parent wants—or believes—the child to be.

The child's unique personality, challenges, goals, and dreams are ignored, as the idealized image, that the parent projects, becomes the character the parent interacts with.

The child may outwardly display pride, even narcissism, but internally, they can be filled with self-doubt. In some cases, they remain oblivious to the unrealistic image they have grown up with, and they may think that the image really is who they are because they have received so much support and applause from their parents and others for the role they have been playing.

In contrast to Paul, who grew up in a family with negative enmeshment, Stewart grew up in a family with idealized enmeshment, and, like Paul, Stewart suffered for it.

Stewart is the third of four children. His father was a former Marine, who later became an engineer, and his mother was a teacher. The parents' relationship was civil and distant, and by the time Stewart was 12 years old, his parents divorced.

Shortly after, Stewart's mother began viewing Stewart as an emotional substitute for her former husband. She started asking him to rub her shoulders or feet. She also began calling him endearments, such as "Stewey" or "Golden Boy." This behavior from his mother, which intensified after the divorce, had actually begun when Stewart was at an early age.

Stewart remembers his mother leaving the door open when she took baths, a habit that began in childhood but continued until he was seventeen.

Once his parents divorced, his mother would have parties

with her girlfriends, women who he sometimes ended up sleeping with. These experiences both aroused and shamed him, leading to self-loathing and filling Stewart with low self-esteem.

When he was with his father, however, Stewart was confident and helped around the house with chores. But Stewart's father also viewed Stewart as an extension of himself, being so focused on his son's success that Stewart felt pressured. Stewart felt he must be the "good son" so that his father wouldn't be disappointed. Stewart did whatever his father needed, in order to please his father, even if it meant setting aside Stewart's own ideals and dreams. He so strongly wanted to be the son his father wanted him to be.

A few years ago, Stewart hit rock bottom, when, struggling with alcohol addiction, he lost his job as an executive for a successful high-tech company. After treat-ment in a rehab facility, Stewart came to me. We began working through the ways that his mother's suffocating attentions and poor boundaries had traumatized him, leading him to become stuck emotionally. After practicing techniques—those I present in Part II of this book, Stewart began to grow emotionally and discern the ways in which his self-defeating adult behaviors were rooted in his coping efforts to adapt and survive as a child and adolescent.

Today, Stewart has completely restructured his life, and he is choosing to live according to his own wants, needs, and reality.

Stewart's life story is a classic example of abuse from idealized enmeshment, or what Mellody terms, "false empowerment." Both parents used Stewart for their own needs. As they did so, he didn't feel neglected or abused in any way. Instead, he felt important, special and empowered. But these inflated feelings of self-worth became problems when he grew older as he struggled with trying to remain in the limelight while realizing he did not have a sense of Self. He had never had a chance to develop that Self when he was so busy conforming to the self his parents invented for him.

Both Paul's and Stewart's experiences are forms of parental enmeshment. Both are also forms of trauma. While one is covert, the other is overt. But because the wounds of their childhood were chronic, and in Stewart's case, masked by an over-abundance of attention, they did not necessarily recognize their childhoods as traumatic ones—they had normalized their trauma.

As these stories demonstrate, trauma affects a child's development in a multitude of ways. A child has inherent needs that, if not met, will cause the child to adapt in a way that compensates for those lost needs—whether that's by lashing out in anger, as Paul did, becoming self-involved, as Martha did, or self-medicating through addictive behaviors, as Stewart did.

Each of these clients struggled in different ways to obtain the safety, attention, and comfort they so desperately needed. And each suffered as they matured because the behaviors they adopted as children didn't work in the adult world. Paul's angry outbursts didn't make him safer. They jeopardized his safety and intensified his pain. Martha's self-involvement didn't bring her the attention she had been deprived of. Instead, it further alienated the people who cared about her. And Stewart's addictive behaviors didn't bring him the comfort he needed. His addictions intensified his suffering. The trauma these people suffered as children had led them to form protective habits which failed to protect them as adults.

As these stories illustrate, neglect and enmeshment are powerful forms of abuse. But neglect and enmeshment are not the only forms of family-of-origin trauma. Let's consider some other ways that family-of-origin trauma plays out.

CHAPTER 3

EMBRACING THE BELOVED CHILD

O ne of Pia Mellody's best-selling audio books is entitled, *Permission to be Precious.* I love that title—it strikes right to the heart of what it is that the child has been denied, their precious nature. It is important to understand what Mellody means in discussing the nature of the precious child. Before you can understand the gifts and wounds you received or didn't receive during your childhood, you need to understand the nature of childhood itself. This will give us a model or baseline from which to consider our unique experiences. This perspective is like saying to yourself, "If this were a perfect world, and I grew up with well-adjusted parents who knew how to affirm, nurture, give guidance, and set limits, this is what I would have felt like and who I would have been as a functional human being."

As Mellody points out, the nature of a child born into this world is that they are precious and valuable. They have inherent worth the moment they enter their own life. They are miraculous creations of the Divine presence in the world. They have a purpose in our world, the nature of which may remain a mystery, or may manifest itself in remarkable achievements at some point in their lives. That is why Pia Mellody's first Core Area, "Loving Ourselves," is so important—we all have inherent worth and are worthy of being loved. And while we cannot compel others to love us, we can and ought to extend our love to ourselves. But doing so can be difficult for the person who was deprived of love as a child.

The reason it is so difficult is that no matter how miraculous their existence, babies and young children cannot esteem—or regard—themselves. They aren't able to have self-esteem because their brains have not yet developed that self-reflective capacity. It is therefore the job of the parent to nurture a child's confidence and self-worth as they mature, in order to create that sense of self-esteem.

If the parents fail to do so, and the child grows up in a less than nurturing family, as the child matures, he or she will feel inferior to others, undervalued, and disempowered. In some cases, however, Mellody cautions that children who are overvalued by a parent may feel better than others or what she terms, falsely empowered. It's important that a child be valued and esteemed for who they truly are, and not for who they have been falsely imagined to be.

Many parents believe that one or more of their children have failed them in some way, or, on the contrary, that the children are the most amazing humans to ever have been born. Either view is mistaken and damaging to a child. All children have their gifts, but these gifts don't make them better than others; just as all have their shortcomings, and these shortcomings don't make the child less than others.

Inherent worth is not based on performance, attributes, or who loves you. Inherent worth is, as the word says, *inherent*; it just is.

If a family system can't foster the practice of valuing the child inherently, the child will grow up either feeling disempowered and shamed, or they will grow up to feel falsely empowered, which is to say, grandiose and better than other people. Dysfunctional families that can't respond to a child's needs might either attack or ignore the child, or they might overvalue and indulge the child. Either extreme is damaging.

Functional parents, on the other hand, help clarify and meet the child's needs by affirming, nurturing, setting limits, and giving guidance. Unfortunately, many of us don't receive such parenting. When a family is unable to support a child's value, the child starts believing that they are messed up. The child will then try to gather self-esteem from external sources. Children can also come to believe that they are better than others by watching their parents act contemptuously of others. They internalize the message that others are inferior and that they, themselves, are inherently superior. Both are manifestations of poorly developed self-esteem.

All functional esteeming comes from functional parents cultivating confidence in their child throughout their life, and from the child, in turn, internalizing this practice as their own self-perception. But what happens when that functional esteem is not cultivated? In the two stories that follow, you will see how one child, who was emotionally neglected but materially rewarded, grew up to feel undervalued and disempowered, while the other, who was never corrected, grew up to feel overvalued and falsely empowered.

THE UNDERVALUED OR DISEMPOWERED CHILD

Like Martha, who grew up with an abundance of her material needs met but her emotional needs neglected, Tom grew up in an affluent family, but he was emotionally neglected. The last of six children, Tom's parents paid little attention to what he was up to. His father was a diplomat. As such, his parents focused on their life of entertaining, helping others, and maintaining their image. But behind the image they presented to the public, life at home was no party. As his father focused on being an international ambassador for the United States, his mother focused on the social responsibilities that came with her role, relegating much of her parental responsibilities to domestic help.

At her best, Tom's mother was a gracious hostess who reveled in her social life and the popular parties she threw. At her worst, she was angry, shaming, and controlling and prone to fits of rage. She would ignore Tom as long as she could, until he did something to upset her. Then she'd aim her anger straight at him.

In contrast, Tom's father was intelligent and accomplished, but at his worst, he was narcissistic, arrogant, and insulting. When Tom would get into trouble, his father would be sure to let him know how badly he'd screwed up. Although Tom grew up feeling loved by his parents, he was acutely aware of the dichotomy between the social image his parents projected, and the volatile reality that characterized their home behind closed doors.

While he was young, Tom was regarded as a normal but mischievous child. As the child of a diplomat, however, he had lived in many places around the world, which, while providing him a rich cultural experience, made it difficult for him to form lasting friendships or to feel secure in any of the many homes they occupied. Unfortunately, his parents didn't seem to recognize their son's increasing loneliness, nor the struggles he faced from having his home life disrupted with such frequent moves. As he grew older, his family moved from West Africa to Thailand, where Tom began to manifest the consequences of his parental neglect.

When he was twelve years old, Tom started wandering the streets of Bangkok and hanging with strangers doing drugs. Busy with their own lives, his parents never kept track of him. When Tom was fifteen his family once again moved to another side of the world, settling in Washington, D.C. There, Tom continued to do drugs, and, not long after, he began drinking heavily, which continued until he was 32. It was then that he got sober and sought treatment.

Today, Tom talks about how lost he was as a child. Despite his life of material comfort, and his family's high social status, as well as his parent's love for him, Tom's parents paid little attention to his safety or his emotional needs. They were so consumed with trying to meet—however badly—their own emotional needs. While his parents were constantly surrounded by society, Tom's experience of life was one of loneliness and isolation, a loneliness that continued to haunt him well into adulthood, despite becoming successful and popular.

From our work together, Tom came to understand that he had been undervalued, and, as a result, felt disempowered. He did not know his own value or power. Over time, he discovered and owned his "feeling reality," which is a state of emotional awareness that legitimizes the authentic feelings a person learns to suppress in an effort to protect themselves. As Tom learned to claim his feeling reality, his sense of Self was also restored, and he now finds joy in his life.

We will return to Tom's story in Chapter 10, as we explore what it means to be a Lost Child, but, for now, I want you to contemplate how emotional neglect affects self-esteem in adulthood, leading to a sense of disempowerment in all areas of life.

Tom is not alone. Many of my clients, who come to me suffering from addictions, self-destructive behaviors, and loneliness, have had childhoods very much like Tom's.

Others who come to me were not neglected or put down. Instead, some were put on pedestals so high that they could only look down on others. That is just what happened to my client, Bill.

THE OVERVALUED OR FALSELY EMPOWERED CHILD

Unlike Tom who could do no right, Bill could do no wrong. Bill's father was a doctor and his mother was a homemaker, with another son from a previous marriage. As Bill grew up, the first born only son of his father, he came to know that he was faultless in his father's eyes. Whatever he did, no matter how little effort he put into it, his father celebrated as if it were a grand achievement. Whatever he did wrong was treated as an insignificant human error. At home, Bill was, quite literally, "above the law".

In contrast to how Bill's father treated Bill, he found nothing but fault with his wife. He would yell at her frequently, in front of the children, and controlled both her and the home. The bad treatment toward his mother, alongside the glowing praise directed at Bill from his father, conditioned Bill to feel better than his mother. This gave him a sense of undue power in the family that soon permeated other areas of his life.

Like Tom, by the age of twelve, Bill began to act out in increasingly bad behaviors. Although he was athletic and was considered the class clown, which made him popular with his friends, he showed little respect for authority. He skipped school, but there were no consequences. He ignored or talked back to his mother, and there were no consequences. By the time he was seventeen, he was arrested for provoking a police officer. When his father came to jail to bail him out, Bill told his father that the police officer was the one who had done wrong by arresting him for no reason. His father patiently listened to his son, and then validated his experience that the police officer had indeed been the one in the wrong. Thus, Bill was once again excused for his bad behavior.

As with the altercation with the police officer, no matter what Bill did, his father found others to blame. This kind of parenting set up a precedent that led Bill to never consider how his words or behaviors impacted other people. In his view, they were always wrong, and he was always the victim. No-consequences parenting and false empowerment became a subtle way of putting him "above the law", where the rules for others did not apply to him.

Bill had a sense of false empowerment, and he overvalued his self-esteem. Even at the time he married, he had never had to live with or face the consequences of his actions. He believed he was better than others, including his wife, and that his very existence gave him the right to control the behaviors of others. These qualities helped him to excel in his profession, where he had great responsibility and authority over others, but they did not help him to succeed in his marriage. Bill's wife, like Bill's mother in her own marriage, soon came to feel as if she didn't matter. His wife felt that she was not a priority for Bill.

Eventually, Bill's failure to prioritize his wife's needs became so great that she was ready to leave if he didn't agree to marriage counseling. In my work with Bill, I helped him see that the power he felt in his relationships was based on a false sense of value—a grandiosity his father had instilled in him, leading him to overvalue himself in comparison to the others, whom he devalued. In our couple's work since that time, Bill has gained great insight and has become a better husband by making the relationship a priority. He has become more empathetic by focusing on his wife's needs and their connection, rather than focusing mainly on his work performance and need for acclaim. Moreover, he now realizes that most of his work accomplishments are not long lasting, but the relationships he cultivates and nurtures stay in his life a good long time.

As these examples show, parents must embrace their beloved children for who they are, not for who they are imagined to be. By valuing or devaluing only an image of the child—whether by putting them down and dismissing their virtues, or by elevating them to unrealistic heights, parents hurt their children's development.

When parents fail to accept and understand a child just as they are, that child then fails to develop healthy self-esteem, and the Core Area of Loving the Self—or what I prefer to call Being Valued—does not develop. When that happens, not only is the child's sense of Self damaged, but so too are their boundaries—which are essential for development in the second Core Area, Protecting the Self.

BOUNDARY SYSTEMS

Just as children are unable to esteem themselves, they are also unable to protect themselves. Children don't have a fully developed boundary system, and they must rely on their parents to protect them physically, sexually, and emotionally. Boundaries act like filters—they filter the information we are able to receive or communicate to others.

While the concepts of physical and sexual boundaries have long been noted by mental health professionals, let's take a look at how Pia Mellody presents these concepts anew. And, as we examine these boundaries, we'll consider how boundaries relate to a child's sense of self-esteem.

An overly porous boundary allows too much information, too much emotion, or too much human interaction, to be received and/or to be communicated or sent out to others. Meanwhile, a too rigid boundary tightly controls what is received, to such an extent that not even love can permeate in or out of it. But it is useful to investigate: just how do our boundaries develop?

Children learn boundaries by watching their parents, and also by the experiences children have when interacting with others. If the parent is dysfunctional with their own boundaries, their children will absorb this dysfunction. Mellody notes that there are two polarities we find in such dysfunctional families when it comes to boundaries.

On the first polarity, there is either an absence of boundaries, what she refers to as being *boundaryless*. Also, along this side of the spectrum are situations where the boundaries that do exist are weak—what I like to call *porous boundaries* **or** being thin-skinned.

The other polarity is a state of people having such rigid boundaries that they erect virtual walls between themselves and others. I often see these rigid boundaries manifest between a parent and their child.

When there are no boundaries in a family, the parent exudes too much emotion, information, or even physical connection toward the child, or may invite too much in. In some ways, Bill's father exhibited no boundaries by exuding too much attention and reverence for his son.

In the second example, of rigid boundaries in a family, the parent lets little to no positive emotion, information, or physical contact reach the child. Tom's family provided for him materially, but virtually excluded him from their lives in every other way. They exhibited rigid boundaries. Either way, the child is trapped in a dysfunctional family.

Functional parenting will demonstrate and teach boundaries within a family system. Physical boundaries encompass the right to control how close a person can get to you and whether or not they can touch you, or your personal property, without your consent. Children need their parents to closely monitor these physical boundaries with others, boundaries that protect children's bodies, and their physical belongings. Sexual boundaries are especially important for children and young adults, which is why they need to be supervised by a functional parent who will recognize whether anyone is inappropriately touching, staring at, or sexually interacting with their child—and that includes relatives, family, or friends.

Children by nature want to be loved, and, in regard to basic needs, if they are not being valued in a family system, many will be drawn to someone who freely gives them attention—even if it is harmful and inappropriate attention.

Lastly, and importantly, psychological boundaries also protect and promote healthy development. Pia Mellody refers to these, in her book, *Facing Codependence,* as "internal boundaries." Children are like an open door. They can't shut out verbal abuse when they are young, and once they get older, they adapt to this abuse by creating psychological walls to hide behind, which lessens the pain of criticisms. Examples of these walls include indifference, subordination, hostility, and acting out with antisocial behaviors, such as those Tom learned.

Children are also like sponges; they feel and pick up everything that is going on around them. They are acutely attuned to the environment, and, not being able to distinguish between their own reality and the environment that surrounds them, they absorb the environment as if it is their reality. For the purpose of my work, I define an individual's reality as how they give meaning to what they see happening. It starts with their senses bringing in information. Then, depending on a person's age, they will have a thought. And later, their thoughts will create a body sensation. These sensations will in turn become felt emotions that can then shape their behaviors. As the person grows, they learn their psychological boundaries by watching what is happening in their immediate family. A parent's job, especially when children are young, is to teach children how to protect and contain—and thereby grow and develop—their thinking and their emotions.

A functional system is where the parents have a healthy boundary system in place, and they adhere to it—without turning that boundary system into a series of impenetrable rigid walls that shut out the child completely. If there is no functional boundary system, a child will feel as if they are standing alone on a battlefield with a complete lack of protection. Or they may feel they are standing behind a system of walls, which are made up of fear, anger, politeness, or silence. Either way, the walls or their own solitude protects them at a cost. That protection is an illusion, because such isolation leaves the person unconnected to life or to others, and therefore in danger.

Conversely, when a child has no boundaries at all, they are set up to be an unprotected victim or to victimize others. The worst-case scenario is when they become both the victim and the offender. One part of them is set up to be a victim because they are unprotected from attacks, and the other part is doing the attacking and being offensive.

To better understand these boundaries, let's take a closer look at how healthy boundaries function in families and in social relationships.

HEALTHY BOUNDARIES

Boundaries are essential for any relationship. Boundaries contain and protect the body, control distance and touch, and they filter information and communication coming in and going out. Healthy boundaries form a system of limit-setting that protects a person from being a victim and contains a person so that she or he is not offensive to others.

The purpose of psychological (or internal) boundaries is to contain and protect a person's sense of Self, when they are interacting with other people. When internal or psychological boundaries are used functionally, they help establish our sense of Self, how we give meaning to the information we receive, our emotions, and what behaviors we do or do not do. When physical or sexual (external) boundaries are being used properly, they protect our personal property, our bodies, and our sexual intimacy. There is a difference, however, between setting a boundary and setting a limit.

Social/psychological, physical, and sexual boundaries define what we will and won't allow in respect to our different relationships. We might discuss politics with our friends, but not with our coworkers. We might not hesitate to discipline our own child, but we'd be crossing a boundary if we disciplined someone else's child. We might not think twice about giving an expensive or personal gift to someone we love but giving an expensive or personal gift to someone we've just met would be crossing a social boundary. Imagine receiving an expensive piece of jewelry, some sexy lingerie, or a book on social manners from the new neighbor who just moved in down the street! They'd be crossing a boundary—a boundary that might not exist for a spouse or close friend, depending on the gift and the occasion.

A limit, on the other hand, is not something so flexible. Instead, *it's the line of unacceptable behaviors we impose on ourselves and on others.* If it's our child, we set limits as to what they can and cannot do, before having consequences enforced. If it's a spouse, we set limits as to what we will and won't put up with before we're heading to a couples therapist for help. And with our parents, as we mature, we might set limits on what they can and cannot say to us, demand of us, or do in front of us, depending on the nature of the relation-ship and our histories.

You might have an alcoholic parent, for example, and your limit is that you will not see them if they've been drinking, but you grudgingly put up with their cigarette smoking and their cussing. You've set your limit—no drinking in your presence. Marriages, no matter how strong and long lasting, have plenty of limits, and they vary depending on the people in the marriage. Most strong marriages are based on clear limits—no emotional or physical abuse, no betrayals, no addictions unless the addict is getting treatment, no secrets regarding finances or other serious matters.

If these unacceptable—off limits—behaviors continue, or the limits are constantly being violated, the limit needs to turn into a bottom line. A bottom line is like an ultimatum; it means that if someone doesn't stop the behavior, you are out of the relationship.

The point is everyone needs boundaries that define *the nature* of their relationships, and limits as to *what they'll put up with* in those relationships.

People with clear boundaries typically set clear limits with the people in their lives, and don't tend to get exploited or abused—at least not for long. If people violate their boundaries or go beyond the limits that have been set, they say something. If the person persists in violating those boundaries or defying the limits, they'll do something—even if it means ending the relationship.

If it's a child who has ignored the limits that have been set, they will discipline the child or, in extreme cases, get professional help for the child—because they understand that the developing child needs clear limits in order to thrive and have a healthy sense of Self.

Conversely, people with poor boundaries often set poor limits. Having poor boundaries, they may overshare intimate details of their lives with coworkers and others who they've just met. Similarly, having poor limits, they may let their children do whatever they want, eat whatever they want, and break whatever they want. They may let their spouse abuse and betray them over and over again, just as they may abuse and betray their spouse over and over again. They have no clear boundaries that distinguish one relationship from others—anything and everything goes in all relationships. Such people will also likely have no limits as to what they'll put up with; they tend to live in chaos, because chaos is all they know.

Establishing healthy boundaries and setting reasonable limits is good for our relationships because every time you overextend yourself, you resent it. If you find yourself "hating" someone you love, such as a spouse, friend, or child, because of something they are doing or saying that adversely affects you, it may very well be an indication of not setting appropriate boundaries and limits. But it's also important that limits are not a way of controlling others. Setting a limit means, "If you do this, these are the consequences, and these are the reasons: because those behaviors are contrary to my values or sense of Self." Not, "You cannot do this, because I am the boss."

Boundaries are where the wounds of trauma most clearly manifest. Healthy boundaries help the child develop healthy self-esteem. Clear, appropriate boundaries are so essential, in fact, that Pia Mellody has identified several types of boundaries that shape healthy relationships and self-esteem. By taking a closer look at these boundary systems, you can better understand the role your own boundaries play in your wounding—and in your healing.

CHAPTER 4

IDENTIFYING OUR BOUNDARIES

B oundary systems take many forms, and we all have multiple boundaries that overlap and even conflict with each other. The more we are able to identify our boundaries, and to determine how we hide behind them—or how we fail to establish them, the better able we are to recognize the many ways in which our childhood traumas affect our current relationships. By now, you understand the basic concept of boundary systems, but let's take the concept one step further to explore some specific types of essential boundaries.

EXTERNAL PHYSICAL BOUNDARIES

Setting an external physical boundary means communicating, "I have the right to control how close you get to me, whether you get to touch me, and whether you have access to my personal property." Personal property includes things like computers, wallets, phones, purses, or our rooms. There may be people we share these things with, but there ought to be plenty of people we don't grant access to such personal items. These things represent your privacy, and to cross the boundaries of these personal things, or physical places, is an invasion—a disrespecting of your privacy. This constitutes a boundary violation. It's not okay.

Similarly, personal space is how close someone can stand or sit next to you, listen to your private conversations, or expose you to an illness. Personal space might vary by culture, age, or gender—in some cultures, people might press up against each other as they wait in line, and they may think nothing of it. In others, a personal space of three to six feet might be normal. Stepping inside these invisible boundaries can be perceived as a threat, unless it is invited.

Similarly, we have certain friends who we invite into our private conversations, and other friends we keep more distant. We might sit very close to family members of our own gender, but more distantly from family members of another gender. And we might accept that our spouse and children will expose us to their illnesses, while we resent when a coworker does so.

Personal physical boundaries vary depending on the culture, context, and the people involved, but everybody has them—even though some of us may need some help to clarify and to enforce our physical boundaries.

EXTERNAL SEXUAL BOUNDARIES

An external sexual boundary is a form of a personal physical boundary, but it is much more clear and unambig-uous. Having an external sexual boundary means knowing, "When someone is approaching me sexually, I have the right to control when, where, how, and who is going to be sexual with me. In return, others have the right to control when, where, how and whether they will consent to a sexual advance or suggestion, and I must respect their choice."

When people cross our sexual boundaries uninvited, however, we might become confused, and in many cases fearful. Someone who is clear on what their sexual boundaries are will have no trouble saying to the person that they must stop. Someone less clear on those boundaries, or someone who feels they lack inherent power and self-worth (or who has been deprived of love and attention), might resist in less assertive ways, and might even give in against their will—without clearly communicating that the behavior is unwanted.

The most extreme example of boundary crossing is rape, where no amount of resistance or forceful communication will be able to prevent the brutal violation of your body. If that has happened to you as a child, it is important to deeply understand that what happened had nothing to do with your boundaries or limits, and everything to do with the other person's shameless, cruel, violent—and criminal—actions.

INTERNAL BOUNDARIES

In addition to the external boundaries we set in our lives, there are internal, or psychological, boundaries. An internal boundary is to your psyche what skin is to your body. It keeps the bad stuff from damaging what's inside of you and prevents what's inside of you from leaking out. Pia Mellody indicates that there are two important parts of an internal boundary system. The first part, Mellody calls the "listening boundary" (and I term the protective boundary). The other part she calls the "speaking boundary" (which I refer to as the containing boundary).

One way to understand how internal or psychological boundaries work is by looking at the polarities that can operate in a dysfunctional state. I am guessing you have had these experiences, probably long before putting words to these interactions. For example, in a dysfunctional state, we might be quick to blame, or we might explode at the people we love when we are annoyed, frustrated, or angry. We might insult them or accuse them of "always doing this" or "never doing that," just because they have said or done something that we didn't like. We all do it, but in a dysfunctional system, such accusations become habitual ways of interacting when under stress. If these bursts of emotion are our boundaries acting in a dysfunctional state, how, then, can boundaries act in functional, healthy ways?

THE PROTECTIVE BOUNDARY

The protective internal boundary protects you and filters information and feedback you receive from the people and the world around you. When the protective boundary is working functionally, you are curious and listening to understand what someone is saying to you. The boundary—your filter—allows you to hold yourself in high positive regard, even when others are giving constructive criticism, saying negative things about you or being hurtful. And if what someone is saying is true, you take it in and experience your feelings about it—at your own pace and with your own discernment.

If what someone is saying is not true, you have the choice of not letting it in; you can let it roll right past you; and you realize it reflects the person speaking, not you. If it is true, you have the choice of reflecting on what it means. If it is positive, it can enhance your sense of Self, and, if it is negative, it can help you reflect on how you can improve—without it diminishing your sense of Self.

We all struggle with managing the comments made about us, or the perceptions others have of us, and sometimes that struggle can be painful. When a person says something to me about myself, I ask myself, "Is this true or not true for me? Or is it partially true, but not completely true? Do I need to get more information about what they are saying?"

Of course, it's far easier to accept the positive things people say about us as true, even when they aren't, than it is to accept the critical comments, even when they are. But for some people, it is harder to accept the positive comments than the negative ones. Such people have been so conditioned to view themselves negatively that, when someone praises them, they reject the praise as false praise. Similarly, some people are completely unable to accept even the most benign negative criticisms about themselves, even if the comments are true. Telling such a person that they look tired could prompt a furious reply. Suggesting that the dinner they made was good, but not as delicious as the dinner made the night before, could send them into a downward spiral of depression. Those with a healthy protective boundary would, instead, react with good humor, good-natured agreement *or disagreement*, or simply let the comment pass. Those with a weak or nonexistent protective boundary would be unable to do so. We refer to such weakened or nonexistent protective boundaries as being "boundaryless in the protective boundary."

BOUNDARYLESSNESS IN THE PROTECTIVE BOUNDARY

To speak of being "boundaryless in the protective boundary" is another way of saying someone is "thin-skinned." If you are boundaryless in your protective boundary, then, when someone says something the slightest bit uncomfortable, it feels as if that comment penetrates you. Whatever the intent of the speaker, their comments are interpreted in the worst possible way, as if their words were a deep and deadly wound. It isn't your fault if you misinterpret the information. It's just the natural response to not having yet developed a healthy and functioning protective boundary.

Another common, but often less discernible, way that a boundaryless person experiences the absence of a strong protective boundary is through failure to differentiate between someone else's emotional state and their own. For example, if you have a weak or nonexistant protective boundary, you may take on what another person is feeling, making it your own internal state. Their anxiety becomes your anxiety, their distress becomes your distress, and their joy becomes your joy.

To a certain extent, this emotional contagion is normal in our close relationships. If our child is sad, we feel sad for our child, because we want our children to be happy—and because our protective boundaries are more porous for those we love. If a spouse is excited about a new job or a new opportunity or achievement, we share in their joy. But taken to the extreme, the person who has a weak protective boundary cannot modulate their own emotions. They are completely reactive to whatever is being felt or said by the person or people around them. Such a person adapts to the same emotional temperature as the person next to them. If that happens, the person is experiencing boundary failure. He or she has no filtering going on. Within a second of being around someone else's negative emotions, the person feels affected and becomes uncomfortable.

The protective boundary helps determine whether the comments we are hearing about ourselves are about us, or about the person speaking. The abusive spouse or parent who is continually criticizing is really communicating something about their own weaknesses and insecurities, not the person they are speaking so harshly to—but that doesn't mean the person who receives such criticisms is not feeling the pain and shame of the feedback.

Determining whose issue it is, is an essential component of

using the protective boundary. Being human means, we all see things from our own standpoint or perspective, as we gain greater Self Awareness, and functionally use the protective boundary, we come to recognize what is our stuff and what is the other person's stuff. Boundaries are the practice of Protecting the Self. The protective boundary is the key step in which to create a sense of Self. But sometimes, the protective boundary becomes so impermeable that it is no longer a boundary, but a wall. And when that happens, you become walled off in your protective boundary.

WALLED OFF IN PROTECTIVE BOUNDARY

According to Pia Mellody, being "walled off in protective boundary" is when you are protected by your boundaries so that you don't personalize everything. On the other hand, since no information can pass through the impenetrable walls you've erected, you also can't be influenced. You are unable to have empathy for someone else because you have shut down. When you are behind a wall, you are no longer listening or curious. You've established your reality and are unwilling to change it. People, ideas, even experiences, are all viewed as threats.

There are several types of walls that can be erected in the protective boundary: walls of anger, words, preoccupations, silence, worry, depression, humor, and seduction. For example, some people are verbally gifted and can talk poetically and insightfully on any topic—but their eloquence with words is so cleverly designed that no one can challenge what they're saying, and no one dares. Others use humor to keep reality and pain at bay, like the funny friend who always has a wisecrack or a witty observation to keep the group laughing, the one who turns any moment of sadness or negativity into something funny. The problem is, they aren't always using humor to lighten a difficult situation—they may also be using humor as a wall or defense, so that no one can ever get too close.

One of the most difficult forms of walling off other people is silence. Whether giving someone the preverbal "silent treatment," or shunning them completely by not speaking or interacting with them in any meaningful way. Such silences prevent anyone from getting close or intimate, while communicating to others that they are not worth interacting with.

Depression, a very real biological and psychological disorder, can also be another way to distance people. No one wants to be around a depressed person, and a depressed person usually takes no initiative to be around others, nor to engage in meaningful conversation or interaction. When that happens, the depressed state can become a shield that walls off other people. And, the longer the depression continues, the higher and more impenetrable the wall.

Not all walls are unpleasant, however. Some walls can be quite pleasant, such as people who use humor as a wall. Another pleasant wall might be the overly cheerful "Polly-anna" who does not want to be bothered by any negativity. This person might whistle a happy tune while the roof is caving in. They act seemingly blind to any problems, no matter how urgent or important. Such an optimistic person might be admirable to a certain extent, but if taken to extremes, their optimism is just another way of covering their ears and closing their eyes and screaming, "I can't hear you!" Because they can't. They're too scared to face reality, so they create a false Shangri-La to live in—and they expect you to live in their land of make believe, as well. The person who erects a pleasant wall is not mean; they're just not taking it—or you—in. They're in their own world, not the real world.

CONTAINING BOUNDARY

In contrast to the protective boundary, which filters information received (what we hear), the other form of Internal Boundaries is what Mellody calls the "Speaking Boundary" and I call the "Containing boundary." This boundary filters the information we transmit to others, that is what we say (out loud or in writing).

The containing boundary protects family, friends, and other people from you. This part is about staying respectful and not dumping your emotional baggage onto others. That means you don't rage at others, you don't put them down or call them names, and you don't blame them for their mistakes or your own mistakes. While everyone has cracks in their boundaries and occasionally does rage, blame, or insult others, those who do so regularly have failed to develop a healthy containing boundary.

The function of a containing boundary is to help us control our emotions and master our stress. In so doing, we cherish and preserve our relationships. The containing boundary is also how you set limits on yourself. It is a way to create an internal "pause" button. By giving yourself time for your emotions to settle down, you get your prefrontal cortex—the executive functioning part of your brain—back online.

In some cases, people develop functioning containing boundaries in public, interacting in social settings with grace, diplomacy, and even charm. Yet among those they are close to, the boundaries are stripped away. In contrast to their public restraint, in private they insult their spouses, children and other family members, and blame them for everything. The reverse is more rare. It seems those who have clear containing boundaries with family members do not typically shed those boundaries when in public.

An increasingly common way in which people practice using their containing boundaries differently in different settings is the person who rants and rages online in social media, blogs, email, or other (usually anonymous) internet platforms. Such people may be kind and respectful to their friends, family and those they meet in public settings. But online, they adopt a different persona altogether. Protected by the distance of the internet, they abuse people, either indirectly—by sharing negative views of public figures, or directly—by attacking specific people online in a public forum. Their containing boundaries are stripped away by the anonymity and distance technology provides them, and in many cases, they are completely unaware of the deep pain they may have caused others. Some become surprised and ashamed when they learn that there was a real person who suffered real pain because of their actions. Others remain indifferent, having felt empowered by the opportunity to express themselves free of their containing boundary, while not having had to face the object of their rage in person. Because the internet dehumanizes communications in many respects, boundaries become more permeable.

The containing boundary also acts to filter the pain and sadness we share with others. It is one thing to tell the people close to you that you are feeling hurt or sad, but to share that same information with people you don't have a close relationship with—someone you just met, or a work colleague, for example—can leave you and others feeling uncomfortable. In my practice, and even in my daily life, I encounter people who do just that—they respond to the rhetorical greeting of "How are you?" quite literally. They answer in such detail that people flee, and then they wonder why people seem to avoid them.

Most people, however, recognize that sharing too much with others is unwise. Telling acquaintances how much money you have and make, discussing your sexual habits and relationships, or disclosing confidences that others have shared with you is generally not appropriate. Discretion is what we display when we can use boundaries. Using our boundaries is a form of respect for other people.

The minimum of loving anyone, Pia Mellody points out, is being respectful. You must express your thoughts and emotions in a diplomatic way so that others you are in a relationship with can know you, genuinely, deeply, and safely. While there are different degrees of porousness in this boundary, depending on the relationship, even among those closest to us, it is important to have a healthy containing boundary. But what happens when that boundary is weak or missing altogether?

BOUNDARYLESSNESS IN THE CONTAINING BOUNDARY

People who lack clear containing boundaries tend to share their emotions and thoughts with other people without any appropriate filtering. They dump their emotions onto anyone who will listen—and on many who try not to listen.

Like the ones who respond to "How are you?" with excessive detail, or those who rage at strangers for the slightest offense, or those who tell people they just met about how much money they do or do not make, people who lack a containing boundary always encounter social problems. As Terry Real has described, "Lacking a containing boundary is like the barf bag approach to intimacy!" This oversharing behavior is a type of offender role, and it is called "boundaryless in the containing boundary."

This unfiltered communication is a form of a "one-up" position. The speaker is showing they are better than the other person and therefore entitled to discharge whatever thoughts or feelings they have on someone, meaning the rules of communication don't apply to them. If you engage with such a person, they will still require *you* to go by the rules. For example, a person who lacks containing boundaries may wail at the injustices they've suffered, and talk and talk about their wounds and difficulties, but when someone else tries to contain them, to get them to stop talking about their woes or to see their problem in a different light, the speaker becomes furious. They feel they must be the one to control the conversation, not the other person. And should the other person try to share their own emotions or difficulties, the conversation usually comes to an abrupt halt—only one person gets to talk, and only one person is expected to listen.

WALLED INSIDE YOUR CONTAINING BOUNDARY

As you can see, it is important to have a containing boundary, but taken to extremes this boundary becomes a wall. Turning your boundary into a wall, making it so inflexible and impenetrable that you share nothing with anyone, prevents meaningful intimate exchanges with others. The person who has transformed their containing boundary into a wall does not share what is important to them and avoids expressing emotions. No one ever gets close enough to them to really know who they are—and thus, no one ever gets close enough to hurt them.

Being walled inside your containing boundary is especially common in males, who often grow up being told that emotions aren't manly, but women can erect these walls, as well. When anyone erects walls in place of boundaries, it creates deadness in a relationship, due to a lack of the emotional and intellectual intimacy that would normally characterize a healthy relationship. This deadness is something that my client, Cynthia, knows all too well.

CYNTHIA'S STORY—BOUNDARYLESS IN CONTAINING AND PROTECTIVE BOUNDARIES

Cynthia was a first generation Russian American, the youngest of two children and the only girl. She grew up bilingually, speaking Russian as her first language and English as her second.

Her father was a construction worker, heavily involved in his union. He was a hard worker, and, though he loved his family, his work and union obligations left him with little time for them. Shortly after Cynthia's birth, her mother got pregnant again, but the baby died at birth. As a result, Cynthia's mother was depressed for most of Cynthia's younger years and was unable to provide her daughter with the nurturing she needed.

When Cynthia was six years old, her mother was diagnosed with breast cancer and died a year later. Cynthia's father became the sole parent and breadwinner in the family. She was left at home with an older brother, twelve years older than Cynthia.

When she was still young, Cynthia's brother would yell at her and humiliate her. With no mother to protect her, and her father working all the time, Cynthia was subject to her brother's bullying and constant name-calling. When her father did come home from work, he seemed unable to set practical limits with his son, nor to establish consequences for the boy's behavior. As a result, the abuse continued for another five years. With little intervention on her father's part, Cynthia had to defend herself, which she learned to do exceedingly well.

By the age of twelve, Cynthia was able to yell back, scream, shame, and bully her brother in return. She could threaten and punish her brother within seconds of perceiving a threat from him. She had let in too much of his contempt and shame, and she had been so abused for so long that she just retaliated.

She had been the unprotected victim for years, and now it was her turn to be the offender. There was no concept in her family of *relational respect,* or respect for other people.

Consequently, as time passed, Cynthia found herself letting out too much of her emotional turmoil, without any containment for those emotions. This boundaryless behavior has had enormous consequences for her in her adult life. When she came to me for help, Cynthia was having difficulty sustaining relationships with friends or with potential partners. In our work, we concentrated on learning how to use a containing boundary.

A containing boundary is a boundary which contains emotions but doesn't deny them. It was important for Cynthia to acknowledge her emotions and address them over time, but it was equally important that she contain them, so that she wouldn't overwhelm—or even frighten—others with the force of her emotions.

Among the techniques I taught her, one which was particularly effective for Cynthia when she was in a heightened emotional state, was learning how to develop her containing boundary by pausing, breathing, and counting to ten before speaking. This intervention allowed her nervous system to settle and to become more respectful in her personal relationships. When she does let too much out, she is able to go back and make amends.

Cynthia was not only boundaryless in her containing boundary; she was boundaryless or porous in her protective boundary. A protective boundary protects us from the emotions, words, and actions that others direct our way. A healthy protective boundary provides filters that we use to evaluate the credibility, legitimacy, and accuracy of the information we receive. In contrast, a weak protective boundary leads us to accept everything we receive as equally valid, regardless of its merit. Cynthia had an exceptionally weak protective boundary. She took in too much and absorbed it personally without filtering it, without determining whether the message she was receiving was true or not true. Then, due to her nonexistent containing boundary, she let too much out. Her entire life became a cycle of receiving wounds and hurling back her aggressions. She took too many things personally because she didn't have a parent to protect her. She was as defenseless as a very young child. She needed an adult to step in.

In contrast to Cynthia, who was boundaryless in her containing boundary, my client Howard was walled-in, in both his containing and his protective boundaries. He suffered greatly as a result.

HOWARD'S STORY—WALLED-IN IN CONTAINING AND PROTECTIVE BOUNDARIES

Howard grew up in southern New Hampshire, born to a working-class family with traditional gender roles. His mother cared for the home and children, and his father was always working. His father was also a functioning alcoholic who did not help in raising the children. Viewing himself as the breadwinner and boss, Howard's father expected his wife to be silent and subservient to him. Feeling powerless, as an uneducated, working-class man, Howard's father viewed anger as a marker of strength, and his domination at home his only power. Consequently, any resistance from his wife or three children was met with anger, shouting, and shaming—because it challenged the only power he felt he had.

Howard was overweight as a child and was bullied throughout grade school. When he would come home after being bullied all day, he often found himself bullied by father. If his father had been drinking, he would yell at Howard about his lack of performance at school. Howard internalized his father's shaming and became depressed. By the age of twelve, he had developed walls in his Protective boundary and Containing boundary to keep himself safe and learned not to share anything personal with anyone.

Perhaps it was one vivid memory of his father's abuse that most triggered the formation of these wall-like boundaries. When Howard was twelve, his father picked him up from an event, clearly intoxicated. Howard and his mother begged his father not to drive home. His father ignored their pleas, got behind the wheel, and yelled at them for an hour as he drunkenly drove them home, gripping the steering wheel and wobbling on the road. Howard was certain his father's drunken driving would kill them all.

This type of behavior from his father created walls in Howard's psyche. Terrified and shamed by the abuse, his response was to erect rigid, impermeable boundaries so that nothing could get through the protective walls in his mind. He had no choice but to erect these walls to protect himself. His mother—perhaps terrorized and abused herself—never intervened when his father would yell. Howard continued to use these walls to protect himself during therapy, becoming reluctant to open up, to share the deep wounds he had suffered, or to relive the emotional conflicts he had endured.

Howard was in a freeze state when he began therapy with me. As a child, he couldn't fight his father because he would be punished. And he couldn't flee from his father because that would also be cause for punishment. Consequently, he froze— and remained in that state throughout his life. But as we worked together, Howard began to explore the traumatic wounds of his childhood, and he began to thaw.

Today, Howard still struggles in intimate relationships in regard to sharing himself and being vulnerable emotionally, but he is learning to take greater risks and to use new ways to protect himself in all of his personal relationships.

One technique he learned, which we will explore more fully in Chapter 12, was what Pia Mellody describes as, "having your own back." I call this technique "Standing in Your Truth." Mastering this technique made it possible for Howard to feel safe to talk about himself yet still feel that he could protect himself. "Having your own back" is an intervention that Pia Mellody proposed in order to allow clients to have a voice and to speak up without fear of being abused. As Howard practices this technique with me, he is getting much better and feels that he is being heard.

Howard is an example of being porous in the protective boundary when very young—by internalizing his father's and the bullies' abuse. Eventually he walled-in his protective and containing boundaries in his adolescence, making these boundaries impermeable. When he learned, in his adolescence, to wall off in his protective boundary with his father, he experienced being impenetrable and felt nothing.

Using a strong protective boundary is a great defense

strategy against verbal or physical abuse, because nothing anyone says can affect you. Using a strong containing boundary is a good offensive strategy, because no one knows what you're thinking. However, if these boundaries become too rigid and inflexible, they transform from boundaries to walls. When that happens, the adaptive benefits they provide become maladaptive. What once helped you now hurts you and limits your growth. By learning how to dismantle these walls and how to erect healthy boundaries in their place, you can begin to heal.

Unfortunately, healthy boundaries can be rare, partic-ularly among people who were traumatized or faced extreme adversities as children. Pia Mellody's conceptualization of these boundaries has been invaluable in my own practice, as I've worked with clients to address their boundary issues. Many of my clients have faced challenges with their psychological or internal boundaries. Many of them also struggle with physical boundary violations when they are enraged and reactive. Some of my clients' family of origin histories involve all three boundary violations in their upbringing, which has in turn chronically damaged their ability for self-protection in their adult lives. Yet even people so direly affected by trauma can learn to create healthy, functioning boundaries.

CHAPTER 5

KNOW YOUR REALITY AND DISCOVER YOUR NEEDS

A s you learned in Chapter 4, the creation of Self comes from our sensory organs—your ears, nose, eyes, tongue, and skin—bringing information to your brain. We then form thoughts, based on how we have assigned meaning to the information our brains have absorbed. These thoughts and meanings combine to form stories in our minds about why something was said or done, and about what it means to have done those things, and what that tells us about who we are and what kind of place the world around us is. All these stories and meanings combine to produce body sensations that register as an emotion—or multiple emotions. Lastly, there is a behavior that manifests. Through these steps we create our reality.

We will be talking more about how to know your reality, in

Part II, but in this chapter, we are going to explore the third and fourth Core Areas: "Knowing the Self" (meaning to be real or authentic) and "Caring for the Self" (or fostering interdependence, as I refer to it). These two Core Areas, so essential to a healthy sense of Self, are often the most neglected by parents. A child's sense of reality is created by their parents, and, when a parent fails to bring their child to life emotionally, or when they demand that their child act in a certain way, in order to make the parent comfortable, the child ends up not knowing who they are. When the child has no inherent boundaries, which must be taught by the parent or caregivers, that child tends to become chameleon-like, adapting to their environment, changing to conform to what others expect. The result is crazy-making—the child feels fractured, their mind and thoughts feel not so much their own as the mind and thoughts of many others.

Knowing the Self, the third Core Area, (which I discuss more in depth in Chapter 8), is essential to a developing human. To foster knowing the Self, fostering interdepen-dence is key. Neither self knowledge, nor independent identity and thought, come easy to the child who doesn't get what they need from their parents.

Children are inherently needy. They are born with needs—the need for nourishment, warmth, comfort, and touch. As they mature, children need guidance, emotional connection, education, and material comforts. Many of their needs become wants, such as wanting toys to play with, or cookies to eat. Providing for all a child's needs, without teaching them how to provide for themselves, creates extreme dependence.

Meanwhile, providing for all of a child's wants leads the child to never feel fulfilled, to always want and want more. Yet the parent who neglects their child's needs, and rarely, if ever, addresses their child's wants teaches their child to be needless and wantless altogether, or to desperately seek other ways to satisfy needs and wants—ways which are frequently damaging, as in the examples that follow.

THE NEEDLESS AND WANTLESS CHILD

One of the Core Areas Pia Mellody discusses is "Caring for the Self," or taking care of our own needs and wants, especially in relationship with others. Yet many traumatized children cannot do that. Mellody's concept of the "Lost Child" includes the needless and wantless child—the child who subordinates his or her needs and desires to others. Susan was just such a child. She grew up in the suburbs of New York City, the second daughter born to a privileged Jewish family. Her mother was unhappy with her marriage and spent her days of wealth and comfort in her home, smoking and drinking, while the children were neglected.

Susan's father was a journalist with a degree from an Ivy League school. He would often come home from work and get into big fights with Susan's older sister. Susan remembers watching them yell and scream at each other, a scene which so disturbed her that she became quiet and withdrawn. Her depressed mother would do nothing about the arguments, which worsened, as Susan's sister got older. Susan remem-bers saying to herself that she would never be like her sister, who would respond to the fights by taking out her anger on Susan.

Very early on, Susan became determined to be so good and perfect that she would cause no conflict or stress in the family and her father would not yell at her. She spent countless hours alone in her room. She became the quiet, accommodating child, making no demands, and caring for herself as much as she possibly could.

This pattern of being good and perfect continued not only until she left for college, but throughout her life and into her marriage and motherhood. Then, when she was in her mid-fifties, her mother died, her husband asked for a divorce, and one of her adult sons who was developmentally challenged needed her to help financially support him. Through all the stress this scenario entailed, Susan continued to strive to be perfect, picking up all the pieces from her mother's death, her husband's divorce, and her son's challenges. Eventually, however, the strain became unbearable, and she came to me for help. She had lived a life taking care of others, but finally, she realized, she needed to take care of herself.

Susan's quest for perfection was rooted in a childhood fear of conflict that would arise if she made mistakes or crossed her father. As a result, she grew up to demand so much perfection of herself that she could never live up to her own standards. She had become needless and wantless. A child who is needless and wantless will not be able to figure out what they need or want, as no one has ever asked them to discuss their desires. Such people just respond to whatever demands are made of them. In Susan's case, by focusing on perfection and control, she matured beyond her years. As she grew older, by focusing on the needs of others, she could keep her own needs at bay.

While that approach was adaptive during her childhood, because it did help her to avoid conflict and to excel academically, by the time she reached adulthood, those same habits became maladaptive, because they were unsustainable. Susan could only do so much to try to tackle every crisis, and as much as she was capable of doing, all that doing eventually wore her down.

Another way that children adapt is by accepting parental responsibilities, such as caring for younger siblings, preparing meals, cleaning the home, even caring for the parents, so that the child's home life remains as normal as possible. Being needless and wantless is a reality that may never have even crossed a growing child's mind, due to parental neglect. Instead, like Susan, such people, as they grow, take pride in their maturity and take equal pride in their success at pulling themselves up "by their bootstraps." But such self-reliance comes at the cost of a childhood, and, later, at the price of sacrificing or losing their own emotions and needs.

In the case of Tom (in Chapter 3) who was emotionally and physically neglected, but was provided with material comforts, he responded with rebellion. Tom would quite literally do anything he could to get attention. In the opposite example, we see what happens when a neglected child does just the opposite: suppresses their needs altogether and never asks for attention—finally reaching the point where they no longer know how to.

THE ANTI-DEPENDENT CHILD

Kathy grew up in West Virginia. She was two years old when her mother, a grocery store cashier, divorced her father, who worked as a baker. Kathy's father remarried when Kathy was four, and, a year later, Kathy's mother remarried. Kathy was shuttled back and forth between her mother and father as each parent focused on the new families they were forming.

Her father's new family included two stepsons, about ten years older than Kathy. One of the stepsons began sexually abusing Kathy. Like many abused children, she feared telling anyone. The abuse did not stop as Kathy grew older, but instead, it continued for many years.

Kathy's mother, unhappy in her new marriage, became depressed and struggled financially. Afraid that if she told her about the abuse, Kathy would only add to her mother's stress, she suffered alone, telling no one what was happening. When she was eleven, however, she swallowed a bottle of aspirin in a desperate cry for help, ending up in the hospital. Despite this alarming act, her mother never visited her in the hospital nor talked to her about what was happening.

After she was discharged from the hospital, Kathy realized that her parents were not there for her. She became anti-dependent in her life, attempting to rely on herself alone. But the stress of the sexual abuse, which had finally ended, culminated when she was sixteen, and she told her mother and stepfather about what her stepbrother had done to her. Unfortunately, they didn't believe her, and they told her that even if it did happen, Kathy had no need to worry since it was no longer happening. Kathy retreated further into her world of self-sufficiency and silence.

When Kathy finished high school, she moved out, and found a job, presenting as a very competent, mature young woman, who eventually married and had children. Yet Kathy had no voice in her marriage, and would go about taking care of herself, never asking others for what she needed. She was a responsible mother and wife for years before she realized that she had to ask others to help with her needs and wants.

By the time she came to me, Kathy felt dissatisfied with her marriage; she had difficulty articulating her needs; and she wanted to leave her husband to create a new life for herself. After our work together, Kathy came to recognize her needs and she found her voice. She is now assertively working on her marriage of 20 years, and she is currently earning her graduate degree in counseling psychology.

Kathy's story is all too common. The parents she needed as a child were unavailable and their neglect not only made it possible for her older stepbrother to sexually abuse her, the abuse was compounded by Kathy's parents' indifference about it once Kathy did speak up. When children learn that their cries for help are met with silence—by the parents who are supposed to protect them—they are unlikely to rebel, as opposed to what Tom did. Tom had learned that his rebellion got him attention. Kathy had learned that calling for help, through rebellion, got her none. Like so many children whose cries for help go unheeded, she had learned to stop expecting any help at all. Children like Kathy grow up before they are ready.

In contrast to Susan, who so feared the consequences of imperfection that she exhausted herself striving to do everything and be everything, or Kathy, who was so neglected that she learned to take care of what she needed alone, some children respond to their dysfunctional families by learning to take no risks at all. In families that don't allow for mistakes, children may react by learning never to try anything new or difficult.

THE OVERLY DEPENDENT CHILD

When children are too dependent, they convince others—if not themselves—that they cannot do ordinary things and that they need help to do almost everything. They manipulate others into doing for them. They use strategies such as doing a poor job with household chores so that a parent will intervene and do all the chores or asking for help with homework in an effort to get someone else to write down all the answers in the guise of "helping." The dependent child shows little interest in learning to master these tasks themselves, and, as they grow older, they seek partners who will take on a parental role and who will assume the major—and often the minor—responsibilities of life.

Peggy grew up in a small Midwestern town, the only child of parents who married young to escape their own painful histories. Peggy's dad was a foreman in a factory that created products forged in fire. This made the factory unbearably hot, even in the dead of winter. Peggy's father would come home from work exhausted and irritable. Her mom worked as a clerk at the local grocery store. Peggy stated that although her parents would fight often, it was the raw disappointment in their shared life that stood out for Peggy when she reflected on where she has come from.

Peggy's father came from an angry alcoholic home where he learned that real men work and survive by finishing their day having "another cold one." Her mother grew up in a large family and was often neglected by a preoccupied dad and depressed mom.

As a result of her parents' own traumatic childhoods, Peggy found herself being parented by a disinterested alcoholic father and a mother who compensated for her childhood (and marital) neglect by making sure that her daughter got the love and attention that she never received.

As Peggy grew up, she and her mother were each other's best friends, and they would shop, cook, clean, and spend all their time together. Peggy recalls that if she struggled in any area of her life, her mom would handle it for her. Whether it was a problem at school, a homework assignment that she couldn't quite figure out, a conflict with friends or her father, her mom would quickly step in and take over. Peggy now understands that her mother fostered a "learned helpless-ness" that led Peggy to believe that if she couldn't do something, her mom would always save the day. By the time she started college and was separated from her mother—for the first time, Peggy felt overwhelmed with fear that she couldn't handle things on her own. After one difficult semester, in which she spent countless hours in tears on the phone with her mom, Peggy decided to move home and attend a nearby community college.

It was there she met a handsome young man who was strong and confident. She fell in love, and, a year later, found herself married and moving away from her mother. The challenge of this transition was great, and it wasn't long before she became overly dependent on her husband, just as she had been with her mother.

Unfortunately, her husband manipulated her dependence, telling her what to think, what to say, and what to do. He came from a deeply religious background. He had been raised to believe that men are the authorities in the home and are not to be challenged. As a result, Peggy struggled through her marriage, as her husband became increasingly emotionally abusive—not only toward her, but toward their two children, as well.

Once Peggy entered therapy, she began to explore her false belief that she was incapable of making her own decisions. She learned that she had the capacity to stand on her own, even when it was difficult, because there is growth in struggle. As she grew more confident in her ability to make decisions, she made the decision to divorce her husband. Her confidence has grown since her divorce, and Peggy is now enjoying a more independent life, one which may be challenging at times but is ultimately rewarding and joyful.

RAISING OVERLY-DEPENDENT CHILDREN

William has been my client for a few years. He is a wealthy, successful man with two sons. While he was married to his first wife, he was the traditional breadwinner and his wife was a stay-at-home mom who did most of the child-rearing and parenting. William played a subservient role in the marriage and pretty much did what his wife said, supporting her in most things while the boys were growing up.

Due to their parents' wealth, the boys received the best education, and they lived in a gorgeous home in a great neighborhood. Most of their needs were well exceeded when it came to food, shelter, clothing, cars, medical care, education, and recreation.

What was missing from William was a commitment to teaching his sons how to create friends, foster relationships, earn money, save money, and provide for their own needs and wants as they matured. Instead, William enabled his children by giving them everything they wanted, rather than providing guidance or teaching them how to provide for themselves or setting reasonable and reassuring limits they could learn to internalize.

William had created overly dependent children who never learned to meet their own needs or to launch their own lives. Consequently, even after his children had grown, they were still dependent on him for virtually everything in their lives, which was becoming so stressful for William that he felt overwhelmed and increasingly resentful of the sons he loved.

Through our therapy, William realized the consequences of his parenting style, and he realized that giving so much had become a burden for him—as well as a handicap for his sons. Over time, William has come to see how he has enabled his sons in their over-dependency. Today, he is successfully setting firm limits on supporting his grown children financially, buying them gifts, or providing them with vacations.

As these stories demonstrate, children are born with innate needs and natural limitations. If a child's needs are not met, or they are punished for their limitations, they will adapt behaviors and thought patterns that become maladaptive as the child grows into adulthood. But, because a child has practiced these adaptive responses and repeated them over many years, their brain has learned to respond to new stimuli through this same series of patterned behaviors. The good news is, patterns can be altered and changed.

DEPENDENCE AND PERFECTION IN YOUR OWN LIFE

Did you recognize yourself in any of these stories? Almost every survivor of family of origin trauma has had their sense of independence and dependence affected by their childhood experiences. Think about how you relate to your spouse or other family members, or even your coworkers and friends. Do you rely on them to do things you can do perfectly well yourself, if only you would try? Or do you have to do everything yourself, afraid that if someone else does it, you will be dependent on them? Of course, a certain amount of independence is healthy— being able to cook your own food, support yourself financially, and change a tire if your car breaks down demonstrates responsibility and maturity. You may rely on others to do these things for you but having the skills to do them yourself if necessary is a healthy sign of independence. Some dependence, or asking others for help, is also healthy. What I'm talking about here are dysfunctional patterns of dependence or independence that manifest in multiple areas of your life, that lead you to become chronically dependent, needless, or wantless, or conversely anti-dependent in your relationships.

Similarly, if you are a perfectionist who never finishes things because each thing must be perfect, you may find yourself "getting by" on little sleep, not trusting others to do anything as well as you. You may end up doing everything yourself and then resenting it. If so, you probably live with chronic anxiety over what might happen if, one day, you should fall short of perfection. And you may believe others ought to live up to your high standards, thus continually judging them harshly, or feeling compelled to let them know they fall short.

Yet there is no such thing as perfection in our lives. We are human, and we need to embrace our humanity. Doing so keeps us from condemning others—and keeps us having compassion for ourselves. In other words, your quest for perfection has produced some profoundly imperfect con-sequences in your life!

If these scenarios resonate with you, if you've identified ways that you are chronically dependent, needless-wantless, or anti-dependent, or overly concerned with presenting a pleasing image to the world, then you will benefit from giving some thought to your childhood. Were you punished or ignored for making mistakes? Were you applauded and idolized no matter what you did or did not do? In what ways were you forced to grow up before you were ready? In what ways were you forced to remain a child long after you had matured?

At this point, you don't need to do anything more than start thinking about these patterns and memories. In Part II, we will delve into the techniques for addressing these legacies of childhood trauma, but for now, just reflect, and read on. In the next chapter, we'll consider what happens when the patterns look like no patterns at all. Sometimes behaviors are taken to extremes. We'll explore these extremes and how they manifest in adulthood.

CHAPTER 6

OPERATING IN THE EXTREMES

C hildhood is marked by a wondrous imagination and playfulness that leads children to be naturally spontaneous. When children experience their spontaneity, they are experiencing their essence. In following his or her spontaneity, the child is having an experience of themselves without feeling self-conscious or feeling shame. Sadly, however, if a child is severely traumatized in the first years of life, they will not be able to experience this spontaneity—their own spiritual essence. That is why Pia Mellody's fifth Core Area, learning to moderate or control ourselves, especially in relationships with others, is so important.

If the natural spontaneity we experience as children was quashed or uncontrolled, we will face difficulties in our adult relationships. Pia Mellody has helped me to understand the role spontaneity plays in trauma—and in healing. Mellody suggests that children express and experience their "real" self in spontaneity, which includes a profound sense of their joy in life. In a functional parenting system, the parents teach the child appropriate behavior and appropriate timing for spontaneous experiences. But if the parents don't nurture and prize this spontaneity, and instead attack the child's behavior as being "chaotic" or "immature," the child becomes emotionally numb or overly mature. If a child's spontaneity is shut down too much, when they are adults, they will withhold their energy in their intimate relationships, which will have a deadening effect on themselves and others.

In contrast, Mellody suggests, if children are raised without any limits to their spontaneity, they will learn to live in a state of chaos. As adults, she suggests, they will be drawn to relationships that lack control. They will feel free and spontaneous initially, which will excite them, but over time these relationships will become chaotic. This pattern can overwhelm their partners, and the relationship will have a chaotic rollercoaster effect.

Functional systems can be created by learning how to establish and use boundaries to contain this spontaneity, but not to stifle it. Respect for a child's development comes by appropriately controlling spontaneity while allowing exper-iences and feelings to be authentic. In all too many cases, however, the child never learns these boundaries, and their spontaneity is not properly nurtured. My client, Brenda, grew up in such a boundaryless and chaotic household.

CHAOTIC SPONTANEITY

Brenda was the third child in a family of Russian Jewish immigrants. Her father was a businessman, and her mother was a teacher. When Brenda was very young, her mother was in college and her father was always working. Brenda was primarily left in the care of a nanny who essentially parented her. Still, Brenda was a happy child. She was inquisitive and playful and loved to dance, sing, and draw. She lived a life of creativity.

When she was seven years old, however, Brenda's father was in a car accident and was paralyzed below the waist. After this incident, her father became angry and increasingly focused on himself. He was frustrated with being in a wheelchair, and he became preoccupied with his pain and misery. Brenda's mother was sad and overwhelmed, caring for her three children and disabled husband, so Brenda tried to help her mother by doing everything she could to make her father happy. Ultimately, however, Brenda felt helpless to do so; her father was stuck in a state of hopelessness and despair, and her mother was stuck in her own state of unhappiness.

As the years went on, Brenda's parents were so pre-occupied with their own problems that they were unavailable for Brenda's needs. Throughout her adolescence, Brenda's mother let her do whatever she wanted to do. At the age of thirteen, she was smoking marijuana openly at home and having boyfriends stay overnight in her bedroom. Her mother tolerated anything Brenda did, while her father remained wrapped up in his world, paralyzed not just physically, but psychologically.

Because there were no limits set for her at home, as Brenda

grew older, she had no concept of setting limits in her own life or relationships. Everything in her life was spontaneous—her feelings, her actions, her words, and her decisions. Having been creative as a child, she matured with this creativity partnering a freedom to do anything at all, without restraint or containment. Unfortunately, that combi-nation did not develop her creativity, but, instead, effectively imprisoned her life.

Brenda tells me today that she is afraid of relationships because the ones she has "are very intense relationships and I lose my sense of Self." Brenda lacks containment in her relationships—she cannot contain her emotions or set limits with the people in her life. Today, she struggles with moderation in her relationships, her creative life, her diet, and mostly her emotions, but she is finding greater strength and resilience as she confronts the patterns of her childhood and the ways in which she is replicating these patterns into adulthood.

CONTROLLED SPONTANEITY

In contrast to Brenda's childhood of 'anything goes,' Sally, who grew up in a traditional Chinese family in a large city in the Midwest, learned to fear any display of her spontaneous Self. Her father was a cook in their family-owned restaurant, and her mother was the waitress and bookkeeper. Sally herself helped out in the restaurant. Her early beginnings were hard because her parents had an arranged marriage and Sally saw how unhappy her mother was in a marriage to a considerably older man.

Her mother was a perfectionist who Sally recalls as, not only unhappy, but cold, critical, and resentful. Sally's father was passive and withdrawn. Sally has few memories of her father being loving to her. At a very early age, Sally learned to shut down her spontaneity, because it was not something her mother would approve. Sally rarely experienced joy or happiness, and mostly knew only fear and dread. On top of it all, as the child of immigrants, whose first language was Chinese, Sally made no friends as she grew up, feeling like an outsider in her community and school. To compensate, and to please her parents who expected her to succeed, she shut down spontaneity entirely and applied herself to excelling in her studies.

When Sally was fifteen years old, her father died. Her mother then left Sally and Sally's brother to marry another man. Left all alone with her brother, Sally tried to take care of herself and to finish school. Her hard work paid off, and Sally received a significant scholarship to an Ivy League college. Yet instead of feeling joy at the opportunity, she remained shut down and depressed, feeling dead inside. When she got to college, Sally felt under such pressure to excel and to fit in that she became suicidal.

Fortunately, that was when Sally sought help and began the hard job of exploring her feelings. She had been so over-controlled by her mother, that she became closed down emotionally and was rigid in every aspect of her life. Having joy and happiness was not in her life experience. Now married and a mother herself, Sally still struggles with being too controlling and shut down, especially when it comes to her children. She is learning, however, to become more flexible, forgiving, and spontaneous. She struggles not to replicate her mother's parenting style.

SETTING THE THERMOSTAT

What Brenda and Sally have in common is that they both were living in the extremes. For Brenda, her spontaneity had never been contained, so she learned to live on the extreme edge of her impulses. Her emotions, her actions, and her relationships were always high drama. Her life provided her great excitement, entertainment, and intensity, but also left her with extreme feelings of disappointment, unhappiness, and anger. For Sally, who had learned to live in the polar opposite extreme, shutting down her spontaneity stifled all her impulses. Her emotions were so deeply buried that she was often unaware of them at all. Her actions were carefully strategized, and her relationships were so void of emotional depth and intimacy that she avoided them altogether. She felt so disconnected that she literally considered ending her life—because it was a life that had no 'life' to it—no freedom, no expression, no Self.

Pia Mellody's call for moderation of the Self is especially needed here—what I describe as "setting the thermostat" to help establish and control the right degree of moderation. Brenda and Sally needed moderation in their spontaneity. One of the most common issues I see my clients facing is how hard it is for them to be balanced and moderate in their lives. Many of them try repeatedly to solve relationship problems but become handicapped in their efforts because they are living in the extremes. In other words, they don't know where the middle or balanced position is—nor how to get and remain there.

Living in the extremes, we are either totally involved with every detail of our lives and relationships, or we are totally detached. Neither position enables us to assess our problems effectively, much less to resolve them. The result can be that we become, either so effervescently happy that we avoid any possibility of experiencing a negative emotion, or so miserable we cannot recognize the joyous facets of life right before us. My clients living in extremes either take a baseball bat to a broken TV, or they do nothing at all to fix it. They either have a family drama over what their teenager is wearing or what their spouse served them for dinner, or they sit around doing nothing while the kids are using drugs. The parents are drinking to the bottom of every bottle, and the bank account is so 'in the red' that bankruptcy looms around the corner.

When I see these clients, I think of my metaphor of the busted thermostat that needs to be recalibrated for the family to live in comfort. But recalibration of the Self is no small task. We can't just call someone in for service, write a check and call it fixed. It's something we have to work on, over time, and with attention.

Children learn how to cope with trauma by watching how their parents or caregivers live in these extreme patterns of living. Struggles of living in the extremes manifest in four different areas: our bodies, our thinking or cognition, our emotions, and our behaviors. Each area comprises a fundamental part of our lived reality and together, they determine how we give meaning to what we experience.

How might these extremes be experienced in your own life? Observe your daily habits, how you express yourself verbally, gesturally, and symbolically; how you behave in social interactions; and how you respond to problems and conflicts.

Do you dress in the extreme, by wearing loud colors and styles that can't be missed when you walk down the street? Or do you dress in such muted colors and such conservative styles that no one should notice you at all?

Do you modify your body with extreme piercings and tattoos, or do you avoid any adornment at all beyond a simple watch or studded earrings no one is likely to see?

How do you interpret the world you live in? Do you see all problems and solutions in black and white? Is there only one right way and one wrong way, and is your own way always the right one?

Do you allow for any ambiguity or moral relativity, knowing it is a complex world we live in? Do you allow for others who share your worldview to differ in some respects, or do you see any mark of difference or ideological im-perfection as unacceptable and a mark of betrayal?

How do you respond to conflict? Is the first sign of conflict an indication that the relationship is over? Does a conflict at work mean you're ready to engage in battle? Or do you go out of your way to avoid any conflict at all, not seeing it, not hearing it, not responding to it, and erasing any possibility of facing it by eliminating the source—or running from it altogether?

How do you approach relationships? Do you see people as either good or bad, and sort them *in* or *out* of your lives accordingly? Do you trust everyone? Or no one at all? If so, how does that square with what you allow for yourself? Do you let yourself have "good" qualities and "bad" qualities, recognizing that you are complex, multifaceted, and wondrously human? Do you then deny others these same complexities and contradictions?

How do you view yourself? Do you see yourself as a good person, and do you reject any suggestion you might have bad qualities? Or do you see yourself as worthless, and therefore, do you reject any suggestion that you might be otherwise? And no matter how hard you try to acknowledge your goodness, do you inevitably fall back to your baseline of viewing yourself as worthless and unlikely to amount to anything at all?

If you recognize yourself in these questions, you are feeling your emotions, and perceiving your world and your Self, in the extreme. And if that's the case, these extremes are interfering with your life in a multiplicity of ways. Here are a few of the ways your emotions are adversely affecting your life.

HOW THE EXTREMES MANIFEST IN THE BODY

- Exercising for hours every day, or never exercising at all
- Eating only healthy, organic foods, or eating mainly high-fat, sugary, salty junk foods
- Eating hardly any food, or eating constantly
- Wearing baggy clothing to hide your body, or overexposing your body by wearing too little or too tight clothing
- Wearing loud and flashy styles that can be seen from across a crowded room, or wearing such conservative,

standard colors that no one will notice if you're standing right in front of them

- Spending countless hours (and money) grooming yourself in the mirror several times a day, or not paying any attention at all to what you look like
- Bathing scrupulously and keeping every inch of your body meticulously clean, or rarely showering or cleaning your body at all
- Being preoccupied with every bodily sensation, or being completely unaware of any sensations in your body
- Going to the doctor for every little ache and pain, or never going to see a doctor—even when there's a problem that just keeps getting worse

HOW THE EXTREMES MANIFEST IN OUR THINKING

- Planning and organizing every detail of your working day and week and making sure you never deviate from the plan—no matter what comes up, or not planning, not organizing anything—just going with the flow
- Trying to figure out what everyone around you is doing or thinking just in case it affects you in some minor way, or never considering what others are doing or thinking unless it affects you in some major way
- Always talking and never listening, or always listening but never taking your turn to talk
- Sharing everything about your life with others down to the most minute detail, or never sharing anything about your life—not even major life events
- Viewing everything as black and white, good or bad, us or them, and allowing for no ambiguity, complexity, contradiction or moral imperfection
- Viewing the past, present, or future as utopian and perfect, or viewing it as so bleak and despairing that not even winning the lottery could change your mood for long

HOW THE EXTREMES MANIFEST THROUGH EMOTIONS

- Letting every emotion overwhelm you and letting your feelings be known to one and all, or feeling and expressing no emotion at all
- Experiencing only adventure, seeking fun and romance

constantly, or experiencing only sadness, loneliness, anger, or fear

- Feeling a single emotion overpower all other emotions, such as constantly feeling angry and resentful; or avoiding a certain emotion at all costs, such as never letting yourself feel anger or resentment
- Feeling love so intensely that you'd rather die than live without it, or feeling no love at all for anyone or anything

HOW THE EXTREMES MANIFEST IN BEHAVIORS

- Constantly cleaning and organizing your home, or living in filth and cascading clutter
- Always arriving exactly on time—or early, or being chronically late
- Planning everything you do in your spare time and being inflexible or upset if something unexpected arises, or never planning anything and being spontaneous in everything—from what you eat, to when and where you go, to how you have fun
- Needing to control all social situations and relation-ships, or never taking control and letting others make all the decisions

I'm sure that whatever your traits and tendencies, you've noticed yourself in at least some of these examples. We all have them, but people who suffered trauma as a child typically have a number of these traits and can spot their patterns right off the bat. Traumatized children learn these traits from their parents or caregivers. In families where there was a lot of screaming and few rules—or what rules that did exist were constantly broken, where continual dramas escalated, the children are likely to grow up to live in the extremes. Some will live in the extreme of spontaneity. Others will tend in the opposite direction. Some, like Susan (in Chapter 5) respond to such chaotic environments by shutting down and seeking extreme control in their lives.

Others, who were traumatized in families where emotions and behaviors were rigidly controlled, are likely to live on the extreme of suppressing their emotions and behaviors—unless, like Tom, they learn to rebel at such control. In short, we tend to replicate our parental patterns, *or* we tend to rebel by adopting the opposite extreme.

The bottom line is that parents or caregivers who live in the extremes produce children who live in the extremes, and parents or caregivers who live in balance, moderating their emotional expressions and behaviors, produce children whose emotions and behaviors are in balance.

Chances are, if you're reading this book, your parents, and you, have been living in the extremes. The origins of why this might have happened to you come from developmental trauma. Either you were exposed to traumatic abuse or traumatic neglect, and, in the process, you learned to either tightly contain your spontaneity, or you never learned to contain it. In a family system where you were required to contain your spontaneity or authentic Self too much because you had to take care of a parent or parents, or had to avoid conflict with your parents at all costs, you were required to assume a heroic role. You needed to be hyper-responsible. There was no room for spontaneity because spontaneity was too risky. The shutdown of your spontaneity—your innate Self—over time can show up later in life as an internal deadness and sense of feeling drained. The result can also leave you feeling so fearful of that deadness that you constantly seek excitement or intensity in every aspect of your life—you seek risk-taking behaviors and adventures in order to bring your Self "back to life."

To contain ourselves appropriately, as Pia Mellody cautions, we need to practice boundaries with others. When we use walls in relationship to others, it shuts down our spontaneity too much, and we withhold our energy, as a result, our relationships inevitably have a deadening effect—they don't feel authentic, we don't value them, we may even resent them.

When we are intimate without boundaries, we can feel free and spontaneous—but we also need to learn who we can and should trust, and with whom we should not be free and spontaneous in our daily lives. For those who grew up without any boundaries, allowed to have free rein in their spontaneity, failing to establish boundaries in certain relationships—such as work colleagues, neighbors, and others for whom sharing everything is not a good idea, we may well find ourselves in one conflict after another.

As Pia Mellody's teachings emphasize, all children need to be taught how they should and should not act in regard to their emotional spontaneity in order to sustain a moderate and balanced emotional life in adulthood, one that fosters healthy and rewarding relationships. That means that each child needs to be taught boundaries, and if they are not taught these boundaries in childhood, they face an even greater challenge in adulthood, as they reconstruct their personal boundary system. Fortunately, reconstructing your own safe personal boundaries is a feat that can be done.

Part II

The Primary Core Practices

CHAPTER 7

GETTING STARTED ON YOUR OWN JOURNEY

Remember the central narrative of Dorothy and *The Wizard of Oz* I presented at the start of this book. Well, you've now made it across the poppy fields, so to speak, in your own journey to recovery. You've learned about some of the mistakes that parents make in failing to provide their children with the most basic emotional or material needs. You've learned how parents can fail to instill in their children appropriate boundaries. And you've seen how mistakes in parenting can damage children's ability to form healthy self-esteem. You've also learned how these family dynamics result in lasting impacts on the children, impacts that persist well into adulthood.

No doubt, you have recognized yourself in some of these stories, and have had to face some tough truths about some of the things that happened to you throughout your childhood. You may realize that, like many others, you weren't always valued, protected, or validated. You didn't always have your needs met, or you weren't taught moderation. That realization can be alarming. Or you may have realized that you were valued and loved, and although most of your needs were met, there were times when they weren't—because your parents were suffering from their own wounds. Maybe, as a result, they couldn't be there for you when you most needed it.

Take a moment to think about how these wounded places from your childhood manifest in your life today? Do they feel open and gaping, in need of immediate attention? Or do they feel buried, hidden beneath the surface, but throbbing, nonetheless? How do you go about healing these areas of trauma?

In Part II, we shift from discussing these traumas, to discussing how to heal, drawing largely from the work of Pia Mellody's Five Core Areas, which I've revised here as the Five Core Practices. In Chapter 7, I'll show you how to use the first two Core Practices—"Loving the Self" and "Protecting the Self"—for healing in your everyday life. You'll find that using these practices will give you a powerful tool to help alleviate the pain you've suffered since childhood. You've already been introduced to Mellody's Five Core Areas (in the Introduction and in Chapter 1, where I discussed childhood woundings). Let's take a closer look at the Five Core Areas as they relate to the well-being of a child.

To understand what comprises a healthy functional childhood, we must first look at the nature of a child. All children are by nature needy—they have essential needs, beyond the basic human needs of food, clothing, and shelter, in order to grow into healthy, functional adults. These needs are best understood as the Five Core Areas of Wellbeing, which together constitute a measure of health for any child growing up today.

THE FIVE CORE AREAS OF WELLBEING

1. <u>All children need **to be valued.**</u>
   When children are not valued, they become depressed, and they feel worthless. As they grow into adulthood, they will internalize this depression and sense of worthlessness as their core identity.

2. <u>All children need **to be protected.**</u>
   When children are not protected, they will be hurt, as well as damaged, emotionally and physically. The lingering effects of this damage persist into adulthood and are manifest as a sense of vulnerability and/or a mask of toughness.

3. <u>All children need **to be validated emotionally.**</u>
   When children do not have their emotions acknowledged and respected, they will struggle with understanding themselves. As they mature, they will learn to quash certain emotions, and overexpress others.

4. <u>All children need **to have basic human needs met.**</u>
   When children do not have their basic needs met, they

will struggle to survive. By identifying the needs that were not met in childhood, the adult learns that certain behavioral patterns are an effort to fulfill these needs.

5. <u>All children need **to moderately express feelings and behaviors**</u>.

   All children must learn how to express themselves, but to do so in moderation, neither totally concealing nor totally revealing everything they feel and think. It is critical that children be allowed to express themselves emotionally and to sometimes be spontaneous, But, if they are not taught healthy containment, or are not taught control of their spontaneity or emotions, children grow up to either be overly controlled or to be out of control.

The Five Core Areas of Wellbeing are the basis for understanding what children need, and for seeing how the maladaptive patterns that we exhibit as adults relate back to a lack of one or more core needs being met. The maladaptive patterns become reinforced by the life stories we tell ourselves, and stories we project onto the outside world, as we grow. To rethink such patterns, I recommend practicing Compassionate Self-Awareness or Mindfulness, focusing in on the first two Core Areas, which are "Loving the Self" and "Protecting the Self."

As you gain awareness in these areas, you will gradually shift your self-perception. You will begin to draw on healthy boundaries almost automatically. Practicing Compassionate

Self-Awareness is essential, because, before you are ready to move on to the three other Core Practices, you will need to spend some time on the foundational underpinnings of repairing and restoring the damaged Self. We start with "Loving the Self," because—after all you've been through—you deserve this love, and only you can give it.

CORE PRACTICE #1: LOVING THE SELF

Many people tend to think self-esteem is something that you attain by being loved and admired by others, by having great wealth or beauty, or by achieving great success. Such good fortunes, some believe, inevitably lead to positive self-esteem. Conversely, lacking good fortune, the same logic presumes, leads to low self-esteem. But here's the thing—that's not where self-esteem comes from. Self-esteem is an inside job—it comes from work you've done internally. Self-esteem, according to Pia Mellody, is *the ability to hold yourself in warm, positive regard _despite_ your imperfections and humanity.*

This concept of Loving the Self, or Self-esteem, is at the heart of all the other practices you will be learning to master. We all need some degree of Loving the Self to start our healing—no matter what our trauma. Indeed, the greater the trauma, the more likely it is that we will turn our pain against ourselves, so the more important it is to release that pain by Loving the Self.

Healthy self-esteem is an internal sense of "I am enough, and I matter." It is a sense of abundance, or believing "I am enough, just as I am." It is connection to the world and to others, spiritual in nature. It is recognizing, "I matter, regardless of my past."

Having healthy self-esteem means that you embrace the belief that your essential worth is no better, and no worse, than anyone else's. Just as you learned that children are innately precious and have value, here you will learn that adults have essential worth too. Your worth is not something that must be earned; it is a given, an innate quality you possess just by being. It can't be decreased or increased; it just is.

As you learn to acknowledge your inherent worth, you will come to know that your gifts don't make you better than others, just as your weaknesses don't make you less worthy than others. Your gifts and your weaknesses just define your humanity—your humanness.

Years ago, the concept of self-esteem, in traditional therapeutic interventions with people who were depressed and feeling constantly ashamed, was thought of as a way to bring them up from shame to feeling better about themselves. Many methods were based on cognitions that were illogical and helped them reason their way to feeling better. But in most cases, these approaches failed to work, because they resulted in temporary fixes. The wounds were not addressed, so people's self-esteem inevitably still suffered.

In contrast, the other polarity of self-esteem is a feeling of grandiosity or believing oneself to be better than others. This inflated perspective was seldom explored, or it was seen as a problem in the therapeutic environment only. Yet grandiosity in relationships is offensive and judgmental. Living in the extreme of grandiosity creates a "one-up" attitude and a feeling of being '"above the law" as if the rules don't apply to you, but to others.

If you have developed a sense of Self that is grandiose, you are living under an illusion every bit as damaging as low self-esteem or inadequacy. As painful as it may be, you must view your sense of Self honestly, so that you become aware of the subconscious foundation on which you've built your life. This awareness of a human, imperfect yet worthy Self is critical to understanding that living in either extreme polarity is dysfunctional. Let's take a look at the different faces of self-esteem, so that as you begin the first technique, you'll have insight into your own self-perception, and will have a strong foundation to build on.

DIFFICULTY RECOGNIZING HEALTHY SELF-ESTEEM

Unhealthy self-esteem shows up as carried shame or grandiosity; the core energy of which is contempt. Shame is feeling inherently 'less than' other people or putting the Self in a "one-down" position. When feeling shame, you feel diminished. With carried shame, which I will explain later, in Chapter 11, the beam of contempt is turned inward toward the Self. In contrast, grandiosity is feeling better than others or putting the Self in a "one-up" position. Grandiosity feels uncomfortable to others, but seductive to the grandiose individual. It often shows up as contempt for others or offensive behaviors toward others, as well as irresponsible behaviors in relationships with others. With grandiosity, the beam of contempt is turned out toward others.

Another form of grandiosity is perfectionism. Perfectionists may not realize it, but, by demanding perfection of themselves, they judge others for never being as perfect as the ideal the perfectionist carries constantly in mind. What the perfectionist is essentially communicating to others is, "I know the right way to do this, and you don't." Since they are working extremely hard to be perfect, they remain distant from any feelings of their own imperfections.

Imperfection, in the perfectionist's view, is failure. If they fail to achieve perfection, they view themselves as failures. According to that logic, if others fail to achieve perfection, they are failures. Perfectionism allows the wounded person to distance themselves from their emotions and to not experience their own shame—which they would feel if their imperfections were exposed.

Instead, perfectionists constantly stay in the "one-up" position—until they fail to achieve perfection, at which time they tumble far, far down to a state of worthlessness. In other words, the perfectionist can never truly face their own true Self as long as they pursue perfection, because as the saying goes, no one is perfect. We are all human, and as such, we are inherently imperfect.

Among the many ways we manifest our self-esteem, there are three ways that stand out as the most common, and these are performance-based, attribute-based, and other-based. Here's how each type is expressed:

PERFORMANCE-BASED SELF-ESTEEM

Performance-based self-esteem is exactly what it says— what we do determines our value. Someone with performance-based self-esteem believes, "I have worth because of what I do." Whether a doctor, a schoolteacher, a homemaker, or an artist, the person with performance-based self-esteem ties their identity and worth to feeling proud of their accomplishments and successes. Of course, it is perfectly healthy to feel good about accomplishments, and to celebrate your gifts—you should indeed be proud.

The problem is, performance-based self-esteem only lasts as long as you are performing. If you lose your job, retire, or are unable to continue in your profession, you could fall hard into the depths of depression. That is why performance-based self-esteem is so fragile—it is dependent on continued success no matter what else happens. Performance doesn't have to change your essential sense of worth, however. You truly have value, no matter what you do for a living or what you achieve in your life. The challenge is to own that value, to incorporate it into your essential sense of Self.

ATTRIBUTE-BASED SELF-ESTEEM

Attribute-based self-esteem may exist alongside performance-based self-esteem. It is based on what you *have* materially, whether physical attributes or wealth and possessions, rather than what you do. Attributes can also include your children and their successes, your spouse or other relationships, your social status, or your family history, such as being born into a well-known wealthy family. The person with attribute-based self-esteem thinks, "I have worth because of what I have."

In fact, our culture is largely attribute based. We are encouraged to value beauty and to invest a great deal of money to acquire and maintain it. Similarly, we are encouraged to have beautiful cars and spacious homes and to belong to desirable social circles, prestigious clubs, and a leisure class. We have been manipulated into thinking that, if we have these things, we have value, whereas, if we don't have these things, we lack value. This view can be so ingrained in our thinking that we go into great debt to look younger than we are and to live beyond our means. When we embrace this view, no matter how many things we accumulate, we never have quite enough—there is always something bigger, pricier, flashier, that we strive to acquire in order to maintain our self-esteem.

Unfortunately, such attributes, like performance, only last as long as you have them; the danger comes when you lose them—and we do lose many of them. The beautiful face will grow old, the perfect body will change shape with age, great jobs can become layoffs, the expensive car wears out, and even social status can diminish over time.

When we begin to lose our attributes, we scramble to replace them with new attributes—plastic surgery, new things, anything to bring attention to ourselves. Sadly, a never-ending cycle of acquisition and replacement never brings true peace or self-validation, but always brings momentary highs, followed by everlasting, recurrent lows.

OTHER-BASED SELF-ESTEEM

One of the most deceptive—and tenuous—forms of self-esteem is other-based. Other-based self-esteem is the feeling that "I have worth because you say and think I do." Pia Mellody points out that this type of self-esteem can be a form of love addiction. People with other-based self-esteem think: "I matter and have worth because someone else (a romantic partner or spouse) says I do."

Of course, when someone we love and care about, loves and cares about us in return, it gives us a great sense of value and confidence, and it can be profoundly enriching. But if our whole self-esteem is founded on how someone else values us, we are just as fragile as if our self-esteem were based on performance or attributes. If that person becomes angry with us, loses interest in us, or leaves us, we believe we have no value, and we have a self-esteem crash. The person with other-based self-esteem believes that they cannot see and hold their worth without the other person conferring it on them.

As these examples illustrate, self-esteem can be fragile, and, in many cases, fraudulent. Yet, when healthy, self-esteem can bring us security, comfort, peace, and great reward. Central to establishing healthy self-esteem is looking inward. Here's a way to do that.

PRACTICING COMPASSIONATE SELF-AWARENESS

I've developed a series of techniques based on Pia Mellody's work, which should help you to develop healthier self-esteem. To get started in your journey to healthy self-esteem, you will need to learn a mindful technique of moment-to-moment compassionate Self-awareness. This way of looking at yourself without judgment—good or bad—is essential for getting started on to the journey of healing.

Compassionate Self-awareness means observing yourself with curiosity, not contempt. Cultivating this observing Self will become the foundation of growing your "functioning adult

Self" (a topic which will be discussed in depth in Chapter 9).

Over time, compassionate Self-awareness will become a constant practice, so normalized into your daily thoughts that you won't have to think about doing it—it will become as much a part of your consciousness as breathing in and out.

But it will not be easy initially. We tend to react to our thoughts of Self with a range of judgement—from feeling 'better than,' to 'less than,' to self-loathing. If practiced regularly, however, the judgments will fall away, and, in their place, you will find that you can examine your Self, including your behaviors, thoughts, emotions, and past actions, with impartial curiosity. And when we are curious about ourselves, we become open to infinite possibilities.

To begin, reflect honestly—without judgment—on whether your self-esteem tends toward the "one-up" position, or the "one-down" position. Do you see yourself as smarter, better, or superior to most people you encounter? If so, you are in the "one-up" position.

Conversely, do you tend to think you aren't as smart, or as attractive, or as successful, or as good as other people? Do you think most people look down on you? Or, do you look up to them? If so, you are in the "one-down" position.

For most of us, our self-esteem is a mix of both the "one-up" and the "one-down" positions. In certain contexts, we feel superior to others, and in other contexts, we feel inferior. Neither are accurate assessments of who we are. Both positions can be shifted with a practice of compassionate Self-awareness.

COMPASSIONATE SELF-AWARENESS MEDITATION

1. Compassionate Self-Awareness begins with becoming aware of your thoughts, emotions, and body sensations. It can be practiced at any time, in any place, but, for now, just sit in a comfortable, relaxing spot. Close your eyes and observe your thoughts. Don't engage with them or judge them. Just acknowledge that they exist. Then let them go.

2. As you do so, become curious. Notice: What are you feeling? Anxious? Annoyed? Impatient? Angry? Whatever your emotions, just observe them, as you did with your thoughts, without judgment.

3. What are your physical sensations as you observe these thoughts and emotions? Do you feel certain muscles tightening? Can you feel your heart beating? Do your legs or hands or fingers begin to fidget or shake? Does your jaw clench? Just observe the physical sensations that accompany your thoughts and emotions. If you can, relax these body parts as you become aware of them, but don't judge them, and don't worry if you cannot relax them. Just let them be as they are.

4. Now, cast your gaze more broadly, and view yourself in the world, both spatially and temporally. See yourself as an integral part of this world, engaged with others. Who are you—in relationship to these other people? Who are you—over the course of history? Consider your life history as it has unfolded. Don't judge this history, however traumatic it may have been. Just notice details.

Can you see your life in terms of any of the blessings you've been gifted? Do you have sight? Do you have the capacity to walk? Do you have the ability to think? No matter how tragic your story, reflect on all these gifts and how they have helped shape your story. Let your story unfurl before you like a beautiful flag. See yourself as the protagonist in an unfinished, unfolding, yet amazing story. All of these experiences, encounters, and emotional depths comprise your story and have made you who you are today—a survivor, and yet more than that. You are a creation in progress, and the artist of your own creation, as well.

5. Now, take a few deep breaths, slowly inhaling and exhaling, and, with an exhale see if you notice your body able to settle more deeply into your seat—chair, couch, pillow, mat—connected to the ground. Notice what if feels like as your body settles. As you embody this calm, place your hand on your heart. Now gently send the warm energy of positive regard to your Self. Perhaps envision this warm regard as warm rays of the sun on your body.

6. Now, as you open your eyes, return to your essential state. Begin to orient to the room and the place where you are seated. Become again aware of your thoughts without judgment, without worrying whether you did the meditation right. Try to hold on to curiosity rather than judgment and continue to send yourself warm regard. With open eyes, see if you can embrace your gift of being human.

This technique is one you will repeat many times, in many contexts, and, as you do, you will find that you can revert to it with ease whenever you feel stress or emotional turmoil. Don't be alarmed if you can't do this right away, it is a process. I recommend that you record yourself reading the meditation and start using it on a daily basis. Here are a couple of examples of how you can put it into practice. Let's start with bringing yourself down from the "one-up" position.

BRINGING YOURSELF DOWN FROM THE "ONE-UP" POSITION

I live in Boston, and the drivers here are notorious for being aggressive and contemptuous; and that snarly attitude has even left its mark on me. If I am following a slow car or one that appears lost, not sure where or when to turn, I notice I become impatient and find myself slipping into a "one-up" position, calling them names (to myself), judging these other drivers as inferior to me. But having practiced compassionate Self-awareness for many years, when that happens, I notice what I am feeling and where I am in my body. I gently intervene by bringing myself down, saying, "I, too, have been lost before while driving, and this person is only human." Then I take a few breaths and if my irritation lingers, I add, "I do not need to be in judgment and contempt of them, because they deserve the same compassion that I will give myself the next time I am lost." Again, I breathe and bring myself back to a position of compassionate Self-awareness. This awareness is the healthy place for me to be.

The key here is to notice when you are going into a better-than state, when you start building up judgmental energy. I find that many clients in my practice live in this "one-up" position. They have difficulty bringing themselves back to the "same as" place or centered place. The practice involves noticing the thoughts that are taking you from your sense of awareness off to a place of judgment. Then, when you notice that happens, you can bring your thoughts back to center—back to the body and being human—rather than staying in judgment and contempt. Staying in a judgmental position is like a train going off the rails—you will become dangerous to yourself and anyone else in the way.

BRINGING YOURSELF UP FROM THE "ONE-DOWN" POSITION

Susan was a client who struggled with feeling "one-up", but, more often than not, she also felt "one-down". She grew up in the western suburbs of Chicago, where her father was a successful businessman. The neighborhood they lived in was middle to upper class, and her high school reflected the wealth of the community. As a teenager, she based her self-esteem on her physical appearance, and, no matter how nice she looked, she never felt that it was good enough.

She viewed movie stars and models as the standard of acceptable beauty, weight, and fashion, and she felt inadequate because she could never match them. She felt "one down" because she felt she looked too heavy by comparison to these professionals. She would tell herself, when she saw their images, "She is so thin and trim, and I'm so fat." Or Susan slipped into the "one-up" position by feeling grateful she wasn't "as fat" as someone else. The constant comparisons to others was torturing her, so she came to me for help.

As we worked through her thought patterns and past history, I had Susan regularly note how she felt in her own body. I encouraged her not to judge her body as either good or bad, but merely, as a body. Over time, instead of comparing herself to others, I had her practice saying to herself, "I feel healthy and comfortable in my body, and I accept the body I have been given, as I take care of it through eating healthy, exercising, and dressing appropriately."

As she began to master this affirmation, I gave her another one to consciously repeat to herself, "I breathe and hold myself with warm regard." This gentle reminder has helped her to feel comfortable in social settings, neither feeling shame for her own looks, nor contempt for how others look. She now pays greater attention to the soul inside each body—and the soul inside her own.

If you, like Susan, find yourself continually judging yourself in comparison to others, your moments of struggling will become less intense with healthy self-esteem practice, and your capacity to recover will feel easier. This way of holding yourself gently becomes a moment-by-moment practice that is essential to use every waking hour. It may sound difficult to conceptualize a constant state of self-awareness and Self-Love. However, if you pay attention to your inner dialogue, you may see and feel the significant fluctuations of how this inner dialogue brings you up and takes you down. Every time you go to the store, to a friend's house, or to work, every time you drive your car, visit your family, or—you name it, this fluctuating "one-up"/"one-down" dialogue starts in. The way to start focusing on these fluctuations is to, again, be curious about what you are observing. Do not be judgmental.

FINDING THE CENTER POSITION EXERCISE

Start with a thought, such as "I have inherent worth."

Then reflect on how it is experienced physically. Is there warmth in your heart? Anxiety in your nervous system? Do you relax or tense up?

Identify the primary emotion you are feeling. Is it love? Anger? Sadness? Again, don't judge. Just identify the emotion that accompanies the physical sensation.

How do these thoughts and emotions manifest in your behaviors? Do you shake your fist and cuss at the cars that are moving too slow for your patience, or skip meals for fear of gaining weight—or eat far too much to self-comfort? Reflect on the ways in which these behaviors are tied to your thoughts and emotions around your sense of worth.

You will discover that life starts to change when you commit to using the healthy self-esteem practice moment by moment, in your daily life. This discipline unlocks the mystery of loving the Self. Next, you'll need to protect that Self.

CORE PRACTICE #2: PROTECTING THE SELF

Just as the Core Practice Loving the Self is central to healing, so too is Protecting the Self. We protect the Self through healthy boundaries, and, as you learned in Chapter 4, there are a multitude of boundaries that we draw on to protect the Self. Yet boundaries can also become walls. Being boundaryless and using walls can prevent us from living fully. Just as it is essential to have healthy self-esteem, it is essential to have healthy boundaries.

In Chapter 4, you learned about Pia Mellody's work on External and Internal Boundaries. There are two types of External Boundaries—physical (distance, personal space, privacy) and sexual. You learned that she suggests that Internal Boundaries are psychological ones and are comprised of two parts. First, the outer, protective boundary, filters information we will allow in—to see, hear and feel. And, second, the inner, containing boundary keeps us from being offensive to others— it contains our emotions, thoughts, and comments so that we don't dump on others inappropriately.

You also learned, in Chapter 4, that you can become "walled off" in these boundaries, keeping any information from coming in or going out, just as you can have overly porous boundaries that let virtually everything in and out. Now you will learn how to use Self-compassionate awareness to establish healthy boundaries.

Boundaries are particularly important if you want to have healthy relationships with other people, particularly intimate relationships or partnerships. In primary relationships, it is critical to establish these healthy boundaries, and to become aware of the ways in which your own boundary issues are preventing you from having healthy relationships with other people. Here are some examples of how you can put the boundary practice into action.

USING A FUNCTIONAL PROTECTIVE BOUNDARY

Imagine a friend tells you that you can be distant and

uncaring in your relationships. If you are confident after filtering whether it is true or not true for you, let it slide over your boundary like water pouring across your skin. If it is possible that it is true for you, however, open your boundary and take it in. Don't judge the idea, just observe it. As you do so, you will have feelings about the observation, but don't reject those feelings. Just acknowledge and experience them. By considering and observing the information and your feelings without fear or judgment, you begin to develop a healthy boundary that protects your self-esteem. It isn't necessary to take any action at this point. Just consider it. Being mindful of the observation your friend shared with you is something you may want to look at later. This feedback is not something that changes your worth as an individual; it only emphasizes your humanity and provides you an opportunity to grow.

Another person says you are moody and controlling and difficult to be around at times. You feel this is true for you; you know you're moody and bossy with your friends. Feel your anger and search below that emotion to the more vulnerable feeling such as shame. Take it in and tell yourself, "I am enough, and I matter, although I can be moody. I am no greater than or less than anyone else." Then choose to work on it while holding yourself in high regard. Perhaps you might want to improve your self-care, so you are not so moody. If the comment is unclear to you, and you aren't sure why your friend would say this, ask for more data from different sources and until you have more data, don't fully take it in.

Investigate further. If it is not true for you, it is infor-mation about the person who is giving it to you. Don't take it personally.

Work hard to keep it out of your personal psychological space. When you feel it poke and probe your psyche, push it out gently but assertively. Just tell the thought to go away. It will likely come back, but, if you keep rejecting it, that nagging thought will eventually stop knocking.

Make room for the information that is true, even if discomforting, but don't give space to the information that isn't. Your time and your mind are too precious for such thoughts. By engaging your mind in this technique, you are practicing compassionate Self-awareness. Practiced regularly, this protection of your psychological space will help you to develop strong yet flexible, healthy boundaries.

THE BOUNDARY PRACTICE IN ACTION—USING A FUNCTIONAL CONTAINING BOUNDARY

My husband can misplace his belongings. He loses his wallet, phone, shoes, and other belongings on a regular basis. I used to find them and put them back or move them out of the way. He would regularly be frustrated and blame me for moving his things. He would say, his irritation rising, "Where did you put this or that?" and I would respond with my own irritation rising. But one day I realized that I was committing a boundary violation by moving his personal things around. I wasn't respecting his privacy—his physical boundaries—when I moved his things.

So, I committed to not touching and moving his things anymore. Now, when he can't find things, I know his frustration is about him. I use my containing boundary, even though I want to lash out, to instead respectfully tell him to stop blaming me, and that I have no idea where his things are. I take a deep breath, count to ten, and imagine something like spandex material holding me in, yet still honoring the emotions that are occurring. Later, I use my containing boundary to be moderate when I ask him not to blame me, and when I ask that he take accountability for his own stuff.

This example uses both the protective and the containing boundaries. The protective boundary protects me, as I realize that he is blaming me for something I am not doing. I recognize that this is about him, and I don't let it in. Then I call on my containing boundary to moderately and respectfully tell him to stop blaming me, lower his voice and take responsibility for his things.

How might you learn to incorporate this same technique in your life? When putting Pia Mellody's teachings on boundaries into action in my counseling practice, I begin by having my clients engage in compassionate Self-awareness. You can practice this technique yourself. Here's how:

FINDING YOUR BOUNDARIES EXERCISE

As you reflect on your thoughts and your emotions, consider yourself in relation to others. Just as you reflected on your Self in the "Loving the Self" practice, now reflect on the boundaries that separate that Self from others.

What about your physical external boundary? How close do you let people get to you physically? Do you let people get physically close to you at all? Or do you always maintain a distance. If so, your boundary has become a wall. Reflect on how and when you maintain a distance from someone. Don't judge yourself, just observe yourself.

How close do you get to others when you're interacting in a social setting? At what point do you begin to feel uncomfortable if someone comes too close? Do you stand close, just inches away? Do you stand close to members of the opposite sex, and at a distance from members of the same sex? If so, you might be exhibiting a poor physical boundary in respect to the opposite sex.

Or is it the opposite—do you feel comfortable getting physically close to members of your own sex, but recoil at the opposite sex? Both of these scenarios are about assessing—without judgment—how your external physical boundary is operating.

Do you let people get into your personal things? Do you let people touch or handle your personal property? If so, who? Everyone? Or no one? Do you go to excessive lengths to guard your personal property, wary of anyone approaching or entering your home, seeing or using your things? Or, do you welcome complete strangers into your home and share your computer, possessions, and personal property with anyone who asks?

How clear is your external sexual boundary? When being approached with touch or sexually, do you feel comfortable setting limits? Or, do you feel uncomfortable saying "No," even when you want to stop someone or something that is happening? Do you initiate hugs and touches? Do you feel comfortable giving someone a hug goodbye? Or, do you avoid even so much as a handshake? Think about the ways that you greet people. Do you have a healthy external sexual boundary, knowing when to hug or touch someone appropriately, or do you erect walls that prevent you from touching or hugging even your own child?

Do you readily gaze upon or touch others in a sexual manner, before they've made any indication of attraction? Do you speak sexually to others who have not signaled an interest in doing so? If so, your external sexual boundary is poor.

Or do you never flirt? Are you never able to approach others sexually? If so, you may have erected—not boundaries, but—walls.

Now turn to your internal boundary, which has two parts. Let's begin with your protective or listening boundary. Do you react to everything you hear? Do you internalize every comment as about you? Do you interpret neutral comments as insults to you? Does the slightest comment suggest to you some kind of disparagement or threat? If so, your protective internal boundary is weak.

Do you ignore any possible constructive criticism? Do you block your ears to any input? Do you have little to no interest in what others have to say about their lives or problems? If that is the case, you have erected a protective internal wall, not a boundary.

What about your containing internal boundary—in other words, the things you say: do you say whatever comes to mind, without regard for how others might feel? Are you brutally honest, quick to blame, and always ready to curse, threaten, yell, or otherwise let people know what you think? Frequently doing so reflects a poor containing internal boundary.

Or, do you keep every thought close to your chest, never

sharing anything about your personal life? Do you avoid expressing any emotions? In this case, you've established containing internal walls.

As you go about your daily life, when you find yourself in social situations, reflect on these boundaries. The first few times you'll need to review the exercise and do it in private. But, as time goes on, you'll find that you can do it automatically and in the context of social interactions, as in the example where I was bickering with my husband over his personal property. You will begin to automatically recognize the ways in which you are erecting walls, or, conversely, not employing *any* boundaries, or when you *are* exhibiting healthy boundaries in appropriate situations.

Like the Compassionate Self-Awareness Meditation, the more you practice, the more ready you will be to make changes, and the more natural those changes will become.

SOME FINAL NOTES ON INTERNAL OR PSYCHOLOGICAL BOUNDARY VIOLATIONS

As you engage in compassionate Self-awareness practice, you will notice that you are starting to uncover the gifts that come with recognizing and putting into practice your boundaries. Anytime you are in a relationship with someone, and they are being offensive, or are acting as if the rules don't apply to them, you will start remembering the way that boundaries work.

Part of using your practice of loving and protecting your Self is addressing such violations with anyone in your life who is being disrespectful—who is acting out internal boundary violations on you.

Whenever someone is blaming, shaming, being sarcastic, yelling, screaming, name calling, lying, breaking commitments, or telling you what you should be feeling, thinking, or doing, they are violating your internal boundaries. Stay on the alert and stand up for yourself when your internal boundaries are violated.

Make sure you don't violate your own containing boundaries as you do so. Don't rage, don't scream, just make it clear that you have reached your limit. Stop interacting, until and unless the other person reins in their own boundaries and begins acknowledging yours.

Most importantly, if you have been traumatized in the past, you will discover that when you lose your physical, sexual, or internal boundaries, you will have a trauma reaction—a process mental health professionals term *dysregulation or* entering into a reactive state. Some people call these reactions "triggers." Whatever you call them, they will take you back to an emotional state or memory from your past, and you will find yourself reliving the traumas. Therefore, being aware of your boundaries and using them is paramount.

On the following page, please see my chart entitled *Internal Boundary Assessment.*

The chart[2] will help you integrate the material in this book specifically focused on internal boundary assess-ment. As you look at the chart, in order to get a real sense of your internal or

---

[2] From Pia Mellody, *Facing Codependence*, HarperOne, revised 2003 adapted Jan Bergstrom.

psychological boundary profile, imagine how you interact with someone who is very close to you. Once you can assess your profile, start to notice yourself, with curiosity and nonjudgment, as you interact in close relationships.

I invite you to download this chart, as well as the others you'll find in this book, at:

forms.MountainStreamPublishingCompany.com.

Internal Boundary Assessment

	Boundaryless	Walls	Functional
Protective (Listening)	Completely reactive and porous to others' thoughts and emotions; takes in the blame. Takes everything that is said to them personally. Thin skinned.	Never listens to what is important to others; avoids empathy, connection and reciprocity. Uses a wall so no information gets in. Uninterested.	Sorts through what others are saying and feeling; ONLY takes in and has feelings about the truth as they know it. Realizes if it is not true for them, it is information about the person talking to them.
Containing (Talking)	Reactive and says whatever comes to mind and does not contain emotions; gives the blame. Can be unbridled in their talking.	Does not tell others what is important to them; avoids expressing emotions. Stays shut down and protected; unknown in relationships.	Talks clearly, but in a political and diplomatic manner; releases their emotions with moderation. Present in relationships, balancing talking and listening.

*Adapted by Jan Bergstrom, LMHC from the work of Pia Mellody

Implement the steps for focusing that I outlined and get practicing. I tell my clients that protecting the Self in this way is like going to the boundary gym. It is only from steady practice that your muscles get stronger!

In the next chapter, we turn to three more practices based on Pia Mellody's Core Areas. These three, I call the Secondary Core Practices. As you incorporate each Core Practice into your daily life, you'll find that your relationships improve, your mood shifts, and your sense of Self grows stronger and healthier. And then you'll be ready to master even more effective techniques that help you heal.

CHAPTER 8

CONTINUING YOUR JOURNEY

After you have been engaging in daily healthy self-esteem practice and protecting the Self, with focus on boundaries, you have become ready to incorporate into your daily practice Pia Mellody's next three Core Areas. Each will help you discover your true and potential Self in ways you never thought possible. Because childhood trauma is so wounding, the traumatized child learns to survive—at the cost of being, and growing into, their authentic Self.

When we are focused on survival, we are unable to relax into our lives. As a result, a state of hyper-vigilance follows us, sometimes keeping us on high alert, other times playing in the background, a barely perceptible but constant state of preparation for any possible threat that might come our way. That's no way to live, but it's the way any child who has been traumatized by their family of origin learns to live. Now, however, you can truly relax, because these Core Practices will help you return to the Self you left behind.

In this chapter we will be working with the practices I call, Knowing the Self, Taking Care of the Self—and Interdependence, and Balancing the Self. Let's begin with Knowing the Self.

CORE PRACTICE #3: KNOWING THE SELF

Pia Mellody's third Core Area involves knowing ourselves by creating a sense of Self. But just how do you do that? Who are you? If someone asks you that question, chances are you might answer in terms of your profession, your relationships, or other material details. You may be a mother, a father, a husband, a wife, a lawyer, a banker, an artist, a chef, a machinist, a soldier, a doctor. You may add to that your nationality, religion, race or gender, but all of these identities are relational—they are who you are in relationship to people, to your job, to political nations, religions, genders, or other institutions. These relational identities are social identities, and such identities may well be central to who you are as a person, but they don't strike to the heart of who you are. Who are you?

Answering that question honestly is difficult, because most of us never really reflect on the answer. But when I am working with clients, once they have become comfortable with the Primary Core Areas, I focus on getting them to think through the question of who they are as the next critical step to their healing journey. To get them started, I have them contemplate three questions:

Who am I?

Am I authentic?
What is my sense of Self?

To answer these questions, I have my clients explore their authentic Self—meaning knowing yourself as the soul who inhabits your body. Knowing your authentic Self begins with your sensory organs. What do you see? What do you hear? What do you taste? What do you smell? And most importantly, what thoughts arise and what emotions do you feel and what sensations do they create in your body?

By thinking of yourself as a sentient being, a process of embodiment, you are able to bring in information about the world through these senses. You can begin to see yourself as an agent in your own life—capable of giving meaning to that world. Humans are the only species that confer abstract meaning onto objects and actions. That unique capability is remarkable, and we continually create—or make meaning—without even realizing it most of the time.

You now are able to perceive something through your senses, turn that perception into a thought, give meaning to that thought, have emotional responses to that meaning, and finally, to have physical reactions or behavior to that emotion.

Let's think for a minute about taking a step outside. As I write this, it is very hot outside, so hot that the flowers are dying. If I step outside, I feel that heat on my skin, I see the dried grass and the wilting plants, I feel the scorching pavement through the soles of my shoes. Those sensations lead me to think, "This heat is uncomfortable. I don't like it. I want it to be cooler." If I am in a foul mood, those thoughts can turn to, "Why is it so damn hot? When will it cool off?" I might curse God or bemoan climate change.

If I am in a good mood, my thoughts might continue to, "I am so thankful the sun is shining! I have some cool shade in my yard, and some beautiful flowers. This weather is glorious! I think I'll fire up the grill and eat outdoors tonight!"

By giving meaning to the thoughts—such as "It is uncomfortable," or "I want to blame God, this heat is so bad," or, conversely, "This is wonderful; the sunshine feels good; this is a good day for cooking and eating outside."—I feel emotions. Those emotions are subjective emotions arising as an aftereffect of the thoughts that arose from my perceptions. And physical impacts can be further effects of emotions. If I feel anger or discomfort, then my emotions might manifest in my body as elevated blood pressure and heart rate, tense muscles, a clenched jaw. If I feel joy and gratitude, those emotions might manifest as lowered blood pressure and heart rate, a reserve of energy, or relaxed muscles.

The point is, the objective world that is just outside my door is filtered through the subjective lens of my own mind and body. My Self is a filter through which the world passes but finding my authentic Self may be a challenge.

That is because people who are traumatized as children will learn to detach from their bodies to protect themselves. They will learn not to feel their bodies, or to use their bodies as shields to protect fragile selves. This detachment and lack of embodiment can manifest in not noticing how you are breathing (holding your breath, taking shallow breaths, or hyperventilating), carrying tension in your neck or shoulders, or not noticing you are hungry or satiated. Not feeling your body's sensations is a reality issue—you are detached from reality. This detachment can cause you to have difficulty feeling the stress associated with any of your basic needs. It can even cause you to fail to take care of your needs. This kind of detachment, or disembodiment, also impairs your ability to feel your emotions. Some of my clients struggle to feel sexual arousal, joy, fear, or anger—they have shut down emotionally as a protective wall.

Resenting the hot day is a way to detach from the discomfort of heat. Tensing your muscles, not relaxing into your body, fixing your face in a stern look or a false smile, are all ways to distance yourself from your body.

Your task, then, is to re-attach your Self to your body. By becoming physically aware of your body, you will become simultaneously aware of your emotions, and the way that those emotions arise from your thoughts. Pia Mellody has suggested that when experiencing an emotion, healthy people notice the emotion, breathe into it, and release the emotion from their body as they breathe out. This is called emotional regulation.

Clients who have been traumatized as children will resist feeling any physically uncomfortable emotions, such as shame, fear, pain, guilt, and anger. There are several ways this resistance manifests—holding your breath, smiling, nonstop talking (what Pia Mellody calls a "wall of words"), or other tactics to deflect attention from the discomfort.

The challenge, when uncomfortable emotions begin to arise, is to raise your awareness of the reality that surrounds you, and to realize your agency in giving meaning to this reality.

Here is a technique I use that can help you return to the reality of your Self and body—a reality you may have hid from, or detached from, long ago.

REALITY PRACTICE

- When you see something or someone and have a thought about it or them, how does it feel in your body?
- Do your teeth clench? Does your face tighten or relax? Does your heartbeat increase or remain the same?
- Does your posture shift? Are your shoulders relaxed or raised? Do your legs shake nervously, or your feet tap with excitement?
- How do you hold your hands? Do you touch a part of your body in a self-soothing gesture, such as rubbing your fingers together or smoothing your hair or arm?
- Become aware of these subtle ways in which your body responds to the thoughts you have.
- Begin to reflect on these physical sensations regularly, when you are in the act of doing something, seeing something, or meeting someone.

Over time, you will begin to notice the ways in which some things make your body tense up in anticipation of something bad about to happen or open up and relax in a state of security and joy.

Sometimes these thoughts and sensations will not be responses to what is actually going on in your present life but will instead be reactions to historical emotional ego states. Trauma has a way of freezing us emotionally, and when we see or experience something that reminds us, even subconsciously, of the past, we revert to the emotional ego states of our childhoods.

Our reactions or triggers are not related to the present situation, but to what has happened to us in the past. It is seamless how quickly we go back to the past. The practice of Knowing the Self involves following these "golden threads" back to their origins in the past and using compassionate Self-Awareness to begin the process of reparenting through self-talk, to those emotional ego states. (More of this process is outlined in Chapters 11 and 12.)

Consequently, as you reflect on your emotional and sensory reactions to your thoughts, ask yourself, "How old does this feel? Does this remind me of something that I experienced in the past?"

If so, remind yourself that the past is not happening to you now, however tender it might feel. By drawing on the protective boundary practice, you can ask yourself, "Is this true for me?" If not, let it roll off of your protective boundary. Don't internalize yesterday's lies. Open your heart to today's truths! If it is true, validate, affirm, and nurture that emotional state. (You can also use the self-talk reparenting process, which will be discussed in Chapters 11 and 12.)

The art of creating your sense of Self is a true creative act—done many ways—which you can master through time and reflection. By becoming aware of your body's reaction to objects and people you encounter, you will create a whole sense of Self that helps you to integrate your thoughts, emotions, and body into the world around you.

Your Self will become a compass to direct you and help you to more authentically understand what is going on around you. Another benefit you will discover is that you come to realize that your own thoughts and emotions guide your behavior. You will be less prone to blaming others for your discomfort, and less willing to accept the blame for others' discomfort. Blame is a dysfunctional reaction that distances us from reality and authentic relationships.

When we have a damaged sense of Self, no one is home, so to speak. As Pia Mellody has observed, we may have the appearance of being in relationships, but we aren't really showing up for them. Our partners will have the sense that there is a lack of connection, even if they can't quite put their finger on what it is that's lacking.

But as you learn and employ this Core Practice, you will begin to discover that the emotions you have experienced in response to external stimuli are emerging from your own thoughts and sensations. As you become increasingly aware of the connection between emotional reactions and events in the past, you gain greater control of your emotions—and hence, you start showing up for your relationships! The following Practice will help you to do just that.

PRACTICE FOR KNOWING THE SELF IN ACTION

The practice of Knowing the Self starts with a mindful practice similar to those described earlier. It is a moment-by-moment practice, as you observe the Self without judgment. In this section, I want you to start thinking less about yourself, and more about your Self. As you become curious and start noticing your sensations, thoughts, and feelings, you will begin asking a set of questions when you encounter any experience or interaction with others.

When I work with couples, if they are in an argument, I teach them to take a time out. The practice of pausing helps you center, ground, and get present with what is going on. Whether you are in a relationship or not, if you have any relational interaction, this technique is a powerful way to reflect on any uncomfortable interaction or event that leaves you troubled, confused, excited, joyful, or angry.

THE 5-MINUTE CHECK-IN

Begin by going somewhere quiet, where you can be alone and focused. Sit quietly in this space of silence and ask yourself these questions. See if you can step back as you view in your mind's eye what just happened with Compassionate Self-Awareness.

1. *What just happened?* Review the scene in your mind. Try to be as accurate as possible in your recollections.
2. *What was I thinking? How do I give meaning to what I saw or heard?* Reflect on what was said during the inter-action and see if you can figure out what thoughts you were having or what you made up about their actions and what was going on for you.
3. *What emotions came up for me? What am I feeling? Anger, pain, fear, joy, love, guilt, shame?* Remember if you only feel anger, try to dig beneath that emotion to discover a more vulnerable emotion. Anger is almost always an

emotion we draw on when we're trying to avoid feeling another emotion.

4. *What was I feeling in my body?* Reflect on any tightness, heart palpitations, pressure, tingling, numbness, or other physical sensations you experienced during or after the encounter.

5. *What behaviors was I exhibiting? What did I do, and why did I choose those actions?* Be honest here, and don't just recall the "positive" behaviors, but those that might be not-so-positive. Remember, the point here is not to judge your behaviors, but to observe them.

6. *What do I need to do or ask for, if anything?* Assess how to put into action what needs to be done to address any lingering conflicts or damage, if anything.

7. *How old was I feeling? Where in my historical past have I felt or acted this way before?* Here I just want you to reflect on the childhood emotional age you experienced during the interaction.

Most of my clients struggle with bringing their feeling and body awareness to the surface. Their trauma, as I mentioned before, has cut them off from their emotions and their awareness of the sensations in their body. This detachment is the result of protective strategies that may have helped during a traumatic childhood. But to heal, they must dig in and become aware of what they feel, emotionally and physically.

That is why most of my work initially goes into restoring the connections between past and present, between mind and body, between physical sensations and who we are. These connections give my clients access to their emotions and a greater range of physical sensations. Many of my clients are hesitant about getting in touch with these places in themselves. I stress the importance of "re-member-ing" themselves. This means putting parts of ourselves back together—becoming aware of our capacity to know the Self, by observation, awareness of thoughts, emotions, body sensations, and behavior.

After all, emotions and body sensations are like a compass—they give you information about what is going on and where you are headed. Many clients only want to feel "good" emotions such as love, joy, or happiness; however, emotions are neither good nor bad. They are just emotions giving more direction to our thoughts and lives. The key is learning how to use them and, thus, receive the gifts they offer.

As mentioned, emotions are useful as an indicator of what you need to do. If your emotions are experienced with a strong, healthy containing boundary, they can become a gift. Using the Core Practice of Knowing the Self, ask yourself, "What emotion am I feeling?" You will find that, by taking that simple step regularly, you are better able to identify your emotions. When you follow with, "What do I need to do now?" you will become clearer on what actions to take or whether you need to do anything at all. This step is also a part of the healthy self-esteem practice; it is an act of loving yourself.

On the following page, I have outlined the Eight Basic

Emotions[3] and the gifts you will receive when using each emotion with a functional containing boundary.

I invite you to download this chart, as well as the others you'll find in this book, at:

forms.MountainStreamPublishingCompany.com.

---

[3] From Mellody, Pia, *Facing Codependence*, HarperOne, revised 2003 adapted by Jan Bergstrom.

Eight Basic Emotions Chart

Emotions	Gifts
Anger, resentment, irritation, frustration	Anger is a gift to give us energy. It can help us grow in our assertiveness. It can strengthen our ability to set limits.
Fear, apprehension, overwhelm, threat	Fear is a gift to remind us to protect ourselves-to have our own back.
Pain, sadness, loneliness, hurt, pity	Pain is an opportunity to grow toward our awareness and healing. It can add to our empathy, compassion, and wisdom.
Joy, relief, happiness, elation	Joy brings hope, appreciation, sustenance, inspiration, and endurance to face life's challenges.
Passion, enthusiasm, excitement, desire	Passion gives us the energy to pursue and honor our purpose in life.
Love, affection, tenderness, compassion, warmth	Love connects us to a higher purpose, to ourselves, and to others.
Shame, embarrassment, humiliation, exposure	Our own shame brings us to our humanity and brings us the opportunity to make amends.
Guilt, regret, contrition, remorse	Our guilt leads us to examine our values and to change or expand how we hold them.

Adapted by Jan Bergstrom, LMHC from the work of Pia Mellody

Finally, the last question I ask my clients in their practice of knowing the Self is the questions of: *"How old are you feeling? Where in your historical past have you felt or acted this way before?"*

This question may seem odd, but it opens a whole new way of looking at yourself.

Once the connecting work of teaching my clients how to attach their thoughts, emotions, and body sensations has begun, I start bringing their awareness to observing their historical Self—or their many historical Selves. I then ask them to try to remember when they may have thought this way or felt these emotions or body sensations before in their lives.

By asking "How old are you feeling?" I help them to observe the Self without judgment and to identify their historical, emotional ego states of being. These emotional ego states seamlessly weave in and out of our reality. Some of these states feel very young, and some feel adolescent.

The younger states can feel good and perfect, whereas the older adolescent states can feel angry and rebellious, as if we are acting out. It is also possible that such emotional ego states can feel shut down and withdrawn. As soon as my clients start bringing new awareness to places in themselves that they have never known or understood, I start teaching about these historical "parts" of themselves that seemingly take hold from nowhere. I teach them how to identify these disarticulated parts, so that they eventually forge a relationship with each part, and they are better able to integrate the parts into their whole Self. As my business partner Dr. Rick Butts says, "Rather than *being* the wound, you get into *relationship with* the wound."

Remember that the Core Practice of Knowing the Self begins with observing the Self without judgment, thus learning to cultivate a more mindful and functional adult Self. Within this Self, we start to find the road to travel down. The cultivation of this Self will bring a balanced and self-regulated state to observe and deal with these historical smaller Selves or parts of Self. Depending on the trauma, we can find ourselves arrested in one of these states in our lives, while thinking that we are in our functional adult Self.

Below is a helpful chart for identifying what ages you may be feeling when triggered or activated. Reflect on these varying emotional ages and the emotions they stimulate. If you identify with any of these emotional ego states, make sure you just stay curious and nonjudgmental.

Emotional Ego States Chart

Felt Age	Emotions and Behaviors
Birth—4 years old	Passive, dissociated, overwhelmed, floating
5—7 years old	Needy, emotional, helpless, empty, at fault
8—10 years old	Simplistic reasoning, perfectionistic, harsh, compulsive, people pleasing, anxious, ashamed, all or nothing, better than, less than
11—18 years old	Abstract idealistic reasoning, entitlement, resentment, unaccountable, better than and perfect, or less than and destructive, worthless

Adapted by Jan Bergstrom, LMHC from the work of Pia Mellody

When you have an interaction with your partner or someone else, emotions can quickly rise to the surface and define the interaction. Sometimes these interactions can be explosive, demeaning, unpleasant, or confusing. When you walk away from a situation, or perhaps ask for a time-out during a very heated interaction, you owe it to yourself to work out what is going on for you. What is your reality, or how did you give meaning to what just happened? Weigh in on how you examined, thought about, felt about, responded to, and decided upon what your truth is.

Recall Paul, who you read about in Chapter 2. Paul's father, a plumber in Boston, was an alcoholic and a mean drunk, who would viciously beat Paul, while Paul's mother, afraid of her husband, did nothing to intervene. Eventually, Paul moved out, became a plumber himself, and by the time he came to me, he was replicating the same aggressive behaviors of his father.

For most of our regular sessions, I had Paul practice owning his reality. I used the questions I had you ask yourself at the beginning of this section. Whenever he had an interaction with others that created a trauma reaction in him, I would have him sit comfortably on the couch, in a relaxed position, and, using his inner resources, find a grounded state of being—with a few words of guidance from me. Then we'd begin.

What just happened? Paul mindfully described a scene of approaching the general manager of a 30-unit condominium construction project who wanted changes made on all units done in a week.

What was I thinking? Paul had thought "What a jerk" the general manager was, because he had all these changes, and he didn't think to tell Paul before it was too late, because the sinks were already installed, and he could not do the new changes.

What emotions came up for me? Paul was enraged and resentful by this treatment from this general manager. I worked with Paul on trying to get under the "invulnerable feeling of anger." Usually, there is a more vulnerable feeling underneath almost all anger.

As he reflected on his anger, Paul got in touch with his pain—the hurt from the way that he was treated. This insight is life changing for really furious clients who get in touch with their vulnerable feelings. They become more approachable, and their situations more workable.

What was I feeling in my body? Paul was feeling tightness, heart palpitations, pressure, and a surge of heated energy all over his body. This question requires that Paul stay mindful of his reality, in his emotions, and in his body sensations. I worked with him on techniques to find the body, find an image, and find resources in the moment that would help him expand his capacity for regulating his emotions during those moments.

What behaviors was I exhibiting? Paul used to start yelling—and swinging—whenever he became angry with someone. After working together for the year, Paul was able to contain his anger, breathe, and start putting words to his upset by making requests rather than rage.

What do I need to do or ask for? Paul learned how to make clear agreements with his general manager, with specific dates for any plumbing changes.   He also learned how to communicate these limits in a relational nonthreatening manner.

How old was I feeling? When Paul looked back at the interaction he'd had with his general manager, and similar interactions from the past, he realized that he was feeling the emotional state of his 17-year-old again, the Self he calls, "Paul, fuck it all."

The exercise above is a labor of love. Paul worked hard at owning his reality. It didn't happen overnight but, rather, it took a full year of hard work before Paul was able to gain insights into the ways in which his battles with his father had stopped him emotionally at the age of 17. By working through his past, Paul came to see that the abuse he suffered as a boy and teen was not his fault, and was instead the result of his father's suffering, not the cause of it. Although he continues to struggle to gain control of his emotions, the process has transformed Paul. The practice of knowing the Self takes time, but it is well worth it.

CORE PRACTICE #4: SELF-CARE AND FOSTERING INTERDEPENDENCE

The fourth Core Practice is self-care, which facilitates a healthy inter-dependence with others. Interdependence involves a give-and-take between two individuals. There are two aspects of interdependence to consider: one is about offering help, and the other is about asking for help with your needs and wants.

First, avoid asking for help when you can take care of the need or want yourself. This action keeps you from being too dependent. However, when you need help, learn to ask for it. Second, decline helping others, by saying "No," if you think you are going to be resentful for helping them do something they can do themselves. Such resentment is called *victim anger.* Taking the action of saying "No," to something you will resent avoids overextending yourself. Also, decline helping if you will enable the person asking for help, because they will become dependent and stay small.

Recall in Chapter 2, we discussed the importance of every child having their basic needs met, and that these needs include, not just the very basics of food, clothing, and shelter, but also several other critical areas. Pia Mellody has identified eleven fundamental needs:

- Food
- Clothing
- Shelter
- Physical Nurturing
- Emotional Nurturing
- Spiritual Practice, or Guidance and Protection
- Education

- Money
- Medical
- Dental
- Sexual Education

Unfortunately, the traumatized child remains unaware of many of these needs, and even if aware, they are often deprived of many of these needs. As the child matures into an adult, they are often unable to provide for their own needs. They have learned to suppress their needs, and as a result, they are not even aware of what they lack. By paying attention to the body, however, they can learn to recognize—and eventually meet—their own needs.

Not being able to meet their own needs, traumatized children become dependent on others to provide their needs, directly or indirectly. How do you know what it is you lack and need? How do you distinguish between something you need and something you want?

Remember, needs are essential for our survival. Without them, we cannot live, or at least, we cannot live as functioning, healthy adults. You may well be alive, but without medical and dental care, you may be too unhealthy—or in too much pain—to work and function in society. You may be living and functioning, but without education, your mind cannot function at its most basic capacity. Without emotional nurturance or spiritual guidance, you may be wealthy and materially comfortable, but your spirit will not thrive.

Our wants give us a sense of abundance and joy, but our needs provide us the foundation on which that joy and abundance can be experienced. Both are essential to a happy and healthy life. While all our needs must be met, our wants should be satisfied with moderation.

The first step to self-care, then, is determining what it is that you didn't get as a child. Take a look at the above list of basic needs, and for each of them, ask yourself if the need was met. Don't dwell on the wants that weren't provided—focus on your needs.

Then, after you've identified the unmet needs, reflect on how these needs are satisfied today. If you did not have medical care growing up, do you get it today, or do you neglect going to the doctor, having your annual exams, addressing health concerns as they arise?

If you did not have an adequate education, do you resist reading and learning today? Or have you sought out that education?

On the following page, please see my chart entitled *Self-Care Chart for My Needs.* I invite you to download this chart, as well as the others you'll find in this book, at:

forms.MountainStreamPublishingCompany.com.

This chart encompasses a list of the 11 Basic Needs for Healthy Living. This is a chart I use with my clients that helps them understand what areas they need to work on for their self-care.

Go through the chart on the following page to see which areas you lack and are *not* addressing. Mark those areas with an X, then read through the list again, noticing which areas you are *not* aware of as an important need. In the next column, mark those too with an X. In the far-right column, mark areas where you feel you have appropriate self-care. Pat yourself on the back for each of those areas! And for the areas that need your attention, start addressing them little by little on a more regular basis. You may need to ask for help!

Self-Care Chart for My Needs

Needs	Needless	Needless and Wantless	Good Self-Care
Food: Eating well?			
Clothing: Appropriate?			
Shelter: Reliable and clean?			
Medical Care: Exercise, healthy weight, sleep, etc.?			
Dental Care			
Education, Learning			
Financial: Money Management			
Physical Nurturing			
Emotional Nurturing			
Spiritual Nurturing, Practice			
Sex: Education, consent and self-knowledge			

Adapted by Jan Bergstrom, LMHC from the work of Pia Mellody

What about your dependence on others? If you did not have your financial needs met, do you depend on others to support you today? Or do you overcompensate by driving yourself to ever-greater financial security, at the cost of other needs, such as rest, healthy diet, or spiritual self-care?

Begin a daily practice of becoming aware of your body and asking yourself if you are meeting your body's needs. Ask yourself inquiring questions: Should I eat? Should I stop eating? Should I exercise?

If you have a health problem, ask yourself if you should go to the doctor. When was the last time you had a dental exam and cleaning? If it's been over six months, make an appointment today. Begin to address your own body's needs. Doing so is the first step to self-care and will help you to gain independence—and interdependence as you engage with others. Being able to take care of yourself and your own body will make it possible for you to interact with others as equals—not as someone in constant need of basic care.

Once you have figured out what you need, reflect on how you interact with other people. You need to figure out what it is you need or want, and then reach out to others and start to embody and express those needs and desires. As you do so, there are three golden rules that Pia Mellody has identified for guidance when interacting with others.

1. Do what you can for yourself, and, when you can't, ask for help.
2. Don't say *yes* when you want to say *no*.

3. Don't do for others what they can do for themselves.

Now let's take a closer look at each of these rules. First, "Do what you can for yourself and when you can't, ask for help." That sounds simple, doesn't it? Well, if you're like me, you've found yourself growing impatient, time and time again, when someone hasn't done something for me that I can easily do myself. For example, I want the grass cut, and I grow angry with my husband for not cutting it—when I am perfectly capable of pushing a lawnmower. I want my son to call me, and I become upset that he isn't reaching out to me—when I can just as easily pick up the phone and call him. These are common frustrations that we all find ourselves experiencing, even though we can take care of them ourselves—and would expend much less energy taking care of our needs and desires, than we spend fretting over them not getting met by others.

But for someone who has been chronically traumatized and thus conditioned to depend on others, an entire pattern of dependency can develop. Another pattern from chronic traumatization, as mentioned earlier, is knowing what you need and want but refusing to believe *anyone* is *ever* going to get it for you. So, you become anti-dependent.

Lastly, in a state of being traumatized, you learn not to look inward on what you need and want, because no one has ever bothered to ask you about your needs and wants growing up. So, instead, over time, you become needless and wantless entirely. We've already discussed the gendered ways we learn dependence—such as men being raised to expect women to cook and clean for them, women being raised to expect men to provide for them financially and take care of home and auto repairs, even doing all the driving and making all the major decisions. Of course, not every couple is so rigidly gendered, but many are. Gender stereotypes can also lead people to become anti-dependent. They may know what they need, but because they have been raised to believe needing something is contrary to their gender, they resist asking for it—such as when a man needs help with putting something together but insists on doing it himself because he thinks that a man should be able to do it himself, or when a woman needs help with childcare but rejects any help because as a "good mother" she shouldn't need help.

People in rigidly gender-stereotyped roles may know what they need, but they will never ask others for help and instead, do for themselves exclusively, even if doing so is difficult, frustrating, and inadequate. To ask for help may not just reflect on them as weak individuals, but as weak men or women.

In addition to these gendered forms of dependency, some people become so dependent on others that they never learn to drive a car—because that's something other people do. They may never learn to manage their money and may be constantly in debt, depending on others—because other people are responsible for finances. They live their lives as if they are still children, expecting grownups to take care of the grownup business.

Well now, you are the grownup. It's up to you to determine if you can do it yourself. So whatever it is that you find yourself growing frustrated about because a need is not being met, ask yourself if you can do it yourself. Then do it—or learn to do it.

What about the second golden rule? Don't say *yes* when you

mean *no.* I can't put into words how important this one is—and how often it is breached. So many times I have heard a husband say, "I can't say *no* to her, or she will pout." (or complain, whine, cry, or whatever). Wives, on the other hand have told me, "If I say *no*, he'll get mad." Often, I hear a similar refrain from parents, who complain that their children are over-indulged—while they are the ones doing the indulging! Just say *no!*

By learning to say *no*, you will avoid overextending yourself. When you are asked to volunteer for the one-millionth time, instead of complaining about all the work, or the fact that you are the one who ends up doing everything, just say *no.* Instead of feeling dumped on, when your friends ask you to host a party you really don't have the energy to host, just say *no.* Instead of feeling resentful, when your spouse asks you to get, make, do something for them, if you really don't want to—or can't—do it, just say *no.*

By learning to say *no*, you will avoid becoming resentful and feeling like a victim without any choice. You do have choices; you do have free will. The more comfortable you become with saying *no*, the more happy you will be to say *yes*, when you really are available to help out—and want to.

Finally, the third golden rule: Don't do for others what they can do for themselves. This is similar to the rule of saying *no* when you mean *no.* If someone can do something for themselves, like handle their own taxes, drive their own car, make their own doctor appointment—you are not helping them by doing it for them. Don't enable them. Instead, encourage them to learn their own independence. As you do so, you'll discover that your own self-care leads to a healthy interdependence, and you'll find that healthy interdependence leads to healthy, happy and calibrated relationships.

On the following page, please see my chart entitled *Self-Care Chart for Interdependence (Interacting) with Others*. I invite you to download this chart, as well as the others you'll find in this book, at:

forms.MountainStreamPublishingCompany.com.

Self-Care Chart for Interdependence (Interacting) with Others

Needs	For Yourself in Relationship when in Relationship with OTHERS, are you able to:		When in Relationship with Others and they are Asking YOU, are you:		
	Ask	Don't Ask	Enabling Them	Resentful	Appropriate Interacting
Food: Eating well?					
Clothing: Appropriate?					
Shelter: Stable, clean?					
Medical Care: Exercise, healthy weight?					
Dental Care					
Education, Guidance					
Money Management					
Physical Nurturing					
Emotional Nurturing					
Spiritual Nurturing, Practice					
Sexual Education and Sex for Procreation					

*Adapted by Jan Bergstrom, LMHC from the work of Pia Mellody

CORE PRACTICE #5: BALANCING THE SELF

We are now at the fifth and final Core Practice that will help you heal from your traumatized past. The last concept is one of moderation and balance in all things. Recall how we discussed, in Chapter 6, the innate spontaneity of the child? You learned that children are by nature spontaneous, and that they act without shame as they experience their own joy.

You also learned that spontaneity must be expressed in moderation as we mature. If we indulge all our spontaneous desires without restraint, we are likely to end up in jail, or at the very least on YouTube! And, if we expressed none of our spontaneous desires or emotions, we would end up being dull and lifeless. It's critical to learn to tap into that child-like spontaneity, but to do so in a healthy, mature, and moderate manner. Doing so balances the Self—it helps make you a whole and happy person, in other words, a healthy adult.

When we are in our own spontaneity, we are experiencing the essence of who we are. Whether it's at work, doing a hobby, socializing with friends, or doing anything with our time, we need to engage in the activity with authenticity. As humans, however, we often engage in these activities in extreme ways— we work 80 hours a week, never taking time to relax, never enjoying a weekend off, much less a vacation. Or, we never spend a day alone, because we must always be doing something with our friends. And when we're with our friends, anything goes! We drink too much, we over-share, we gossip, and we get wild. We become consumed with a hobby to such an extent that our home lives are ignored, our spouses and children neglected;

we don't bathe or take care of ourselves, because we are too busy with our hobby.

These are just a few examples of spontaneity taken to the extreme. Spontaneity can be taken to the other extreme, as well. We might work as little as possible, avoid any pleasurable activities such as hobbies, retreat from society, or never interact with friends.

Either way, you're not experiencing your life with authenticity. The challenge is determining the balance. Again, think of the thermostat analogy. If you are not operating in balance, your thermostat may be out of whack, out of reach, or stuck, and it needs recalibrating to achieve moderation. When we are immoderate, we may be really driven, uptight, rigid, or we may be so loose, far-out, out-there that we offend, shame, or hurt others. So, how do you find the balance?

You engage in the compassionate Self-awareness practice. In the Chapter 7, you learned how to observe yourself without judgment. Now, you can apply that same mindfulness practice to your daily activities in order to begin to recalibrate and find balance. Just as you are learning to observe your habits, your interactions with others, and your thoughts without judgment, now you can begin to observe your daily activities.

Start by looking at your extremes. Ask yourself, *Am I working constantly? Or am I avoiding work and just barely getting by? Am I exercising for hours every day, or am I avoiding any exercise at all? Am I cleaning the house so constantly that not a speck of dust has the opportunity to settle? Or, am I letting everything go, never putting anything away, never shutting a drawer or a cupboard, not washing a dish, not cleaning up a thing?*

Begin to observe the ways in which you have things too tightly wound or too loose and unlimited. Begin to notice if you are spending all your time doing one thing or another, or actively avoiding doing something.

If so, you might think, Hey, I'm a little extreme here!

To find moderation in your life, take an inventory of the broad areas of your life. Reflect on your body, your thinking, your emotions, sensations, and behaviors. Then, write your own list of your life activities and assign them an active value on a scale of 1 to 10, with the number 1 representing areas you put *no* time into, and the number 10 representing areas where you invest excessive amounts of time. Your goal is to bring yourself closer to the middle, where you find moderation. You may be surprised how out of balance you are!

Now that you've begun to practice these Core Practices in your everyday activities, learning the moment-to-moment practice of mindfulness—in your thoughts, emotions, communications, interactions, activities, and self-care, you are ready to take the big leap. You are now ready for learning how to create a functional adult Self! Are you ready? This next chapter might well be the most essential part of your healing journey.

CHAPTER 9

CREATING A FUNCTIONAL ADULT SELF

By this point, you should have a better understanding of Pia Mellody's Primary Core Areas, and how I have used them in the Primary Core Practices for Healthy Living. These Core Practices are the foundational under-pinnings of a healthy life. If you habitually use the methods of the five Core Practices for at least three months, your life will change. Part of creating the functional adult Self comes from living smack dab in the middle of the five Core Areas. By living squarely in the middle of the Core Areas, you will find balance because the Core Areas all have polar opposites—such as being boundaryless or erecting walls. By living in the middle, you will experience health. And now for the good news: you don't need to stop there!

Remember that the work of healing your childhood wounds is a journey and, as "The Big Book" from Alcoholics Anonymous reminds us, changing your life can feel like "trudging the road of happy destiny." Many of my clients get to a place where they feel hopeless about navigating their childhood trauma. They want to give up. However, like Dorothy, we have to get our needs met along the way. After Dorothy endured so many trials and tribulations in her efforts to reach Oz, before she saw the Wizard for the first time, she and her fellow travelers were treated to some self-care, cleansing, and pampering, lots of rest, and good food. They were treated as honored guests. Dorothy needed a respite, a place to feel safe and rejuvenated, to gather her internal resources for the next part of her journey—the part where she would claim the magic broom of the Wicked Witch of the West! In other words, the healing journey is indeed a difficult one, but it is a rewarding one, and one that includes a great deal of enjoyment.

While you may not be in pursuit of a curious wizard or a magic broom, what you are in pursuit of is a transformation. You have been wounded, and you need to heal. In order for any recovery or healing to happen, however, you need a vision of what you are working toward. Like a ship traveling in dark seas, you must have a beacon to guide your way. Therefore, it is essential that before you begin any exploration of your trauma, you find a place in yourself that is grounded, regulated, and operating in a functional state of being. For many of my clients, the mere word "functional" is unclear. Their lives have been so dysfunctional, they have no idea what functional looks like, much less how a functional place in themselves can be cultivated.

What I notice in my practice is that everyone struggles with this concept of an internal grounded place. Due to the nature of being human and imperfect, the impact of any trauma in our lives sets us up for confusion. To gain clarity, you need the help of an internal wiser Self. Fortunately, just as Dorothy had the secret way home within her all along, so do you.

A SPIRITUAL PROCESS

Finding your way to a functional adult Self is often called a spiritual process, and involves experiencing one's soul, or true essence. The soul has a tendency to defend itself against the ego, which wants what it wants and always tries to prevail. Each person's ego is comprised of a series of parts or historical states. I look at historical ego states as borrowed identities. They are an accumulation of all that we have observed and adapted in growing up. Many adults function out of these historical places, thinking it is really who they are, not realizing that the Self they recognize is one of their historical ego states.

Genuine Self comes from using the boundary practice, finding out what is true about you and what is not, and being connected to a greater purpose in your life. Pia Mellody speaks on this topic, often saying that the functioning adult comes from embracing the two truths in one's life. She suggests that God (or the Divine) is truth, and that once you shine the light on your truth, God (or the Divine) is also love, and you release that love, experiencing it as warmth and compassion.

For many, however, the concept of God or a divine presence is problematic. God does not fit with their belief system, and therefore, they reject the concept itself. Yet my own view is that you do not need to believe in a God or divine entity in order for the concept to have value. Every culture throughout the world has some concept of a diety or a universal force that helps us to make sense of our world and conceptualize our place in it.

By believing in a force beyond ourselves, whether that force be a Judeochristian or Muslim God, an eternal soul that is forever reincarnated, or a celestial sky full of physical forces, seeing ourselves as connected to something greater provides us with a sense of purpose—and keeps our egos in check!

Thus, rather than speak of God or the Divine, I prefer to think of a Universal Force—we may not agree on what this force is, we may not completely understand it—but by recognizing a power beyond ourselves, a power that connects all living things across time and space, we can begin to recognize ourselves as crucial components of something greater than ourselves.

From holding these truths, we can begin to cultivate an essential place in the Self—what I call the soul, which is connected to the Universal Force. Living through one's soul feels very different than living in ego. A mentor of mine, Dr. Brugh Joy, used to talk about this process. It is through the process of suffering that the ego is re-appropriated to God or to the Divine, he says (or the Universal Force, as I envision).

When this happens, we make room for grace to fill the soul. Most faiths teach you about what "God" or a deity or panoply of deities give or gives you in grace. However, I refer to grace as the light within us. I will discuss the practice of gratitude, which connect us to grace, in Chapter 13.

USING YOUR RESOURCES

Using your resources is an integral part of cultivating a functional adult Self. By this I don't mean overconsuming material goods, overspending, or amassing a great pile of stuff. A personal "resource" for healing, according to Peter Levine, the creator of Somatic Experiencing Therapy, is anything that helps a person maintain a sense of Self. And, what Levine means by a maintaining a sense of Self, is essentially this: maintaining a sense of inner integrity in the face of triggering events, sites, or memories.

The resources Levine and others are speaking of can be internal—thoughts, mind's eye images, cognitive techniques, such as those that help calm you. Or they can be external— spaces you retreat to, objects you hold or gaze upon, anything that brings you calm—through one or more of your five senses. Internal and external resources can provide you with a more profound capacity for organization, regulation, and grounding.

Think of a resource as a bridge to a deeper connection within yourself. When evoked, these resources can be used to cultivate the functioning adult state.

Starting with compassionate Self-awareness, your internal resources can include pleasant body sensations, positive mind's eye images, places in nature, pleasant mem-ories or events, an object that evokes a positive, warm emotion or feeling, and any cognitive affirmations that do this for you. Once evoked, a resource creates a sense of calm, with a grounded, centered, and balanced state in the adult. This balanced state is the foundation for the functioning adult to begin the reparenting process.

Research shows that when the nervous system is regulated and settled, the brain has more access to the prefrontal cortex, which is the part of the brain that gives us more executive function, enhancing our ability to be in a state of action rather than reaction.

Identifying and using internal and external resources helps a person feel calmer, so they then have the capacity needed to manage or navigate their way through a state of dysregulation.

REPARENTING THROUGH AFFIRMATIONS AND LIMITS

Before we move on to how to create and experience our personal resources for healing, let me say a couple sentences about what Pia Mellody refers to as reparenting through self-talk.

Although this concept of reparenting may sound trite, it is desperately needed by anyone who has experienced childhood trauma. The good news is: the ability to reparent will happen naturally as a result of the consistent use of the Primary Core Practices for Healthy Living (covered in Chapters 7 and 8).

Reparenting requires stepping back from our historical ego states, in order to affirm, nurture, and set limits for our childhood-selves. In doing so, we provide—to our Selves—care we deserved and so desperately needed during the long years of childhood. This can only be done from a place of compassion—compassion for our struggles and for our historical ego states. Reparenting is critical, because you really needed this help, back when you were growing up, and therefore—after long years—you desperately need it now, as these wounded historical Selves show up in your adult life!

We all need reparenting, because no one on this planet grew

up with a perfect childhood. The fact is, we are human, imperfect, and we experience challenges in our relationships. We all need a place in ourselves that implements a wiser, more functional Self when it comes to living our lives. Teaching *how* to reparent will be covered in more depth in Chapters 10 and 11. But before you can reparent yourself, you must first learn to create what Pia Mellody calls a functional adult Self. That functional adult Self creates the foundational base for our journey, and that essential starting place will manifest from your finding and using the resources that I outline below.

MINDFULNESS, OR A COMPASSIONATE SELF-AWARE STATE

A practice of mindfulness starts by finding a self-aware place in yourself that can objectively observe what you are feeling, doing, or saying. Most importantly, this self-aware state must come from a compassionate, nonjudgmental place. Jon Kabat-Zinn[4], the father of mindfulness, defines compassionate awareness as "paying attention, on purpose, in the present moment, non-judgmentally." Do you remember learning about the protective boundary, in Chapter 5, and how your protective boundary filters incoming information for you, when it is functioning well? Well, like the protective boundary in its listening mode, the self-aware state is curious. It is watching to understand what is happening—without any judgment.

Of course, when you first set out to observe your thoughts,

---

[4] Kabat-Zinn, J. Full Catastrophe Living, Bantam, 1990.

you will inevitably find yourself judging these thoughts. That is normal. But as you practice observing the thought, dismissing any judgment, and just acknowledging it, you will find that it becomes easier to detach yourself—and your historical ego states—from the thoughts. They will just be.

So as challenging as it may be, keep checking to see how you are viewing yourself. If the words in your head have judgment, stop them! See if you can go back to a state of curiosity. It is not about what is wrong with you, it is about what happened to you that makes you act as you do. Your task is simply learning to observe what is going on inside you, without being carried away by over-activation, or, on the flip side, losing interest out of boredom.

MINDFULNESS EXERCISE

To get started, find a comfortable space to sit or lie down, with minimal distractions.

1. Start by slowing the pace of your thinking and talking. Become comfortable with silence. Refrain from interpreting any thoughts or directing them toward any subject or emotion. Instead, favor neutral observation. Focus on the flow of thoughts, feelings, and body sensations.

2. Become aware of any sensation, thought, emotion, body movement, or external stimuli that is happening in the room, without judgment.

3. Use detachment, noticing it, without participating in it or getting swept away by it.

4. Try putting neutral language to what is noticed (such as,

"I'm having a thought—some emotion is coming up.")

5. Mindfulness can be directed by following the flow of thoughts, feelings, and body experiences as they unfold. If you find yourself judging or controlling your thoughts, try instead to deliberately focus on one aspect of the experience, such as your breath, gravity, or the sensation of your body pressed against the chair. By focusing on a single, objective aspect of the moment you are in, your judgments about thoughts will slip away.

As you first practice this exercise, you will find that you are easily distracted. You may become restless or pursue your thoughts with judgments and storylines. But, the more you practice, the easier it becomes to just let your thoughts be, to acknowledge them and let them go, as if they are nothing more than floating clouds passing by. It takes time, but it is time well spent, as you find yourself more easily slipping— at will—into a calm and relaxed state.

GROUNDED IN THE BODY

First let's start with understanding the key concept of the *felt sense*. According to Eugene Gendlin,[5] who introduced the term, a felt sense is, "not a mental experience but a physical one. A bodily awareness of a situation or person or event. An internal aspect that encompasses everything you feel and know about the given subject or specific event. This physical

---

[5] Eugene Gendlin, Focusing, Bantam Books, 1982.

experience is the activity through which we understand how we feel in our whole body and mind. In order to heal trauma, we must be able to identify the signals of trauma that are made available to us through the felt sense.

The felt sense blends together most of the information that forms your experience. Even when you are not consciously aware of it, the felt sense is telling you where you are and how you feel at any given moment. The felt sense is relaying the overall experience of your being, rather than interpreting each thought and emotion.

Our physical senses of sight, sound, smell, touch, and taste are elements of our felt sense. Other important information is derived from our body's internal awareness—the positions or postures the body takes, the tensions and stress it holds, the movements it makes, its temperature. The felt sense is influenced, even changed by our thoughts. Yet felt sense is not thought. Rather, it is something we physically and deeply feel.

When I work with my clients as they try to find their resources, I help them tune into this place in themselves—a place that is not defined by their thoughts, but rather includes whole body awareness. From this place, we establish each client's personal resources. Starting with compassionate Self-awareness or mindfulness, we add the felt sense of their body, and it is only then that we are able to establish a grounding and centering practice. Then through grounding and centering practices, they become present and embodied—and you will too.

GROUNDING AND CENTERING PRACTICE IN ACTION

Grounding and centering are day-to-day practices that can reconnect you directly with your personal resources—naturally available in your own body. It is important to reestablish your relationship to both the ground and to your body's center, the place where action and feeling originate. The functions of grounding and centering have been compromised during trauma reactions. In trauma, you lose your ground, so an important part of healing is learning how to find your ground—and find your center—again. As you ground and center yourself before each exercise in this book, you will create a feeling of safety, and a sense that you are in charge. Here is how you do it:

GROUNDING TECHNIQUE

1. Sitting in a chair, gently push the heels of your feet into the ground. Notice the sensations in your legs. Engage and release your leg muscles. Experiment with finding just the right amount of pressure in your feet.
2. Bring your awareness to what your feet feel like, inside your shoes, and/or resting on the floor. Wiggle your toes and name the sensations that arise. Become aware of your feet on the ground.
3. Begin deep, slow breathing—explore "pace breathing" (a term coined by Marsha Linehan[6]), where you slowly inhale, to a count of *five*, completely expanding the rib

---

[6] Linehan, DBT Skills Training, Handouts and Worksheets, Guilford Press, 2014

cage and belly, then slowly exhale to a count of *seven*, until your rib cage has contracted and your shoulders have dropped. Do this at least five times.

4. Gain physical support from a comfortable chair. Bring your awareness to your backside as it sinks into the chair, then feel your back, as it is being supported. Name the sensations that arise. Experiment with slumping over and then sitting up straight, lengthening the spine as you do so. Imagine having a string pulling you up straight. Notice any and all sensations as they arise. Does your back hurt? Are your vertebrae creaky? Can you feel blood circulating, leaving your head, and filling other parts of your body? Do you feel taller? More in control? Become aware of each sensation, whether physical or cognitive. Don't judge these sensations, just greet them.

5. Focus nonjudgmentally on the sensations you can feel throughout your whole body. Start scanning your feet, and slowly move up through your legs, abdomen, torso, into your arms and hands, finishing off at your neck and head. Just allow whatever shows up to be there, as you observe each area.

6. Tense, then relax your muscles. Try using an exercise ball if you have one. Or, try a beanbag, a roll of socks, a crumpled towel—anything that you can hold in your hands or between your legs and squeeze tight: hold for five seconds. Then relax for five seconds. Notice the sensations and the difference between engaging the muscles and releasing them.

Similar grounding practices can be done with movement, such as Tai Chi, Qi Gong, or Yoga. Take a class and see if you can focus on what is happening in your body, moment by moment, rather than thinking about your day or what is in the future. If you start thinking about the past or future, while doing the grounding practice, don't worry. Just gently bring yourself back to your body awareness and breathing.

As with the mindfulness practice, this grounding technique will help you to calm yourself, control your thoughts and triggers, and it will enable you to bring yourself to the present at will—whenever you find your thoughts and anxieties spiraling into the past, or your worries, into the future.

The grounding technique becomes even more powerful when it is combined with the centering technique. This technique is a bit more unique, but every bit as transfor-mative:

CENTERING TECHNIQUE

1. Place one hand on your heart and notice what happens in your body when all thoughts are dropped, and you focus on just your hand. Observe the weight of the hand, its temperature, the sensation of the hand itself and the sensation of it resting over your heart. Notice any changes in your breathing, your heartbeat, even the energy you feel in your hand. Visualize in your mind's eye a warm ball of golden energy swirling around in your hand as it rests upon your heart.

2. Keeping your hand on your heart, gently place the other hand on top of your head. Apply a slight pressure on the top of your head to create a sensation of being grounded

to the Earth. With the hand on your heart, focus on channeling warmth and empathy throughout your body through this hand.

With practice, you will find these techniques help you to gain and remain calm. They will also help you detach yourself from the thoughts and memories that haunt you, as well anxieties about the near and distant future. By learning how to become aware of your thoughts, and—even more so—the sensations awakening each moment in your body, you will gain mastery over your thoughts and emotions, such as fear and worry.

FURTHER HELP WITH GROUNDING AND CENTERING

There always comes a time when you find it hard to stay present with an emotion or a physical feeling in your body. This is totally normal, and you may find yourself wanting to stop your investigation of the material that is coming up. No problem! In fact, it is important to know when to stop and what to do. I recommend healthy alternatives rather than medicating your feelings by eating, drinking, taking drugs, or engaging in self-abusive behaviors. Here are some healthy techniques for staying grounded and centered. You may have heard these suggestions a thousand times, and, like anything we hear a thousand times, they may go in one ear and out the other. But this time, try something different. Try at least three of these exercises, just once. Afterwards, reflect on how your body feels, and how your mind feels. Then do them again, another day. You'll be surprised by the difference such simple activities can have on both your body and your mind.

TECHNIQUES FOR MANAGING DISCOMFORT

1. Go outside and take a walk in your favorite place. If you find your thoughts spinning off into worries as your feet carry you along the pathway, bring your mind back to the moment. Observe the sky above you, the earth below you, the flora and fauna. How many birds can you hear? Can you spot one? Smile at the people you pass. When you get home, see how many moments or observations you can recall from your walk. The more alert you are to the world that surrounds you, the less space there is in your mind for worries.

2. If you have a dog, take your dog for a walk, or go to a dog park. Use the time to truly enjoy your pet's own joy for the outdoors.

3. If you have a cat, stroke its fur, scratch its head, and play with it. There is a reason we call our pets "pets." Just petting the fur of a dog or cat can have a comfort-ing effect on both the pet and ourselves, as our endorphins are stimulated.

4. Call a close friend and reach out for support. If you are in recovery from an addiction, call a fellow member or your sponsor. Be sure to listen and be there for your friend, as much as your friend is there for you. If your friend is unavailable, don't judge your friend. They might be in the middle of taking care of their own needs. Ask them to call when they have more time and call someone else. Remember, we are all struggling. The more thoughtful

you are of your friends' time and needs, the more thoughtful they will be of yours.

5. Work out moderately at the gym or at home. If you haven't worked out for some time, start small. If you find yourself watching TV, use the commercial breaks for short spurts of exercise. Try finding a five- or ten-minute YouTube video you can work out with. If you go to the gym, start with twenty minutes, work up to half an hour, and make your goal a fifty-minute workout three times a week. Don't push yourself too hard. Be gentle with yourself. You'll get there.

6. Dance to your favorite music, journal your feelings, draw or use some medium for an artistic expression of what you are feeling. Indulge in your playful side. You never lost it—you just learned to ignore it as you matured. Express yourself artistically, even if it involves doodling or coloring between (or across) the lines!

7. Move your body—open your arms and spread them out to create a circle. Experiment with expanding the size of this 'container' until it is "big enough" to hold all the feelings and sensations or "all of the parts" of your pain.

8. Use your body to put one palm on the side of each knee: push arms against the outer part of the knees while simultaneously pushing out with the legs. This creates resistance and engages your muscles to fight back, which can give you a feeling of empowerment.

9. If you have a flashback or start to dissociate or "fade out," become aware of your surroundings—what Peter Levine calls "orienting" to the external environment (or

room). This technique can be a helpful way to come back into the room, and thus into the present moment. To do it, just choose three things in the room you like, describe them, and reflect on why you like them.

10. Turn your head and neck slowly as you focus on objects in the window, the wall, the door, the lamp, the bookcase. Or focus on objects that might be comforting such as your most favorite object. What are some of the cues that tell you where you are right now? List three or four of them.

MIND'S EYE IMAGERY

Mind's eye imagery is a technique that draws on images to calm and ground the body. Remember all these resources I'm describing are those internal or external personal cues that help you to find a safe place to return to when you become triggered as you navigate through your childhood trauma.

I usually ask my clients to think of a time in life when they traveled somewhere very beautiful, peaceful, or enjoyable, or a time when they had a favorite animal they loved, or when they connected with someone special and experienced a felt sense of calm, acceptance, grounding, centeredness, and safety.

Once they decide upon their chosen experience (or several experiences) of safety, I ask them to write the experience down, describing it enough to bring it vividly to mind. You might want to do the same. These visual image resources will be used throughout the rest of the book, for many of the processes you will journey through. The experiences you choose to visualize will act as anchors. An anchor gives stability in times of need.

And that is just what you are seeking.

MIND'S EYE IMAGERY EXERCISE

1. While in this grounded and embodied state, sit somewhere where you are comfortable, and close your eyes to contemplate the scenes listed below.
2. Allow yourself at least a minute for each scene.
3. Notice your felt sense or bodily sensations as you bring each image to mind.
4. See if you can put words to your body sensations. Some examples might be: *calm, relaxed, soft, warm, centered, tight, airy, spinning,* or whatever words describe the sensations.
5. Remember, don't judge the sensations—just find a word that best describes the sensations you feel as you contemplate the scenes that follow. Here are the scenes:

- Sitting on your favorite beach listening to the ocean waves
- Hiking up your favorite mountain, reaching the top, overlooking a beautiful valley
- Looking across the Grand Canyon and the river that flows through it
- Being on a tropical island
- Sitting in a cozy cottage with a warm fire burning in the fireplace, the snow gently falling outside

Did these scenes calm you? Excite you? What changed in your internal state as you contemplated these scenes? Did you find one that brought you instant calm? If you didn't, think of a time when you were traveling somewhere beautiful, or with plentiful nature—a time when you loved what you were seeing and feeling. Now, you have created a room in your mind, a space you can return to, where you can find instant comfort. When stressed, anxious or triggered, go to this place and relax. There's no admission to be paid, no taxes or mortgages you must come up with, no applications to fill out. This place is yours, available to you whenever and wherever you find yourself. Welcome!

Remember that creating and cultivating a functional adult Self comes from using your resources. Your ability to summon and use your personal resources will be essential for navigating your family of origin trauma. The act of resourcing changes your biology by engaging the parasym-pathetic part of the nervous system in a way that can settle your nerves. Once the settling occurs, the prefrontal cortex—the decision-making and acting capacity of your brain—is fully on board. You are creating the environment in which the functional adult Self can thrive. As you do each imaging exercise, you will gain strength and confidence. And you are going to need that strength and confidence for the next step I want you to take on this journey. Your healing doesn't need to be complete, it just needs to be your goal, for what comes next. And what comes next is one of the most important steps you are going to take on your journey. In this next step, you'll discover that in order to go forward, we sometimes have to look back.

CHAPTER 10

UNDERSTANDING YOUR
CHILDHOOD HISTORY

When you have been traumatized or neglected as a child, you often stop growing emotionally. Having entered that flight or fight state in your efforts to survive, you continue to live your life, growing older, yet there is part of you left behind, a part that perhaps fled the scene or maybe just stood still. Most likely, you aren't even aware of this missing piece, because the rest of you has carried on as if everything is normal—even when everything is far from normal. That's why you need to look back in time, before you can move forward in your journey.

My colleague and business partner, Dr. Rick Butts, calls this process of looking back, "getting your story straight." Simply put, you need to understand and see your story in a new light. Your story is your testimonial of the events and people you experienced as you grew up. It is yours and yours alone—although you will be astounded by how many people can relate to your story, no matter how traumatic it may have been. Our life stories are filled with common themes and patterns, which others have also experienced. The more we share our stories is the more we discover that our stories are uniquely our own, and that we are not alone.

Others have suffered and overcome the very same challenges you have suffered and overcome. Knowing that you are not alone will help you as you learn to better understand and tell your story in all its tender pain and remarkable insight. In this chapter, I'm going to show you how to do just that.

I learned the power of exploring my childhood history as I studied with Pia Mellody. Getting my own story straight helped me to gain a unique perspective that has helped me in my work with clients. Looking back on the gifts that I received from doing my experiential trauma work, I realize now that these gifts were not immediate nor apparent. My truths were realized over time. I realized a big part of acknowledging my truth was getting my story straight from childhood, standing in the authenticity of my story without judgment, and embracing some healthy fundamental concepts about growing up in a functional family.

VIEWING YOUR FAMILY HISTORY IN A NEW LIGHT

Before getting your story straight you need to consider some new assumptions regarding how you view your family of origin history. This process is what Dr. Butts calls "rearranging the furniture." This metaphor means using the concepts below to shift your view of your family history, and to look at that history with new eyes. The shifts you make will mean that what you thought was accurate about your history becomes rearranged or changed. Keeping the following concepts in mind will lessen the emotional triggers of your journey, and it will help you to look with compassion and objectivity at your past.

CONCEPTS TO HELP SHIFT FAMILY ORIGIN STORIES

- Parents are human, meaning they are underdeveloped, immature, and had their own material that affected the way they grew up and the way they could parent.
- They chose to become parents and raise children. You were the child and they were the parents. It was not the other way around. They needed to be parenting you rather than having you taking care of them.
- Their relationship—whatever it was—was their choice to be in, and both parents are accountable for the parenting. If one parent was abusive, the other parent needed to step in. If that parent was absent altogether, it was their responsibility to be there for you. When a parent is yelling or shaming, lying to, or being competitive with their child and wanting to win all the time and put them down, that is abusive. The other parent has a responsibility to intervene. When that doesn't happen, the parent who fails to help is abandoning their child, or throwing the child "under the bus," due to their lack of intervention. Their relationship is adult business, not yours to fix or mediate or compensate for. Their relationship is a template that you

will use in your grown life when you get into a relationship. Good or bad, it is what becomes familiar.

- It was never your fault as a child. Children growing up require a lot of affirmation, nurturing, guidance, and limit setting. You needed to become attached and to feel a sense of safety and connection. If that didn't happen, your parents are accountable. If your parent struggled with the issues of their life, they needed to get help rather than ignore your needs or expect you to fix and heal them. For the most part, parents are well meaning; however, if your needs were neglected, they did *not* do the best they could.

Your parents were your first relationship or higher power as a child. The patterns they established will play out throughout your whole lifetime. If your relationship with them goes unexamined, you will be stuck repeating these patterns. It is best to understand how these patterns dictate choices of partners, jobs, and friends, as well as how we respond to authority and intimacy.

But how do we break free from such patterns? How do we examine and shift the relationship we have with our family of origin history? The truth is, we do it daily, in the many ways we tell and retell our personal histories in the course of our lives. But the key to getting your story straight, and rearranging your furniture, is doing the exercises in this chapter. So, grab a pen or pencil and let's begin!

1. The first exercise is to identify the roles you played in

your family by using the Family Roles Chart.

2. The second exercise begins with filling out the assessment, "Growing Up in My Family Questionnaire."

3. The third exercise is to create your family history timeline.

4. There is a final exercise that is available on my website. It is the brief version of the Developmental and Relational Trauma Assessment. To do the exercise, you can download the form, fill it in, and use its key to further deepen your understanding of your story.

By following these four steps, you will discover that you have a whole new perspective on what really happened in your family.

The process is like writing a novel. Imagine you are writing a novel. As you write, you realize that there are parts that don't ring true, or seem off, or don't fit the whole story. You need to take a look at those parts, cut out what doesn't ring true, and polish what remains, until your story is honest and clear.

As you reflect on your story, you will find that defenses come up about looking at your own past. There may be some serious repression and dissociation that may cause you to resist feeling the experiences and emotions from your own history[7]. You will also likely experience three other responses that we all struggle with. Minimization occurs when you reduce the significance of

---

[7] If you find that this resistance becomes a chronic experience, then you might need help from a professional who works with childhood developmental trauma.

what happened. Denial arises when you become certain that nothing is wrong, but the evidence suggests otherwise. Finally, you may experience delusion. Delusion arises when someone is presented with the facts but is unable to assign proper meaning to them or to take appropriate action, such as to undertake actions a therapist may suggest.

In my own healing journey, I had to learn, in the telling of my story, to let go of judgments I had made about myself. I had to learn to look at my story objectively, from the distance of maturity. I looked back on my past, and I saw it for what it was. I saw myself for what I had truly been, in childhood, a little girl in need of safety, love, and security. I had needed to be understood and protected. And I had needed to know that my parents would protect me.

Once I got my story straight and rearranged my furniture, I began a journey of deepening my understanding in the areas where I had not fully developed my story.

As I did so, I began to realize how the immature places inside me had kept me behaving, in my adult life, the way I had behaved as a child. Once I saw the historical patterns playing out in my adult life, I was horrified. I then started on the next step of the journey, which was to mindfully notice what I was doing, and then replace each destructive behavioral pattern with a functional one. As I learned to do that, I started feeling a deeper, wider experience in living my life.

What I discovered in reflecting on my own story was that, in the beginning of my life, my mother was unavailable to me. Her depression and preoccupation with suicide made it impossible for her to be there for me. My father was also unavailable to me, because he was traveling for his work and would be gone for weeks at a time, leaving me and my brother alone with our damaged mother, and a woman who did the cleaning and laundry for us. I was lost in school, as I struggled with PTSD— not knowing that's what it was, at the time, because the disorder wasn't yet understood—and lost in my anxiety, which became a form of Obsessive-Compulsive Disorder that manifested as constant thoughts that I was going to die. The morbid thoughts stemmed from my mother's repeated attempts at suicide.

As I grew older, however, I became my father's confi-dante—he had essentially used me as a surrogate spouse in my teen years by discussing his frustrating relationship with my mother, and by showering me with expensive gifts, such as clothes, jewelry, and lavish vacations. Because my mother wasn't emotionally available to him to share his thoughts, I became that person he would confide in—which frustrated my mother because she saw that I was getting all that attention from my father. In response, she became increasingly critical and controlling of me, viewing me as competition with her for my dad's affection and regard.

For years, I had interpreted my teen years as full of scapegoating abuse from my mother, but not from my father. He adored me, and I adored him. Yet as I worked through my own therapy with Pia Mellody, I came to realize that, by using me as a surrogate for my mother, and by confiding in me as one would a spouse, my father was actually objectifying and falsely empowering me. I was indeed feeling very special and adult like—a role that is sometimes labeled "The Hero Child," which you'll read more about in this chapter.

Only by recognizing the emotional neglect I suffered—from *both* my parents when I was young (a position called "Lost Child"), *and* the enmeshing abuse from both of them in my teen years (in the family roles of "Hero Child" and "Scapegoat Child")—was I able to begin the journey of healing.

THE FAMILY SYSTEM

It isn't just your own childhood that you need to reflect on when getting your story straight. It's your entire family system. The family systems theory is a theory introduced by psychiatrist Murray Bowen. Dr. Bowen suggests that individuals cannot be understood in isolation from one another, but rather as a part of their family, because the family is an emotional unit. Families are systems of interconnected and interdependent individuals, none of whom can be understood in isolation from the system.

According to Bowen, a family is a system, in which each member has a role to play and rules to respect. Members of the system are expected to respond to each other in certain ways according to their roles, and roles are determined by relationship agreements.

Within the boundaries of the system, patterns develop, as each family member's behavior is caused by, and causes, other family members' behaviors in predictable ways.

Maintaining the same pattern of behaviors within a system may lead to balance in the family system, but it may also lead to dysfunction. For example, if a husband is depressed and cannot pull himself together, his wife may need to take up more responsibilities, in order to pick up slack. The change in roles may thus maintain the stability in the system, but it may also push the family toward a different equilibrium. This new equilibrium may lead to dysfunction because the wife may not be able to maintain this overachieving role for a long period of time. She may become angry, directing her anger not just at her husband, but also at her children, or she may internalize her anger, directing it toward herself—possibly through addictive behaviors, sleep deprivation, or her own depression. The children in such a family may be neglected, abused, or subjected to stress levels that lead them to develop their own coping mechanisms.

In another example, suppose the parents don't have any major issues, but one of the children does. If one child in a family has a major physical or mental health challenge, behavioral problems, or is involved in some type of activity that consumes one or both parents' time (such as being involved in sports or other competitions that require the parents to devote a great deal of time or money to one child), the other children may be neglected and become resentful of the extra attention their sibling receives.

Emma was just such a child. Her older sister had a terminal illness that consumed her parents' time. As Emma reached her teens, her sister's illness had progressed to such a dire state that her mother plummeted into a deep de-pression, which then turned to profound grief when Emma's older sister died.

Although Emma knew her mother loved her and had good reason to be so focused on her other daughter, Emma felt so neglected by her mother—and so sad to lose her sister—that she developed a serious eating disorder that nearly killed her.

Meanwhile, her parents' marriage deteriorated, as often happens in the wake of a child's death, because each parent was grieving in their own way, and unavailable for each other. Emma's younger brother, who had once been a source of emotional support, began acting out, getting into trouble with the law (in his own efforts to gain attention), and their once close relationship was all but ended. Soon Emma found herself recuperating from her eating disorder virtually alone, her family having fallen apart.

Although she did recover from the eating disorder, she entered adulthood with a shattered sense of Self. She didn't feel valued or loved, she didn't feel she had a right to ask for more from her parents, given their grief, and she felt frightened of the adulthood before her. Consequently, she dove into her work with such a singular focus and drive that she barely even let herself sleep. She worked constantly, aiming for great wealth and acclaim, while never allowing herself to just enjoy her life. By the time she sought help, she was not only a high-powered executive, but she was a wife and mother herself, with no time for her family, no time to enjoy the wealth she'd earned, and no time for her aging parents.

It was only when Emma's own daughter confronted her about a lack of involvement in the family that Emma realized she was replicating the family patterns she had learned as a child. She realized, too, that she was still reacting to her parents' focus on their dying child, by trying desperately to achieve great heights so that they would turn their attention toward her.

As Emma's story demonstrates, each family member brings to the family their own issues, challenges and needs. The Self that develops in a family context is one that has been shaped by multiple relational dynamics. Whether you were an only child raised by a single parent, or whether you came from a large close-knit extended family, you were shaped by these dynamics. Thus, one of the best ways to begin understanding your past is to gain an understanding of how the emotional system has operated in your family system.

One way to find clarity in this process is to chart your family tree, identifying each person, and then exploring the branches that extend from your key family members. Genopro® is a useful online tool that can help you chart your family tree. You may find that, using some of the genealogical sites online, you will also discover family histories you never knew, and these in turn, may shed light on certain family dynamics that originated in past generations.

By studying your own patterns of behavior, and how they relate to those of your multigenerational family, you will discover new and more effective options for solving problems and for changing your responses to the role you were unconsciously assigned by your parents. Let's look at three of the more common roles that Pia Mellody describes in her model—the Hero Child, the Lost Child, and the Scapegoat Child.

THE HERO CHILD ROLE

The Hero Child is the proverbial "golden child" in a family, such as Stewart, in Chapter 2. Recall that Stewart's mother and father became so enmeshed with him that his mother turned him into a substitute for her husband, after their divorce, going so far as to leave the door open when she bathed. She even encouraged him to date her friends. His father also put him on a pedestal and thought Stewart could do no wrong. The trademark of the Hero Child is that he or she is enmeshed by one or both parents.

The Hero Child learns to try to mitigate family conflict—often by excelling in everything they attempt. The Hero Child hopes that by excelling in school, sports, music, or whatever they do, they will make their parents proud, and everything will change. The Hero Child may frequently intervene to manage conflicts in the home, and he or she becomes good at controlling out-of-control situations. The Hero Child also focuses on achieving performance, control, and perfection. Such children may end up in Ivy League schools, regardless of their family background, achieving stellar academic performance by studying extremely hard. They may be prone to extreme anxiety, because they fear making any mistake. They often assume far more responsibilities than most people can handle, because they fear no one will be able to do something as well as they can. They tend to not have their own sense of Self, as they are too busy controlling and managing what everyone needs done in the family.

The upside to the Hero Child role is that these strengths carry these individuals—through their teen and early-adult years—toward being successful, organized, initiators and leaders. Hero Child individuals are likely to be self-disciplined and goal-oriented as well as sensitive to others.

David was one such child. The third child out of four, David grew up in Maine, where his father was a manager in a transportation company, while his mother took care of everything at home. David, the second son in the family, was the favored son. He grew up being the family's golden boy. His older brother was the black sheep, who got into constant arguments with their father, but David avoided any conflict. He remembers his father as being lazy and chronically underemployed due to a deep lack of confidence. On the day of David's high school graduation, his father lost his job, and David worried about the future: how was David going to get to college? This worry caused David tremendous anxiety, because he felt that he had to take his father's place as the "hero" in the family.

Seeing his father sitting around the house, loafing, while his mother ran the household, led David to make a silent vow to work hard, take care of his family, and achieve success in all things.

In contrast to his father, David's mother was very driven and a perfectionist in everything she did. She was always going somewhere and doing something. She was driven by excelling in her own athletics, and she had a mantra of "Never quit." Her example instilled in David the belief that he had to be perpetually driven himself. Consequently, as a child, and throughout school, David drove himself to excel in all sports and academics, as well as to be a gentleman and respect others. His work paid off, and he became a star athlete who was well regarded in high school. Unfortunately, his mother responded to his achievements by putting him on a pedestal and showering him with attention. She would go to all his games and cheer so loudly he would become embarrassed. She even scrutinized every girl he dated, because, in her mind, no girl was good enough for him.

Today David sees where his drive and self-esteem came from. He realizes that performance isn't everything. And he is now learning to be more relational—to connect more in his relationship with his wife. He is also learning to relax and enjoy his life and to enjoy a sense of Self, rather than to be responsible for everyone.

THE LOST CHILD

In contrast to the Hero Child—on the opposite end of the spectrum—stands the Lost Child, the role I, myself, learned to become, in my younger years. The Lost Child withdraws from the dysfunctional family by living inside themselves. The Lost Child retreats to a fantasy world of books, hobbies, or television, tuning out the real world in favor of the one they create for themselves. While the Lost Child may well channel that fantasy world into a creative outlet—many Lost Children become authors, artists, or actors, their sense of isolation and solitude often leaves them feeling depressed, lonely, or anxious.

In addition to their creativity and rich imagination, other strengths of the Lost Child show up, later in life, as being flexible, easy going, or particularly self-directed and independent. But the adversities they face can be difficult ones, as each Lost Child struggles to find their place in the world.

Jenny's story typifies just how lost a Lost Child can be. Jenny was raised in Boston, the third of six children, and the only girl. Her German-Irish father was a carpenter, and her Italian mother was a homemaker. With six children, each about a year apart from another in age, Jenny's mother was very busy. Jenny describes her father as a manly man, hard-working, yet a man who could be so angry that she feared him.

When Jenny was 15 years old, she was hanging out with a group of kids her father didn't like, and each time she returned home, her father was so furious he slapped her face, while her mother, who showed little emotion and was quite passive toward her husband, just stood there and said nothing.

Fearful of the anger of her husband, Jenny's mother focused on the household and raising the children, while Jenny, as the only girl, was expected to be—and became—her mother's little helper, well into adulthood. Jenny was a good and impossibly perfect child, who did nothing wrong but was instead helpful, even up to her high school years where she excelled in her academics while helping her mother care for the home and children.

Neither of Jenny's parents was paying much attention to Jenny. Neither parent was valuing her, giving her love and affection, emotional nurturing or guidance. She was forgotten in this way. She was disconnected from every part of her life, as she was expected to be an extension of her mother. She hoped that if she could be good and perfect enough, she would be loved and matter to her parents. She instead became very dependent and naïve.

Of course, the irony of her story is that Jenny went to college and met a man who swept her off her feet. Unsurprisingly however, he ended up being like her father. He did not pay much attention to her, and he treated her poorly.

Just as her mother had done, Jenny became busy raising the

children she and her husband had, and she became very passive and accommodating toward her husband, no matter how he treated her. Today Jenny is divorced, and, through our work together, she is more assertive. She realizes how to set better limits about how men treat her, and she is creating a life of her own.

THE SCAPEGOAT CHILD

Finally, there's the Scapegoat Child. He or she is blamed for all the family's problems. Whether it's the child whose tantrums, melt-downs, or rebellions become the family's excuse for everything that goes wrong and everything the parent has failed to achieve, or whether it's the special needs child whose needs become the excuse for ignoring others in the family and neglecting other family needs, the Scapegoat is the one who is pointed at. Whenever a family problem arises, you can be sure the Scapegoat Child's name gets mentioned.

Even when there are some legitimate reasons for viewing the child's problems or needs as being a priority, when a child takes on the Scapegoat role, they develop poor self-esteem, and they learn to internalize their anger—directing it inward.

Individuals who've been cast in this role often engage in self-destructive patterns as adults, abusing drugs and alcohol, engaging in promiscuous and often unsafe sex (even after marriage), and sabotaging relationships, jobs, and nearly everything they set out to do. However, the advantages of this role in adult life exist too. Scapegoats often have extra access to creativity, and they are less prone to denial and more likely to be honest, good humored, close to their feelings, and able to lead—though at times, in the wrong direction.

Daren was a classic Scapegoat Child, one who exhibited some of the worst, and best, features of the family role. Daren grew up in a remote farming area in northern New Hampshire. His mother, who had been married once before, was from a wealthy background, and was a self-described hippie in her day. His father was a salesman and drug dealer. From his mother's first marriage, Daren had a brother, seven years older than Daren, who would torture Daren and his sister with bullying behaviors.

Daren's parents had a wild and crazy start to their marriage, which turned from passionate attraction to passionate hatred. Their marriage ended after four years, with a great deal of fighting and a bitter divorce.

For at least the next sixteen years of Daren's life, after his parents' divorce, his mother and father were constantly suing and countersuing each other. His father would sue his mother for child neglect and then she would countersue with allegations of child sexual abuse. His father ultimately lost his job at a school because of the all the sexual assault allegations, which were unfounded.

Meanwhile, his abusive half-brother Brian, would be left at home with Daren and his sister while his mother would take off with different men for the weekend. During those weekends, Daren was tied up, stuck in a closet, and tied to a basketball stand by his older half-brother. There were even times when he and his sister were left home alone for a day or two, when he was only five years old, leaving him and his sister to scrounge around the kitchen for food.

By the time he was seven to nine years old, Daren was angry and out of control. He was so wild that he would be thrown into showers by babysitters to get him to stop yelling. Everyone, even his father, who occasionally showed up for visitation, would yell at him to "be a man." No one had his back.

As a result, the family blamed and shamed Daren and talked about what a problem he was and how worthless he was as a kid. Daren was the family Scapegoat. There was nobody to support him. All the family's problems were attributed to Daren's bad behavior. By the time he was a teenager, Daren was so convinced he was bad, that he was drinking at 14 years of age and doing drugs and driving around the countryside with his friends, smashing mailboxes along the road.

Daren was out of control—until he fell out of the side door of a van and smashed his body and face so badly that he was hospitalized. While in the hospital, no one from his family visited him, and, when he returned home, there was no sign that anyone really cared for him. Instead, his mother and father told him that he deserved what had happened to him. The whole family was projecting their problems onto him, and Daren got sacrificed in the process.

Ironically, the Scapegoat is usually the truth teller in the family. No one in Daren's family wanted to own their part in the family drama so they blamed him for their problems thus denying their responsibilities, shortcomings, and problems.

In a classic Scapegoat Child role, today Daren struggles with his impulses to fight or flee tough situations. Through our work together, however, he is beginning to see these parts of himself and how they were formed. By doing so, he is learning to have a new relationship to these parts of himself by reparenting them.

FAMILY ROLES VARIATION CHART

Now it's your turn to assess what kind of roles you took on in your family. Another way I help my clients understand the family roles they were unconsciously assigned is to introduce them to using a Family Roles Chart.

There are really two major timeframes during which roles can be assigned in a family system. These are: first, between 5–10 years of age, and, second, from 11–18 years of age. I don't address the first four years of childhood, because, developmentally, the child is too young to really take on any role that they are aware of.

To make your picture more complete, you can identify certain roles you took on for your mother and others you took on with your father, if that is the case. The same goes for if you were parented by relatives or other caregivers. If you were only parented by one adult, then it is a bit simpler. There are many variations. For now, however, I look at the two primary caregivers.

After reading the previous examples of family roles, try to fill in the possible roles you played when relating to your mother and father (or major caregivers) as a child—Hero Child (HC), Lost Child (LC), and Scapegoat (SG).

On the following page, please see my chart entitled *Family Roles Variation Chart.* I invite you to download this chart, as well as the others you'll find in this book, at:

forms.MountainStreamPublishingCompany.com.

Family Roles Variation Chart

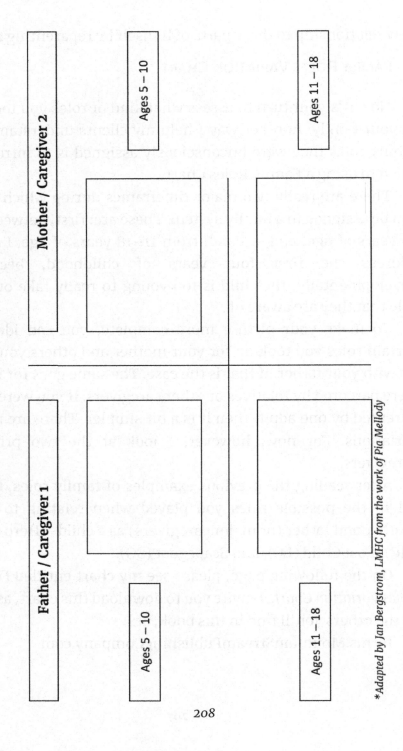

Father / Caregiver 1	Mother / Caregiver 2
	Ages 5 – 10
Ages 5 – 10	
	Ages 11 – 18
Ages 11 – 18	

*Adapted by Jan Bergstrom, LMHC from the work of Pia Mellody

FAMILY ROLES AND RELATIONAL WOUNDINGS CHART

One exercise that I have found to be effective in my practice is to have my clients review my adaptation of Pia Mellody's "Relational Trauma Reactions" which I call *"Family Roles and Relational Woundings in the Five Core Areas"* (on the following page) and which covers the Five Core Areas. I've adapted this chart by showing how acting in one or another of the family roles predicts where woundings may manifest as life patterns that adults keep living and re-enacting. The chart will also help confirm your thoughts on what role(s) you took on.

I invite you to download this chart, as well as the others you'll find in this book, at:

forms.MountainStreamPublishingCompany.com.

Family Roles and Relational Woundings in the Five Core Areas (Distinguishes Where the Trauma Is)

Formation of the Historical/Adaptive Selves Around Ages 5–18

	HERO CHILD / MASCOT	LOST CHILD	SCAPEGOAT CHILD
	Falsely Empowered Child: False sense of Self; identity created for stabilizing the family system	Disempowered Child: No sense of Self, not seen, no matter how hard they try	Falsely Empowered *and* Disempowered Child: Lives in reaction to external happenings
Self-esteem:	Better than others	Less than others	Less than others
Boundaries:	Walled in; invulnerable	Alternates between no boundaries and walls	Walled in; invulnerable
Reality:	Good and perfect; acknowledged and idealized	Good and perfect; unseen and desperate	Bad and "the Problem" in the family
Dependency:	Anti-Dependent: knows no one is there; never asks for much; does it all	Needless and wantless; can be dependent also; often doesn't know what they need	Too dependent; stuck in the system by being "the problem"
Moderation:	Out of control managing; Controlling of others in direct ways	Out of control; manipulative of others in covert ways	Out of control; seen as chaotic and reactive
Presentation and Posture:	Unavailable; passive-aggressive	Yielding; enabling; passive-aggressive; appears powerless	Unavailable; aggressive

Adapted by Jan Bergstrom, LMHC from the work of Pia Mellody

Another way to view your family history is through the Attachment Theory lens. You can try this when you are filling out the second exercise. Attachment Theory was developed by John Bowlby in the late 1960s. It focuses on the importance of "attachment," regarding a person's early childhood development. Attachment Theory claims that the ability of a child to form an emotional and physical attachment to another person depends on how that individual's parents or major caregivers attach to the child.

This form of attachment gives a sense of stability and security, which is necessary to take risks, to branch out, and to grow and develop into a healthy adult. By filling out the questionnaire below, using Pia Mellody's 5 Core Areas, you will see that when a child doesn't get their emotional and safety needs met, they may be traumatized, and the connection or attachment is weakened.

In the questionnaire on the following page, you can begin to assess how much neglect (what you didn't receive) or abuse (what you directly got) affected your childhood. Consider the following questions and circle the numbers that best represent what you experienced in your childhood to create a picture of factors that affected your development.

Rate the different aspects of your experience growing up in your family on the following scale:

1 = Strongly Disagree, 2 = Disagree, 3 = Slightly Disagree, 4 = Slightly Agree, 5 = Agree, 6 = Strongly Agree

Growing Up in My Family Questionnaire and Assessment

Mother or Caregiver 1:

1.	I felt valued by them.	1	2	3	4	5	6
2.	I felt protected physically.	1	2	3	4	5	6
3.	I felt protected emotionally.	1	2	3	4	5	6
4.	I felt protected intellectually.	1	2	3	4	5	6
5.	I felt it was okay to make a mistake, at ages 4–10.	1	2	3	4	5	6
6.	I felt it was okay to make a mistake, at ages 11–18.	1	2	3	4	5	6
7.	I felt my **needs** were taken care of emotionally.	1	2	3	4	5	6
8.	I felt my **needs** were taken care of by physical affection.	1	2	3	4	5	6
9.	I felt my **need** for guidance was taken care of.	1	2	3	4	5	6
10.	I felt, as a child, that I could be spontaneous.	1	2	3	4	5	6
11.	I felt, as a teen, that I could be spontaneous.	1	2	3	4	5	6

Father or Caregiver 2:

12.	I felt valued by them.	1	2	3	4	5	6
13.	I felt protected physically.	1	2	3	4	5	6
14.	I felt protected emotionally.	1	2	3	4	5	6
15.	I felt protected intellectually.	1	2	3	4	5	6
16.	I felt it was okay to make a mistake, at ages 4–10.	1	2	3	4	5	6
17.	I felt it was okay to make a mistake, at ages 11–18.	1	2	3	4	5	6
18.	I felt my **needs** were taken care of emotionally.	1	2	3	4	5	6
19.	I felt my **needs** were taken care of by physical affection.	1	2	3	4	5	6
20.	I felt my **need** for guidance was taken care of.	1	2	3	4	5	6
21.	I felt, as a child, that I could be spontaneous.	1	2	3	4	5	6
22.	I felt, as a teen, that I could be spontaneous.	1	2	3	4	5	6

©*Adapted by Jan Bergstrom, LMHC from the work of Pia Mellody*

Pervasive Neglect / Pervasive Abuse	Neglect / Abuse	Good Enough Parenting
22 – 65	66 – 109	110 – 132

Now add up your score and see what category you fit in: Pervasive Neglect / Pervasive Abuse; Neglect / Abuse; or Good Enough Parenting.

I invite you to download this chart, as well as the others you'll find in this book, at:

forms.MountainStreamPublishingCompany.com.

ASSESSING WHAT YOU RECEIVED OR DIDN'T RECEIVE IN CHILDHOOD

Now that you've completed the questionnaire, think in greater depth of what it was you received or didn't actively receive as a child. Thinking of the concepts I presented in previous chapters, reflect on a definition of "good enough parenting." Healthy parents value and build their child's self-esteem in an appropriate manner. Healthy parents protect their child physically, mentally, emotionally, and spiritually, by assessing situations for safety and by nurturing. In respect to their *own* relationship with the child, healthy parents are alert to this child's need for protection and nurturing. Healthy parents connect to their child by feeling, understanding, validating, affirming, and setting limits. They are aware of and regularly set limits with their child's sense of the world or reality. Finally, healthy parents are aware of their child's needs, and they work consistently to give guidance. They provide for their child's needs, and moderately provide for their child's wants, which will create hope and not deprivation.

Remember, healthy parents must teach moderation as well, in all areas, including behaviors, emotions, thinking, and material acquisitions. Did yours do that?

Now return to Chapter 8, and review Core Practice #4, which lists a child's basic needs. In her book, *Running on Empty*, psychologist Jonice Webb describes three critical components of a healthy parent-to-child connection:

1. The parent feels an emotional connection or attachment to the child.
2. The parent pays attention to the child and sees him or her as a unique and separate person, rather than a possession, a burden, or an extension of the parent's own Self.
3. Using that emotional connection, and paying attention, the parent responds competently to the child's needs.

Sounds simple, doesn't it? Yet few of us ever receive such a healthy emotional connection with our parents. What we receive instead is what Dr. Webb calls Childhood Emotional Neglect (CEN). A parent's failure to respond to their child's emotional needs, also known as Childhood Emotional Neglect (CEN) is something that almost all traumatized children have experienced. The parent may well have loved their child and recognized them as a separate person, but the parent may have been unable—or unwilling—to respond competently to their child's emotional needs.

Or, the parent may have failed to achieve the first component of connecting to their child in that they feel no emotional connection or attachment to the child. This missing connection is often experienced by children who were raised by a step-parent, who may have provided financial or domestic support, but never truly loved or felt any emotional connection to the child of the man or woman they married. Yet even biological parents can sometimes fail to feel this bond with their child, due to their own issues, resentments, or emotional limitations.

Just as damaging are the parents who may have felt an emotional connection but failed in the second component—to recognize their child as a separate person. These parents may have engaged in enmeshment (discussed in Chapter 2), viewing their children as extensions of themselves. These parents either viewed everything their child did as good and perfect, or as shameful and bad. Their children's actions were considered reflections of the parent, and the child was expected to meet their parent's needs, rather than the other way around. Parents who are enmeshed with their children's lives typically have no respect for the child's privacy and boundaries, or they view their child as so perfect that they give the child too much aggrandizement, freedom and independence, never questioning or supervising them.

As you reflect on getting your story straight, think about how each of your parents provided for—and failed to provide for—your emotional needs, based on the three criteria that Jonice Webb lists.

No parent can provide a perfect 100 percent for each of these three criteria, yet the emotionally neglected child received far less than the norm. What percentage did each of your parents provide you? Reflecting on the ways in which your emotional needs weren't addressed in these three areas will help you to understand the woundings you continue to suffer in the five Core Areas of your adulthood.

Reflecting on your own childhood history, assess each of the basic needs listed in Chapter 8. Which ones did you receive or not receive, as a child, and in what amounts—compared to the 100 percent you needed. As you do the assessment, try not to enflame emotional triggers with excessive blame, shame, or self-pity. Observe rather than judge your parents, and yourself, as you do the exercise. The purpose here isn't to dwell in anger or sadness, but to view your childhood from a safe but honest distance, so that you are better able to feel compassion for the Selves within you, and to recognize the ways that your functioning adult Self is responding now to your past childhood quest to have your needs met.

The Family Roles Timeline

This third exercise is one I've found to be especially useful for helping to identify legacies of trauma. When we think about our own traumas, we often forget that trauma can be inherited—much of the woundings we suffer as children have their origins in past traumas that our siblings, parents, grandparents, or even more distant ancestors suffered. To explore the history of trauma in your own family, start by making a timeline. Use an 81/2-by-11 sheet of paper in landscape orientation to create a timeline by drawing a straight line from 0–18 years.

1. Chart significant trauma events on your timeline for your mother, father, and other family members by putting a mark on the approximate spot on the timeline. Add a short note for each event.

2. Below your timeline, note significant events in your family such as deaths, divorces, serious illnesses, or hospitalizations, addictions (and how long they continued), imprisonment, job loss, or other economic impact.

3. Once your timeline is completed, reflect on possible interpretations. Use what you have learned, earlier in this chapter, about functional parenting, for inter-preting the possible impacts of each event.

By reflecting on these events in your life, and in the lives of your family members, you will begin to see that the purpose of getting your history correct, or "getting your story straight" is to make conscious the past traumas of your life. Doing so will raise your awareness as you navigate your future actions and begin to recognize the connections to how trauma is manifest in your adult life. This practice will enable you to be in an action state, rather than a reaction state, thereby creating a new experience of repairing your life.

I would like to address the exercise I mentioned at the start of this chapter. I invite you to download and fill out the *Brief Developmental and Relational Trauma Assessment (DART form)* you will find at:

forms.MountainStreamPublishingCompany.com.

There is also a key, attached to the form. It will give you more information on "getting your story straight."

In the next chapter, I will show you how to move from repairing your old life, to reparenting yourself in your new life. So, get ready for something entirely new to begin.

CHAPTER 11

REPARENTING YOUR HISTORICAL SELVES

You've now reached a pivotal point in your healing journey. You've explored your past, reflected on your boundaries and taken steps to strengthen them, you've cultivated a more functional adult Self and you're learning how to get your story straight and how to rearrange your furniture. You're better able to see your childhood in a more accurate, unfiltered, light. While getting to this point has brought you considerable discomfort, I suspect it's also brought you considerable comfort—by helping you to see that *you* were not the problem in your family, but that the family system you grew up in was unable to give you the nurturing and protection you needed.

Your parents failed you in one or more significant ways and as a result of their failures, you have spent a lifetime trying to heal the wounds their parenting inflicted. Now it's time to reparent yourself. To help you do that, I'm going to introduce you to two essential dialogues—"Reparenting your historical Selves," and "Standing in your truth." We'll get to the second of these in Chapter 12. In this chapter, I'm going to show you how to reparent your historical Selves. But first, let me tell you about Cathy.

CATHY'S STORY

Cathy grew up in a wealthy family in southern Connecti-cut. Her father was a professor at a prestigious university. Her parents had a seemingly perfect marriage and they had created a seemingly happy family. When Cathy turned 12, however, her parents gathered the family in their living room, and they announced they were getting divorced.

Cathy was shocked and couldn't believe it. Within one year the house was sold, the divorce finalized, her father remarried and moved to the Midwest, and her mother remarried and moved two blocks away from their former home—a home where other people now lived! As sudden as all the changes were, Cathy found the transition to be seamless, and she remembers going off to boarding school and not even noticing what it felt like to have her family dismantled.

When I met Cathy, she was going through a divorce of her own, after 20 years of marriage. Within a month of sepa-rating from her husband, Cathy went to her daughter's soccer game where she saw her husband accompanied by a new girlfriend. Cathy grew very depressed. After spending much of her time in the Third Core Practice, checking in with herself, her thoughts, her emotions and feelings, and asking herself how old she was feeling, she was still sad and lonely. Then she decided to go to the barn and visit her favorite horse Barney. She held him, and he nuzzled her. She felt the grounding and affection this horse had for her.

As we worked together, I asked her to find a time in her life when she had felt this way before. She immediately recalled her parents announcing their divorce. She then realized that as much as she'd told herself the divorce had not impacted her, that in truth, she had felt like she was being left behind. Going away to boarding school had insulated her from facing the reality of her family shattering so suddenly. She began re-experiencing the feelings of her 12-year-old Self—the feelings of being left behind.

Once Cathy had put those experiences and emotions together, it all made sense. She began riding her horse, resumed yoga, and engaged in activities with new friends. She was using a cognitive intervention, or Core Practice, called "Knowing the Self." She then used the Core Practice called "Boundaries" and asked her husband not to bring his girlfriend around family events until after the divorce. She also used other Core Practices, such as "Self-Care" and "Needs and Wants." Interdependently with others, she reached out to new friends, which pulled her out of her trauma reaction.

She finally told me, "I can create the life I want!" This is now her mantra when she experiences those feelings again. She comforts herself through this process, which is a way to reparent the 12-year-old girl that was left behind.

How can you begin the process of reparenting? To get started, I'm going to suggest you do something that may sound crazy—start talking to yourself!

REPARENTING YOUR HISTORICAL SELVES—FIRST ESSENTIAL DIALOGUE

For some of you, it may seem silly to hear the term "reparenting your Selves." After all, you only have one Self, right? Wrong. As you'll discover, we have multiple Selves from the past that reveal themselves in our adult lives. And you may think that the very concept of reparenting is a bit odd. Much of this chapter, however, will be about the honest fact that none of us who have suffered childhood developmental trauma, were parented well. Inadequate parenting ends up passed through the generations. When we become adults, and have our own children, we inevitably end up using the parenting model our parents used on us. Perhaps some of us get into deep exploration about how to be a functional parent, and perhaps we even research or read about it. Others will do the exact opposite as our parents did to us, in an effort to not repeat our parents' mistakes. Yet no matter which direction we go, we will find ourselves passing onto our children the wounds we suffered as children—just as our parents did to us. Whichever direction we take, that direction—and its outcomes—point to that fact that we do not have a functional model of parenting and we are swim-ming in our own material.

Recall in Chapter 9 that I defined what a functional adult Self would look like and how to cultivate that Self? This functional adult Self will now enable you to reparent your historical Selves, using self-talk. Another term I use for this process is being relational with your "adaptive emotional ego states from the past." These emotional ego states are like scripts you learned, historical scripts, adapted to the childhood you grew up in. The scripts are so embedded in our psyches that—even for me, after all the work I've done on myself and others—I find they are deeply hidden in my limbic system, and they break out when I am triggered. The same is true for you—which for some of you might come as a surprise. For others, you are so familiar with these young places inside you that they feel energetic and rebellious, just squirming to leap out and take command.

But be careful. What I commonly see substituting for a true functional adult Self is a refined "adaptive adolescent Self." Although these emotional ego states or Selves may look similar, they are substantially different at their core. When someone is behaving from their "adaptive child Self" or "adolescent Self," no matter how well adjusted their communications or behaviors seem, they are still operating out of woundedness and unresolved Core Areas. Their growth and healing have not matured or been adequately completed. The assignment of the functional adult Self, then, is to recognize these historical emotional ego states or historical Selves, and to step in and start to functionally reparent them. The task is a challenging one. These emotional ego states or historical Selves are part of you, even if you don't remember them.

Recall that the ability to esteem yourself with inherent worth from within shapes your humanity, your ability to be intimate, and your capacity to be real. This sense of self-esteem also contributes to how you establish and use boundaries, as well as your ability to maintain a sense of spontaneity. Therefore, it is essential to use your functional adult Self, maintaining Self-compassionate awareness, when you are reparenting your historical Selves.

Self-compassionate awareness happens when you observe yourself without judgment, using a keen curiosity, simply interrogating and noticing what there is to discover about yourself. As you do so, you will be able to step back, to use your personal resources, and to stay regulated and embodied, while reminding yourself that this is a spiritual and intimate journey of embracing your disparate Selves. Another phrase I like to use when describing this process is, "In – To – Me – I – See." In other words, through Self-compassionate aware-ness, you seek *intimacy* with yourself.

In the following chart, adapted from Pia Mellody, "Types of Emotional Ego States," you will discover how invisible and seamless emotional experiences are when relating to our partners, business associates, friends and family. The first two emotional states are present-day experiences we have when sharing with others. The second two adaptive emotional ego states are historical. They arise from your family of origin. Let's start with the present-day experiences with which we are more familiar. The first one is when we are in a well-rested and balanced state when hearing some-one share with us something about themselves and we respond, feeling grounded, present and self-regulated. This emotional state typically occurs when we are in a functional adult Self. In the second present-day experience, when we are in an intimate experience with someone who is sharing their reality or struggles, we can find the same, or a similar, experience in our own lives or imagination, and have empathy for what this person is going through.

HISTORICAL STATES RELATED TO CHILDHOOD TRAUMA

The first adaptive emotional ego states or historical Selves that I work with when I focus on reparenting with my clients are feelings that feel childlike, and familiar from some part of the Self that is related to childhood experiences, whether those experiences are positive or negative. The negative ones can be triggered and show up seamlessly in adulthood without our even realizing where they came from and what they are about. These triggered reactions come from the adaptive or historical Selves that were formed and created to survive the challenging life situations you grew up in.

I believe each person has two, or possibly three, adaptive or historical Selves that are formed from childhood. Anywhere between birth and four years of age, adverse ex-periences can produce a more wounded Self, which is mostly recorded in the limbic section of the brain. The wounding experiences that produce this Self are not remembered, because they are not cognitive. Addressing these wounds requires more experiential and body-based interventions for healing, rather than cognitive or behavioral therapies. In this book, however, I am focusing on the adaptive or historical Selves that are formed from about 5 to 10 years of age, and again are formed differently from ages 11 to 18.

These are the adaptive or historical Selves that need

reparenting, and reparenting through self-talk is one of the two essential dialogues you will need in your journey. If real reparenting and intervention doesn't happen, chances are the historical "Younger Self" and/or the "Adolescent Teen Self" is driving the bus in your life, metaphorically speaking.

Another set of emotional states I focus on with clients are the feelings and emotions absorbed from parents and caregivers as a child is growing up. These emotional states are intricately woven into our historical Selves. Children growing up in a family are like sponges. They don't know how to use functional internal boundaries to protect themselves from their parents' emotions. When a parent is irresponsible with his or her own emotional life, the child of that parent will pick up and carry the parent's emotions. The child will absorb these emotional states—which are usually toxic and extreme—as their own emotions. These emotional states show up to cause problems later in life. They make it difficult for an individual to hold him or herself as having inherent worth and value— especially if the individual was shamed a lot as a child. These emotional states can also cause panic attacks, particularly if the parent or caregiver exhibited extreme fear or panic, or if the parent/caregiver was depressed, causing the child to be hopeless.

The second essential dialogue, which I will discuss later in this chapter, I call "Standing in Your Truth." In this dialog (or self-talk), you tell the parent or offender about those absorbed feelings, and you affirm "Your Truth" as you now know it.

Typically, when I work with my clients, they all struggle with deciphering whether their emotions are historical feelings from the past, which form a part of the Self, or whether they are current functional adult balanced feelings. I give them a simple sentence that can be helpful as a guideline: "If it is hysterical (extreme), it is most likely historical."

I invite you to download this chart, as well as the others you'll find in this book, at: forms.MountainStreamPublishingCompany.com.

Types of Emotional States

Functional Adult Emotional State	A sense of balance and self-regulation, grounded-ness, embodiment, present
Functional Adult-to-Adult Emotional State	A state of empathy between two individuals
Historical Emotional Ego States	Parts of Self that adapted through feelings and behaviors during childhood; can be positive or negative feelings; negative feelings generally relate to childhood trauma
Family of Origin Absorbed/Carried Emotional States	Stressful emotions that were released or detached from by the parents or caregivers; child absorbs and carries in the extreme into their adult life

*Adapted by Jan Bergstrom, LMHC from the work of Pia Mellody

Ultimately, the goal from using the essential dialogues of self-talk—throughout your lifetime—is to heal from your woundings, continually reparenting your historical Selves and learning to stand in your truth by using your functional adult Self. This technique Pia Mellody calls "feeling reduction."

As you know by now, when working with clients I see them as being whole, while hidden beneath a collection of parts.

Everyone has a true Self or spiritual center, known as the functional adult Self, to distinguish it from the disarticulated parts. Even people whose experience is dominated by these Historical Adaptive Selves have access to cultivating a functional adult Self and its healing qualities of curiosity, connectedness, compassion, calmness and living in the Five Core Practices.

I see my job as a therapist to help my clients to disen-tangle themselves from their parts and access their functional adult Self, which can then connect with each part and heal it through self-talk reparenting, so that the parts can be seen and heard and their destructive hold can be released. When this happens, you will enter into a more harmonious collaboration within yourself.

Ultimately, you will be living from action rather than reaction in your life. I have learned to recognize the spiritual nature of the functional adult Self, allowing the practice to be helpful in my clients' spiritual development, as well as their psychological healing.

BEFORE MEETING OUR SELVES

Before meeting their historical Selves or parts, many clients ask me what to do once they notice that they are acting out of a historical adaptive Self. I advise that, when that happens, they should immediately start to notice—step back and view, without judgment—the state they are in. Then, I tell them: ask yourself, again, non-judgmentally, "How old does this feel?"

Once you are aware that your actions are stemming from

your historical adaptive Selves and you can clearly articulate the feelings that accompany those states, the process of reparenting begins by using a series of interventions through self-talk. Three essential skills that I tell all my clients to begin to cultivate, in order to effectively employ these interventions, are as follows:

1. *Nurturing*

   Support and foster the needs of the historical adaptive Self by:
   - Providing for your physical needs (medical, dental, food, clothing, shelter, protection, and affection)
   - Providing for your emotional needs (validation, attention, information, education, and protection)
   - Expressing yourself in a manner that is warm, affectionate and calm, rather than frightening, judgmental, or cold
   - Providing acceptance, guidance, and fostering independent self-care

2. *Affirming*

   Declare and support the truth of the historical Self by:
   - Attachment, bonding, creating safety, and regulation
   - Mirroring and validating your reality
   - Giving yourself time, attention, and protection, such that you "are seen"

3. *Limit Setting*

   Set and enforce reasonable limits on your historical (most likely adolescent) Self's behavior by:

- Enforcing direct consequences, related to the degree of a violation
- Helping yourself to understand the consequences, and learning important lessons on how to be respectful
- Teaching respectful living which creates maturity and accountability

Another way to look at healthy reparenting is through the lens of attachment theory. There are three essential components when you are addressing your historical Selves:

- Feel an emotional connection to that part of you. (You have to feel it in order to heal it!)
- Pay attention to that part, and see yourself as unique, separate from your parents, and separate from others. Appreciate what this part of your Self has done to help you survive.
- Use that emotional connection and attention to re-spond competently to what that part of your Self needs.

DURING THE EXPERIENCE OF MEETING OURSELVES

Ultimately, the historical adaptive parts inside you will experience love by being seen, affirmed, and nurtured. They will begin to feel safe and taken care of, and as such will become integrated into your whole person, rather than each part acting on its own.

During this process, the functional adult Self reiterates and affirms truths, such as those listed below, to the historical or adaptive parts. This is a process of shifting your old childhood paradigms or concepts (rearranging the furniture, as mentioned in Chapter 10).

- You were the child **and** they were the parents.
- Your Mom or Dad did not protect you against abuse. While learning to parent you, they were well-meaning **and** human, **and** they fell short on the job.
- Functional parents work together, **and** if one parent is abusive, the other parent steps in.
- When locked in a good parent/bad parent perception of your mother and father, rearranging the furniture will help you to stop deifying the "good parent" **and** to see their humanity.
- Parents need to be held accountable, rather than blamed for your wounds. Blame keeps us in the victim position and stuck, whereas accountability helps us to move on.
- Your parents were well-meaning, and they were human. You can love your parents **and** still hold them accountable.
- Holding your parents accountable is a process of rightful assignment of responsibility, it helps you in the healing process by shifting the guilt, shame, and responsibility or fault away from you, the child who was growing up. (Accountability is the "rightful as-signment of responsibility" coined by La Shanda Sugg, a student of mine, so that the child doesn't have to keep thinking it was their fault.)
- The best part of your parents would want you to hold them to account for what they did, recognize that they are human and imperfect, **and** they chose to be in relationship **and** have children.

GIFTS FROM A CHALLENGING CHILDHOOD

PUTTING IT INTO PRACTICE

You now have the beginnings of a functional adult Self, now, and you understand your story better. Now, when you get triggered or activated in your present life, you are better prepared to practice some techniques that will help you control your actions and reactions. You will start by asking yourself, "How old am I feeling?" Then, when you have an idea of that age, you will look to find that historical Self, and you will step back to pay attention and reparent through self-talk and nurturing, affirming, limit-setting attention. When triggered emotional states call you, it is because they want to be seen, to be felt, and to know that someone will show up for them.

To help you put these concepts into practice, I want to share with you two examples of reparenting the young Self and the adolescent/teen Self. Remember my story, from the introduction to this book? I discussed what happened to me as a child and how those traumatic experiences ultimately gave me a lifelong interest in working with trauma. Let me use myself as an example of reparenting my younger Self, as a way to help you understand how to do this. When I was four, my mother overdosed on pills, and I found her passed out on the bedroom floor. She was then hospitalized, and while she was gone, my father, older brother, and I were in a serious car accident, which left my father critically injured and hospitalized for several months, leaving me and my brother in the care of relatives.

After my parents came back from their respective hospital stays, it was still another three months before I saw them. My dad still walked with a brace and cane, and my mother's emotional state remained fragile. By this point, I was in kindergarten, and really struggling. I was restless and shy, and uncertain of myself.

Later, when first and second grade rolled around, I had a difficult time learning to read, due to the undiagnosed PTSD. I felt like I was in a fog, and I was so anxious about being called on in school, that I couldn't hear what the teacher was saying. If teachers did call on me, I froze.

On top of it all, I had a lisp and was going to special classes, so the kids made fun of me. I couldn't read, and the adults were talking about keeping me back a year. I had so little confidence that I would just freeze when it came to answering questions or doing work in reading or math or English.

By the time I reached fourth grade, I remember my teacher yelling at me about sentence structures, and again, I froze. I felt so much shame and defectiveness that I would cry. I became so anxious due to my fear of being called on—or made fun of, on top of the chronic belief that I was dying. I was diagnosed with obsessive compulsive disorder.

Decades later, this part of me came up when I began the process of writing this book. My precious nine-year-old Self rose to the surface of my psyche when I received some feedback from an agent about my writing. "Every sentence has to have a noun and a verb to be a complete sentence!" she wrote, castigating me for the grammatical shortcomings of my early drafts.

I dropped into my young historical adaptive Self, and I put my head on my desk and cried. I was no longer my functional adult Self. I was that nine-year-old little girl, being screamed at by her teacher.

So, after I had my cry, wallowed in my anguish, and convinced myself my efforts to write this book were hopeless, I moved to my functional adult Self, where I was com-passionate and curious. I asked myself how old I was feeling. I recognized her in a minute. I sat down in my private office, closed my eyes to start doing the mind's eye work, and I saw her, the nine-year-old inside me.

She was in the classroom, sitting with her head on the desk. In my mind, I walked to her desk, and as I reached her, everyone else in the room disappeared. I took her by the hand, and together, my functional adult Self and my nine-year-old Self walked to a safe place in my office where I could talk to her. I didn't have to introduce myself, as she has met me many times before.

I then started to validate and nurture her by saying "It's okay, you are not stupid. First of all, that teacher doesn't need to speak to you that way. I am here now, and I want you to know that you are worthy. I know you don't believe it now, but you are. I care about you deeply and what you are going through."

I then paused to see how she responded. (Remember this is mind's eye imagination work.) She looked up and gave me a smile. As I scanned her little body, I could pick up her feelings of hopelessness, shame, and fear. I then told her, "I have your back and I am going to help." She smiled more.

I asked her if she had any questions and she said, "Is this ever going to get better?"

I said, "Yes."

Even though I can't rewrite history, just by being there and connecting with her, I created a sense of relief and some hope for that part of myself. I then said, "I can't change the past, but, when you show up today in my life, I can definitely help support and empower you. You will not be alone." I then put her back into my heart for safe keeping. When I was satisfied that my mind's eye work was done for the day, I called my agent and decided to terminate our work together. Instead, I hired a wonderful editor who treated me with compassion and care.

When I work with clients who are discovering new parts in themselves, I have them go through the ritual of bringing the essence of that child version of them into their heart for safekeeping. I ask the client to ask that part of them to join them on their journey in life. Then, if the historical child or adolescent Self says "Yes," I have the client put their right palm up and ask that the essence of that child or teen come into their palm. Next, I ask them to slowly place their hand over their heart. That child or teenage part is then integrated with their adult Self, becoming a conscious part of their identity and being. The client can then be aware of that part's presence and needs for further reparenting as reactions and feelings arise.

Remember, as I said above, the role of the functional adult Self is to reparent with affirming statements, nurturing actions, and limit setting. In my own case, since I have already integrated my child part and my teen part from doing my own personal work about 17 years ago, I do not ask those parts to come with me. They are already integrated. That process of invitation is usually a one-time event.

Another example of reparenting a teen or adolescent Self, comes from the work my client, John undertook. John took my intensive workshop, which is mostly experiential work on learning how to reparent the historical adaptive Selves and to stand in your truth. (I will explain more about Standing in Your Truth, in Chapter 12.) Here's John's story.

John is a 45-year-old successful consultant who has separated from his wife. He grew up in an Italian-American family and was the first child, and the first male child in his family, with one younger brother. John grew up with a mother with bipolar disease and a functioning alcoholic businessman father. When his father was at work, his mother would physically abuse John. The parents had a challenging relationship. They would yell and get angry with each other constantly. When John was 13 years old, he and his brother—who he was very close to—were in a sledding accident, and his brother died.

After his younger brother's death, John felt as if his parents blamed him for the tragic accident. He suffered in agony at both the grief over the loss of his beloved brother, and his parents' belief that he had caused the death—which led him to become increasingly angry.

By the time John was 14, he had become so angry that he was getting into physical fights with his dad. Finally, his rage turned against his mother, and, after getting into a fight with her on the front lawn, he was arrested.

In my intensive workshop with John, we visited his younger child Self and his teenage Self, while mostly focusing on his teenage historical adaptive Self. This part of him was out of control. No one could set limits on him. So, when he went into his past to find the teenage John, he was angry. But underneath all of the anger was intense hurt. He loved his brother, and the shame he felt from his parents was unbearable. To avoid experiencing the shame, he used anger as a weapon, erecting a wall to become invulnerable and to stay away from the pain. Here is John's dialogue with that part of himself.

John was sitting in my group room, as I facilitated his conversation with his historical Self. He closed his eyes, so he could do the mind's eye work. He saw himself sitting on his bed, in his bedroom. He could see his old room and recalled the smells and memories of the room. Then his functional adult Self walked into the room. The adult John began by introducing himself as his grown-up Self of today—important, since teenage John had never met this John before. He started to affirm and nurture his teenage Self, saying, "It's okay—you have every reason to be angry. I totally understand why you are angry and raging." Then he waited to see the look on the face of his teenage Self. But his teenage Self didn't want to talk, so John kept on trying to reach him. "I know how much you loved your brother," he told his teenage Self, "and I know how hard it is to feel that your parents are blaming you. It is not fair."

At that point, teenage John looked up. He was interested. As the nurturing, affirming dialogue continued from adult John to his teenage Self, he got that teenage part to soften and then the tears began to fall. Functioning adult John also confirmed that his parents were out of control and doing nothing about it, and it was all focused on him now. This was an important part of John's work, as functioning adult John needed to feel teenage John's pain, not just think about it as an interesting concept. He ended by saying "I know you don't believe it now, *but you are not at fault.* I care about you deeply, and I care about what you are going through."

As he scanned his teenage body, he could pick up new feelings of calm and hope. He then told his teenage Self, "I have your back, and I am going to be right here whenever you show up in the future. You are not always going to like it, however, because I am going to set better limits on your anger." Teenage John frowned and then acknowledged that the functional adult Self John was right. He then had a smirk on his face and smiled. He was open. So, adult John asked teenage John to join him on his journey in life. The teenager said "Yes," and John put out his right hand, palm up, and asked the essence of his teenage John spirit to come into his palm. When that happened, he slowly placed his hand over his heart. His teenage part is now with him, integrated, where he can be aware of its presence and needs for further reparenting—and especially for setting limits. John had to "feel it in order to heal it."

A MEDITATION TO USE FOR YOUR HISTORICAL ADAPTIVE SELVES

Here's another practice that will help you to reparent yourself by integrating your historical adaptive Self or Selves with your functional adult Self. Find a comfortable and safe spot to sit down. Get into a comfortable position, close your eyes, and begin to relax.

1. Take a deep breath in, to the count of five, and then exhale, to the count of eight. Spending more time in the exhale will allow your body to settle.

2. As you do so, relax and drop further into your couch or chair. Do that at least twice. Notice what feelings or thoughts come up. Notice what sensations you are having in your body. Just allow them to be there, without any judgment, and without having to do anything about them.

3. As you listen, use your mind's eye to imagine that a path opens up in front of you. As you start to walk it, a light draws you forward. As you come into that light, you begin to find your personal resources[8]. You allow yourself to be strengthened and imbued by those resources. Notice and allow a calm groundedness to spread over your body. Feel that calm, knowing that now you are centered, embodied, and connected to your higher purpose or power. You are grounded in your functional adult Self.

4. As you continue to walk along the pathway you come across your old house, and you notice the many details you might have forgotten over time.

5. As you look, the door opens, and a younger version of you is standing at the door. Is it your younger child Self, or is it your teenage Self?

6. You recognize this part of you from when you were growing up. Scan the body of this child or teen Self and take in the feelings and condition of this inner child. Look at the expression on their face. Walk a bit closer and introduce yourself.

---

[8] By resources, I mean the internal or external resources, discussed in Chapter 9, which you have chosen to bring you calm and to help you maintain your sense of integrity and Self in moments of stress or conflict.

7. If it is the young inner child, perhaps get down on one knee to be eye-to-eye with your child Self.

8. After you introduce yourself to this precious part of yourself, greet them in an appropriate way that makes the child or teen comfortable. Perhaps, if it is the first time they have met you, offer a hug, or just a "Hello." Tell them you have lived the same life they have, and you understand the pain, anger, fear, or shame that they are going through. Ask them if they want to go somewhere safe to talk. If they tell you where they'd like to go, follow them out to that safe place.

9. Allow your functional adult Self to gently bring up a difficult memory that your younger Self had growing up. Don't pick the worst one, start out with a more moderate memory. Remember, during the whole conversation, to affirm and nurture them. If it is your teenage Self you are speaking to, remember to let them know you will be setting limits and they may not like it. Allow them to have their feelings. Tell them it wasn't their fault. Tell them that you are here to "have their back" and to "be here for" them. Tell them that you see and feel them now. Ask them if they have any questions for you.

10. Once finished, tell them that they are loved and worthy. Dry their tears or give them a hug if they are okay with that, then tell them you will be aware of them, caring about them, until you see them again.

11. Another option is to ask them to join you on your journey in life and to take them with you. If they say "Yes," then take their essence along by inviting it into the palm of

your hand and then placing your palm tenderly over your heart. If they say "No," leave them in a safe place, until you can come back to visit them again.

12. Finally, as you continue on your journey, leaving the home you grew up in, continue walking down the street, until you find a safe place that you had as a child. It might be a park, a friend's home, or a patch of woods where you took refuge. Whatever it is, go there, and as you arrive, you will sense the calm this place once provided you. Smell the scents and watch the activity going on around you. Find a quiet and safe place to sit down, and as you take a deep breath in—counting to five—and exhale—to the count of eight, you will begin to notice how your body feels.

13. Take each hand and place it gently over your heart, one at a time, checking in to see what that part of you is doing. Just feel the weight of your hand, sending warmth and unconditional love to yourself. If you have integrated a part, notice that sensation and say, "I've got you now." Then in your mind's eye, feel a sense of gratitude for your life and what you have done to get through it. Appreciating all the parts of you, from your past to your present Self, realize that they are a *part* of you, *not* all of you, now that you are grown.

14. End by saying, "I am learning to love all parts of me, creating gratitude in my journey, and being connected to my higher purpose or higher power." Count to five, and slowly open your eyes.

When doing this exercise, I have my clients either record this meditation on their phones or have someone who they are close to and who has a calm voice record it for them.

They can leave some open time on the recording for their dialogue with their child or teen Self. They can listen at any time, when feeling triggered or activated or when they feel they need to talk to the part that is activated. When recording, make sure you go slowly, and pause between sentences, especially in conversation with your historical parts.

I have a worksheet called "Reparenting Interventions," which you'll find on the following page, that shows how to intervene and reparent from the functional adult state, when dealing with each part of your historical Selves. You will notice there is a column for the adolescent teenage Self when they take on the parenting of your younger child Self. Remember the functional adult Self was created to break the dialogue of the teen from parenting the younger Self. If you find your teen is parenting the younger parts all the time, intervene and put limits on them!

I invite you to download this chart, as well as the others you'll find in this book, at:

forms.MountainStreamPublishingCompany.com.

Reparenting Interventions

Younger Child Self	Adolescent Teen Self	Functional Adult Self
When the younger child Self feels less–than and worthless ...	... the adaptive teen Self negatively parents other younger parts of Self by criticizing and attacking, and ...	... the functional adult Self heals and reparents the younger selves by: • nurturing, affirming, being non–judgmental validating and being supportive. • affirming reality for the teen Self yet setting firm limits on their reactivity.
When the younger child Self feels abandoned and left needy and wanting...	... the adaptive teen Self negatively parents other younger parts by neglecting and abandoning them further, and ...	... the functional adult Self heals and reparents the younger selves by: • nurturing, providing good self–care of needs and wants appropriately. • reparenting the teen Self, by using boundaries in relationship with others. • using protected vulnerability in intimacy, asking for needs to be met, yet letting go of outcomes
When the younger child Self feels out of control...	... the adaptive teen Self negatively parents other younger parts by indulging or extreme withholding, and ...	... the functional adult Self heals and reparents the younger self by: • affirming, being non–judgmental, and validating. • using limits to create discernment and safety. • setting firm limits through boundaries and moderation. • enforcing accountability and responsibility. • moving from reaction to action

*Adapted by Jan Bergstrom, LMHC from the work of Pia Mellody

LETTER TO SELF OR TO SELVES

In addition to the meditation for your historical adaptive Selves, I also like to assign my clients a writing exercise as another option of communicating with their historical Selves.

I have them write a letter to their younger Selves. This letter-writing exercise really allows you to appreciate—and even to have deep gratitude for—your many Selves. See what happens when you try the steps below.

Write a letter to your historical adaptive younger Self or Selves—your child or teen Self. Speak from your functional adult Self.

- Thank the child inside you for surviving the way they did. Describe exactly how they adapted to the trauma that they suffered.
- Tell them that they did the best that they could, given the circumstances, and remind them that they were just a child—or adolescent—developing and growing up in a dysfunctional family.
- Let them know that you are now showing up to cultivate and grow your functional adult Self. As you do so, describe, to the best of your ability, what that reparenting looks like.
- Finally, close by letting them know you love them. In your own words, let them know you are proud of them and that you will always be there for them.

FINAL THOUGHTS

The job of reparenting is never done, I'm sorry—and pleased—to say. I'm sorry, because I know it is hard work. However, it does get easier the more you do it. The intensity dies down, and you catch yourself sooner. And I am pleased, because reparenting through self-talk is such an effective healing technique that having it on hand to de-escalate your stress, anger, or anxiety any time, in any place, is such a powerful tool.

There is one more reparenting technique I want to teach you, and that is the second essential dialogue—Standing In Your Truth.

CHAPTER 12

STANDING IN YOUR TRUTH

O nce you have completed the first essential dialogue—
reparenting your historical Selves—you will be ready
for the second essential dialogue, which I call Standing
In Your Truth, or what Pia Mellody calls "Feeling Reduction."
This dialogue exercise is adapted from the work of Fritz Perls,
the founder of Gestalt Therapy. Standing in your truth is a
process of telling your truth to your parents and anyone who
has been an offender to you when you were young, not by
directly confronting them—which could cause further damage
to you and your family relationships—but, rather, through the
use of the "empty chair."

You begin the process from your functional adult Self,
speaking to your visualized image of your parent or caregivers,
not as they are today, but as you saw them when you were a
child. Your objective, in this one-way conver-sation, is to tell
them, honestly and candidly, about the impact their parenting

has had on you, both as a child and as it shows up today.

In this exercise, as you imagine your parents sitting before you, you will tell them what you once needed, and how they failed to provide it to you.

As you do so, you will experience a lifting of shame and guilt. You will realize that so much of your suffering is not your fault. This is not an exercise in blaming your parents. It is instead a process of holding them accountable. Holding someone accountable is a process by which an individual assigns the rightful responsibility for parenting back to the parents or caregivers who were in that individual's childhood.

This reassignment of responsibility releases the adult's belief that the trauma they experienced as a child was their fault. I'll tell you in detail how to do this exercise at the end of the chapter, but first, let's explore how it can transform you.

HOLDING YOUR CAREGIVERS ACCOUNTABLE

What does it mean to hold your parents or other caregivers accountable? As I indicated in the last chapter, holding someone accountable for the damage their actions have caused is basically the "rightful assignment of responsibility," a phrase coined by one of my students, La Shanda Sugg. The reason that you need to hold them accountable is to finally free yourself from the guilt, shame, and pain that you have suffered throughout your life. You were not responsible or at fault for what your parents or primary caregivers in childhood did. They were the adults, and you were the child. The release of this shame and burden comes in the form of energy, relief, and a sense of feeling lighter. Therefore, holding someone accountable for your suffering is a somatic intervention.

In order to hold someone accountable, from the standpoint of your functional adult Self, you may want to use rightful anger or self-protective anger. Anger is a complex emotion, and, while it can certainly be a damaging one, rightful self-protective anger can be empowering, when used well. Rightful anger does not mean yelling, screaming, or being reactive. It is expressed by drawing on your containing boundary, filtering what you want to say, and not letting everything out all at once, or inappropriately. You want to filter your anger, which will bring you into a place of power, where you can be assertive and energized, can stand up for yourself, and can have the strength to set limits. In fact, as you draw on this anger within your containing boundary, you will discover that every time you set a limit with someone, it is an act of loving yourself.

WORKING WITH ABSORBED OR CARRIED FEELINGS

The essential dialogue of speaking your truth focuses on teasing out emotions of others that you absorbed as a child, or, as Pia Mellody coined the phrase, your "carried" emo-tional states. Mellody suggests that whenever a parent or caregiver is being irresponsible with their emotions, either by over-expressing them or by denying them, the child will absorb these emotional states and then carry them into their own emotional life. This is especially true when experiencing absorbed or carried shame. Absorbed or carried shame is problematic for all of us because it clouds our self-esteem and contradicts the practice of holding ourselves with warm regard and inherent worth. It sends the message, "I am bad or worthless."

A key point to realize about absorbed or carried feelings from a parent or childhood offender is that when a parent or caregiver is shaming and criticizing their child, they are engaging in projection. Projecting is the act of casting undesirable feelings or emotions onto someone else, rather than admitting to or dealing with one's own unwanted feelings. Projection happens when the parent hasn't resolved or accepted in themselves what they are seeing in their child, and they then go after the child with a vengeance, blaming the child for the problematic trait or issue.

The child internalizes these messages and feels worthless, defective, or self-loathing, for this shameful problem, absorbing the parents' negative emotions.

When a parent especially focuses on an area that they have not resolved in themselves, the child will most likely grow up to have a "Shame Bind" in the area that they were shamed in. For example, if a mother has a weight issue, she might shame her daughter for eating too much. As the child grows up, the daughter will experience shame around her body image. Whenever anyone mentions her weight or eating habits, she will feel worthless. In her memoir, *Occupy This Body,* author Sharon Suh discusses being force-fed by her anorexic mother, who would not release little Sharon from her highchair, and later the dining table, until she had consumed huge piles of food that were far beyond what any small child could safely eat. As her weight ballooned, Sharon's mother would ridicule her, in front of others, for having such an uncontrollable appetite, while the mother herself so controlled her own appetite that she effectively starved herself. As an adult, Sharon became so ashamed of her body that she over-exercised and under ate, convinced that any lack of control would be evidence of her worthlessness.

Now a Harvard-educated professor of religious studies, Sharon has healed from all the carried shame she endured. She now teaches mindful eating. By writing her memoir, she was able to give voice to the small child within, to affirm her body today, and to testify to the abuse her mother inflicted upon her—by projecting her eating disorder onto her small child.

Another example of projection is when a parent shames or criticizes their son or daughter about the child's school performance. The school performance may be an issue that the parent has not resolved in him or herself, and they therefore project it onto their child or children. Thus, a child feels shamed for their grades and their lack of performance, and later, in their adult life, they will struggle with performance, achievement, or goal-setting, because they will have come to believe that they do not—and thus cannot—perform well. Alternatively, they may become so consumed with their fear of failure that, no matter how great their success, they will perceive their actions as failures.

Olympic skater Tonya Harding is a classic example of a child who suffered from her parent's issues with performance. Tonya's talent on the ice was noted when she was a small child, and her mother was quick to encourage Tonya to become an Olympian. But her encouragement was far from constructive. Even the slightest mishap was cause for abuse, including hitting Tonya with a hairbrush, insulting her, and denying her bathroom breaks. As a result of her mother's abusive actions, Tonya did become one of the greatest skaters the world has ever known, but she also was so terrified of failure that when her competitor Nancy Kerrigan proved to be a favorite of many judges, Harding became tangled in a plot to break Kerrigan's leg. Although the attack injured Kerrigan (but did not break her leg), and Tonya has denied having any knowledge prior to the attack—carried out by a friend of Tonya's boyfriend, Tonya's skating career was over. After pleading to conspiracy to hinder prosecution, essentially admitting to helping cover up the attack after it had happened, Tonya was stripped of her 1994 U.S. Championship title and barred for life from participating in any United States Figure Skating Association events. After the movie, *I, Tonya* was released in 2017, Tonya had her first real opportunity to stand in her truth—by having her mother held accountable for the abuse and shaming that had rendered Tonya so terrified of delivering a bad performance.

While these stories of memoirist Sharon Suh and skater Harding are not examples of people who have used Pia Mellody's techniques (as far as I know), their stories do represent examples of how shaming can be internalized by the child. Each story of projecting behavior by Sharon and Tonya's mothers is a good example of what Pia Mellody calls "carried shame" and the creation of "shame binds" in adult life. What's important to know about such situations is this: *Absorbed shame, pain, or guilt does not belong to you; it belongs to the parent or caregiver who originated it.*

Their issues are something for them to become aware of and to do something about, rather than to continue to project it onto you. The same is true when a parent is in *denial* of their emotions, detaches from emotions, or suppresses them. Either way, sure enough, a child will replicate what they witness in their family, and, as an adult they will demonstrate it through their behaviors and self-perceptions. A shame bind can be actively worked on, and released or healed, by using affirmations, which I will cover in Chapter 13.

Further, Pia Mellody has also identified a "shame existence bind," which she suggests is a more deeply rooted experience. The shame existence bind comes from being born in circumstances where the child is not wanted. Some of you may know that feeling deep down inside, yet you may so conceal it that others around you are not aware of it. The shame existence bind typically arises when a mother never attaches to her child. Or, she does not welcome the child into the world. For those who have suffered this form of shame as a child, you may have grown up to believe that you have no inherent worth but must constantly earn—and prove—your worth to the world. In families and cultures where males are prized over females, the little girls learn from an early age that they are inferior to their male siblings, or they may learn that their parents are sorry a girl was born, and not a boy.

Such children—and later adults—struggle with being on this planet. They often apologize constantly, as if everything is their fault, or they shrink from view and don't speak up, or they give up readily on any potential talents or successes, convinced they don't deserve to be noticed. They may never celebrate their birthdays. They may become embarrassed by any gifts, spend little money on self-gratification, and, in many cases, become people pleasers who devote their entire lives to trying to please others. The shame existence bind is especially challenging, and it is best diagnosed by a professional and worked on with a developmental trauma therapist.

Shame in and of itself isn't necessarily bad. Our own shame or embarrassment is an emotion that leaves us feeling exposed, but tells us that we've gone too far with a certain behavior—such as when you've had too much to drink at a party and behaved badly, or said something you shouldn't have when your containing boundary wasn't quite contained. Shame sends us the message, "I made a mistake," which in turn humbles us. But shame as a passing emotion does not leave you feeling worthless. Such shame merely defines you as being human. You learn from it, and you move on.

In contrast, absorbed and carried shame makes a person feel worthless—in other words, worth *less than* others.

In direct opposition to carried shame, a process I call "Standing in Your Truth" can help to root out feelings of worthlessness. Through this process, you will be able to transform the impact of your parents' parenting—both explicit parenting behaviors and implicit, or implied, parenting messages. The transformation you will undergo by Standing in Your Truth will be truly a game changer. Somehow through the process of standing up and naming your truth—*the* truth of your circumstances—you are able to shed light on your understanding of the emotions you have carried from childhood. This acknowledgment, also called acceptance, energetically releases the heaviness of holding it all in and carrying it unconsciously, buried in your psyche.

MY EXPERIENCE OF STANDING IN MY TRUTH

My own experience standing in my truth was life changing. Typically, in an intensive workshop setting, you work with both parents or your two primary caregivers. But, in my case, I focused primarily on my father. As I mentioned, in Chapter 9, because my mother was so emotionally absent due to her mental illness, I came to idolize my father. He treated me as a surrogate spouse, confiding in me all the problems he was having with my mother.

While working with Pia Mellody, she rearranged my thinking—or "rearranged my furniture"—by helping me to see how my father had abandoned me when my mother was very depressed by leaving me alone with her for weeks at a time. As my father increasingly confided in me, I started to take his side against my mother, which made me feel special, as I was the only girl in the family. He would buy me nice clothes from Saks Fifth Avenue, and I would model them for him. I thought that by having such beautiful clothes and so much attention, I was flourishing! Fortunately, through my work with Pia Mellody I came to recognize that I was not flourishing, but floundering. She told me directly, "Jan, you were not flourishing! You were being objectified and used by your father." Consequently, it is no surprise that I fell into this same pattern later in life, with men in general!

So, when my father came into the "empty chair" I was visualizing, I saw him as he looked when I was a teen. I let him know that I was angry at him for using me in that way and for doing nothing to repair his relationship with my mother. I told him that he also used me as a surrogate spouse by telling me so much about my mother, which had created competitiveness between my mother and myself. I ended by saying I didn't like how he had treated me, and that this resentment showed up in my life through my inability to know how to have a fulfilling and vulnerable relationship with my husband. I explained that I was stuck in the fantasy and seductive phases of our marriage, and that I had a hard time with the attachment phase, because I lived superficially, preoccupied with how I looked and performed as a wife and mother.

Once I'd finished holding him accountable by standing in my truth, I felt released of my concerns about my looks and performance as a wife and mother. My relationships with my family improved, and even my relationship with my father felt lighter and more honest even though he had passed away.

Standing in Your Truth: A Client Example

Before I tell you how to do the next exercise, I want to share another example with you. My client, Betsy, grew up, the oldest of two girls, in a wealthy family in New Hampshire. As with many wealthy families, Betsy was sent away to boarding school at the age of twelve. Her parents thought it would be a good idea for her to have structure in her life.

Betsy was a high achieving student, but she had become very depressed at having to leave her family. Feeling lonely and abandoned, Betsy had come to feel captivated by her psychology teacher, a man who gave her lots of attention. She soon spent much of her time in his office, feeling like he really cared for her.

Eventually, he started having sex with her, when she was only thirteen. When her parents found out about what was happening, however, instead of blaming the man, they blamed Betsy. They shamed her for being so provocative.

While Betsy was in one of my women's intensive workshops, where she was doing the standing-in-your-truth exercises, I noticed that she couldn't get angry at her parents about how they had shamed her. She was so convinced that she was at fault, that she remained withdrawn and depressed while addressing the chairs.

Recognizing her resistance, I asked her to stand up, hold her hands up with her palms against mine, and push them against me. While she was pushing, I pushed back harder into her hands. As I did so, I asked her to push harder and say, "I am angry about how you shamed me, Mom and Dad, when you found out about my relationship with my professor." I continued to push against her, asking her to abbreviate her sentence to them by saying, "I am angry! You shamed me. I was just a vulnerable girl."

As she kept on saying this, she started to feel the sensation of her whole-body energy (which was anger), and she came alive. Once she moved to this state, she could then stand up for herself. She stood up for that 13-year-old part of herself, as she continued the exercise. By the time she had finished, she was in tears and felt relieved to know, deep in her being, that the abuse had not been her fault—that she was not defective. She was beaming afterwards, and she described feeling sensations of lightness and relief. Finally, after all those years, Betsy stopped feeling shamed when speaking her truth.

MEDITATION FOR STANDING IN YOUR TRUTH

Are ready to try out this exercise? If so, find a place in the privacy of your home where you feel comfortable and won't be interrupted. Start by grounding yourself in your personal resources (those you worked on in Chapter 9), so that you are in your functional adult Self.

1. Sit quietly on a couch or chair and imagine an empty chair in front of you.

2. Before your parent or parents appear in the chair, call up the precious child or teen inside of you, and ask them to stand behind you (the functional adult Self), so you can protect them.

3. In your mind's eye, imagine you are telling this child that you are going to meet with their parent, and you are going to stand in your truth. Assure them, however, that you are going to keep them safe.

4. Now, visualize your parent sitting in the chair in front of you. Focus on how they looked and spoke when you were ten years old—or the age of this difficult memory. Remember this is a one-way conversion, and they cannot talk back. They are going to listen. You are in control.

5. Perhaps you would like your parent to sit further away. If so, ask them to move back. If you would like them to move closer to you, tell them to do so. What are they wearing? What is the look on their face? Do they know why they are there?

6. Let them know why you have asked them there. Start by saying in your mind's eye, "I have brought you here to

talk to you about your impact on me growing up."

7. Then tell them about any incident in your childhood where they were abusive to you or unaccountable for what they did to you.

8. Tell them firmly, but within your containing boundary, that you feel anger and pain about it.

9. Then tell them how that wound shows up in your life today.

10. After you finish discussing this event, make sure you say, in an empowered voice, "I give you back your shame," or "I give you back your fear or pain. I won't carry this emotion anymore, it belongs to you." Because it really does belong to your parents to deal with their feelings rather than project them onto you.

11. You can also say, "This is about your struggles with your self-esteem, or body image, or lack of education, or your struggles with money or your profession. It is *not* about mine."

12. When you're done talking, you can take a deep breath and blow the toxic energy of carrying those emotions back to your parents when you exhale.

13. Check in with your body now and see what sensations you are feeling. Do you feel warm, hot, light, relaxed, tight? Or do you feel relief and some joy? Whatever it is that you feel, it is okay. You may feel nervous, or you may feel sadness arise. These are all normal feelings as your body releases pent up energy and resettles.

14. Now briefly check in with your child Self or teenage Self, who is behind you. What emotions are they feeling? What

are they thinking? Sometimes they are proud of you for having their back, and they may feel grateful or safe. Sometimes the teenager really wants to yell or get angry at the parent, and this is when you set limits with them to calm down and be respectful.

15. As you continue talking to your parent or caregiver, notice what they are doing. Do they show remorse, or are they hiding behind a wall and showing no emotion? Either way, when a parent shows remorse, he or she is truly being accountable and releases you from all those tough emotions. When the parent shows no emotions or compassion, then their lack of concern is about them. Don't take that one on. It is their material. You can't do anything about that, it is their life and they have to live it. Pia Mellody says, "Being them is punishment enough.

16. After you have finished your conversation with the parent, another way to move the energy is to imagine that all that carried shame and other absorbed emotions are like black toxic smoke. Visualize this dark smoke draining from your body, starting at the top of your head, moving down to your feet. As it releases from you and exits, it crawls across the floor and enters the parent where it turns to white smoke—which isn't toxic to them. For them, the smoke is healing, as they accept responsibility for the emotions they projected onto you.

17. The next-to-last step is to ask the parent to leave, and to thank them for showing up. Remember you can love your parents and still hold them accountable. If they show no remorse, or have passed away, remember the best part of

your parent would want you to heal from your childhood woundings.

18. Finally, ask your child or teen Self, who is standing behind you to come around in front of you. Observe the look on their face. Are they smiling because you stood up for them? Are they relieved? What is happening? Most of all, you are now "having their back." You are showing up to make them feel safe. This is what embracing your truth does. It helps your historical adaptive Selves feel like they are being reparented. Finally, ask the essence of that child or teenager to come back with you and imagine putting them back into your heart. Remember they are *a part* of you—not *all* of you.

As I end these chapters on the two essential dialogues for a lifetime, I want to stress that you don't have to always sit down and spend 20 or 30 minutes going through these dialogues. You can learn to "practice on the fly," a phrase coined by my dear colleague, Cara Weed. Once you understand what reparenting through self-talk is all about, when you get triggered you will be able to say, "How old is this part?"

And then, you will immediately affirm, validate, or set limits. You will use self-talk to reparent that emotional state or part. In return, when you get triggered and feel worthless, or feel extreme fear, which may manifest in a panic attack, you can tap into that part and empower yourself by saying, "Mom or Dad (or caregivers), I give you back your shame. I have inherent worth, and I deserve to be treated respectfully." Or, you may say, "I give you back your fear. I deserve to take opportunities even though I have some fear of my own. I will not be crippled by it."

These are quick interventions, and, of course, you can always go deeper when you are alone at home, starting by placing your hand on your heart, activating your resources, and sending yourself positive warm regard, before having one of these dialogues.

And most importantly, you are not alone. You will discover that wherever you go, there are guides awaiting you. In the next chapter, I'll introduce you to those guides.

CHAPTER 13

GUIDES ALONG THE WAY

Remember Dorothy? No, she wasn't one of the clients I told you about. She was the troubled young girl from *The Wizard of Oz* who set out to get back home. Along the way, she had setbacks, doubts, fears, and worries, but she persevered—thanks to the many guides who helped her. Whether it was Glinda, the good witch, the wizard himself, or those friends who joined her on her journey, each in search of their own healing. Having others to guide and support us may be the single most important gift we will ever receive.

As you may recall, with the support of her friends, Dorothy ultimately realized that she had the power within her to change her own life all along—just by tapping her ruby slippers together and concentrating on her wish. So, if you want to find that power within yourself, the first place to look for those guides is within.

SPIRITUAL PRACTICE: YOUR FIRST GUIDE

We all come into the world, ready-made to be relational and attached. According to attachment theory, we are created to connect with others and to attach and find safety in our relationships. Whenever you see or hold a baby, you know instinctively that they are precious, innocent, and fully alive when born. They radiate a bright light, reflecting the presence of the divine in their being. As they grow and experience the traumas of life, however, whether through abuse, neglect, or abandonment, their inner light starts to dim. For some, that darkness remains for life. But some will brave moving through that darkness to find and release that inner light once again. Such people, I find, have a longing to return to Self and to experience their connection to others once again.

Pia Mellody defines this longing to connect as a process of creating spirituality in one's life. By that she's referring to a conscious contact with the nature of one's soul.

You may ask, what is one's soul? The soul, Mellody says, is the tiny spec of the infinite inside of you. It is your immortal essence—who you really are, as a person. When talking about your relationship between spirit and soul, Mellody describes the spirit giving life to the body, and the individual soul containing your individualized spirit.

We are settled in our soul, when we are calm, willing to forgive, giving to others, moderate in our speech and actions, and content. We speak our truth and experience a oneness in mind and body. You started your spiritual healing journey when cultivating your functional adult Self, which we covered in Chapter 9. You may not have realized it, but, as you cultivated that functional adult Self, you forged a connection to your soul.

In focusing on the soul, it can be helpful to have a connection to a higher power, such as a divine presence or a higher purpose in our lives. This focus serves to help us embrace our humanity. But I understand that, for those of you who do not believe in God, gods, or a divine presence, opening your heart to a higher power can be troubling. If so, I recommend focusing on a higher purpose in life. As you do so, you will find that this connection to a larger context or higher purpose can help you to find greater meaning in your life.

By having a higher purpose, we discover that the setbacks, obstacles, and—yes—even the traumas, that we experience, are far easier to overcome, because we know that they are not the defining features of our lives. Instead, each experience, positive or negative, is a step toward that higher purpose, or destiny.

The spiritual process is one in which a person becomes skilled at experiencing their soul rather than living in their historical emotional ego states. The functional adult Self grows and gets cultivated through the process of connecting to your deeper Self. Your healthy adult Self is deepened when the spiritual principle of bringing your conscious awareness to soul is activated. According to Pia Mellody, the more a therapeutic intervention addresses a client's spiritual journey, the more successful the treatment.

By having a practice of spirituality which connects us to our soul, we are changing ourselves. We are opening ourselves up to who we are designed to be. We also open to embracing our gifts *and* accepting our shortcomings and imperfections. When we use our gifts for a greater purpose—for more than our own reward, we bring forward benefits to others and to the world.

Sometimes when I'm working with my clients, I discover they finally recognize just how long they have been out of contact with their soul's journey. When that happens, it is because they have been serving their ego. But as they move from their ego to their soul's journey, they begin to experience the emotions of joy and pain in ways they never did before.

The experience is transformative. It is a breakthrough experience of healing the suffering from pain and the disconnection to Self, as well as the joy of being released from that suffering and disconnection—realizing there is a greater purpose to their life.

One of my mentors, the late Dr. Brugh Joy, talked of the process of suffering as an essential part of life. Its purpose is not to punish us, but to guide us. Through our suffering, as we go about living in our emotional ego states, those states are re-appropriated back to the divine or to our higher purpose. There, through experiencing the grace that is given to us, we find our soul.

I look at grace as the divine light within us, and our acts of service and acknowledgment of our growth connect us to that grace. Over many years, I have come to find that being in service to others helps guide me on my journey home, a spiritual journey that I alone take as I heal and grow.

PRACTICING GRATITUDE: YOUR SECOND GUIDE

Another key guide in the spiritual process a practice of gratitude. By having a gratitude practice, you become connected to the source of grace within you. Grace, as I conceptualize it, is different from the religious concept of God. I think of grace as a secret key that shifts your awareness and changes your relationship with life—from one of rejecting the world around you and defending against it, to one of accepting the world as it is, with appreciation for all that it has given to you. Whatever your own faith—or lack of faith—teaches you about grace, you may still find the following practices or exercises effective as a way to deepen your experience.

Most people who have been traumatized as children struggle with this concept of grace. For those who do, it is often because they wonder if grace exists: Why isn't their life filled with grace now? The answer to that question is that our lives *are* filled with grace, at every moment, but we don't always recognize it. A failure to see grace in our lives is due to our lack of perception. Two people can have different exper-iences of life. One is so obsessed with their busy schedule that they can't lift their head from their work for a moment. Meanwhile, another, who is just as busy, looks toward the sky and notices all that is happening up there, as clouds pass, birds fly by, and planes filled with people on their many adventures leave only a streak in their wake. This person notices the flowers in bloom, the smiles on the faces they encounter, the spaces where they feel safe and find comfort. Honoring how you are supported by grace, through the practice of gratitude, connects you emotionally to the flow of life.

I do understand that for those who have been traumatized in life, particularly as children, gratitude may be something that is rarely experienced. After all, how can you be grateful for a childhood of neglect and abuse? Yet that neglect and abuse made you who you are today, and for all the imperfections and flaws you developed in the wake of trauma, you are all the more complex and strong.

You may not always feel strong, but you have survived up to this point despite the battering you've received—and you have come to this book, because you want to grow even stronger. Be grateful for that wisdom you have forged from the wreckage of your past. But there's more to the practice of gratitude than being grateful for the strength and wisdom that helped you to survive your childhood. When we are wounded, sometimes all we feel are the wounds. But I can assure you that no matter how deep your wounds, there is so much more to you—and to your world—to be grateful for. The ability to read these words, to think and reflect on them, to taste a peach, or walk outdoors and see the sky, are just a few of the acts we may engage in every day with little thought as to how profound and beautiful they are— until, of course, we consider losing those abilities. Imagine how you would feel if you lost any one of those abilities—and now imagine how grateful you would be to regain it!

Perhaps you have already lost one or more abilities. Perhaps you cannot walk, or you cannot think as clearly as you once did, or your eyesight is growing dimmer, or gone altogether. Someone may be reading these words to you. Focus your gratitude on the abilities you do have—and on all that you have learned and gained; however difficult it has been—as a result of your loss.

We all suffer loss in life, some more than others, and for you, reader, my guess is your loss is far greater than most. Yet, when we practice gratitude, ending our days by reflecting not on what went wrong or what we don't have or didn't accomplish, but on what gifts we did encounter throughout our day, what did go right, what we do have, what we did accomplish, we find a certain peace and contentment that we otherwise would not experience. That is the place of being connected to the soul—the place you will find yourself during a practice of gratitude, as you acknowledge your healing journey.

To get started on your own practice of gratitude, try the following exercises.

MORNING PRACTICE

Before you even get out of bed in the morning, reflect on one thing for which you are grateful—whether it is having slept well through the night, having had an interesting dream, being woken to the smell of someone making you coffee, or just the simple fact that you did wake up. Then say, "When I am grateful for _____, I feel my connection to life."

DAILY PRACTICE

Next, at different points throughout the day, remind yourself of three good things in your life. Say, "Thank you," to the universe, or to life, for these good things, and allow a feeling of warmth to move from your heart to fill your soul. Imagine your heart smiling back at you. See that heart smile in your mind's eye and receive its thank-you.

You will discover that this practice is like a feedback loop. When you thank the universe for its gifts, a response from the universe—and from your own heart—comes back to you, and new neuropathways are created in your brain. Your brain literally changes, so that good thoughts and memories become automatically triggered by the simple words, "Thank you."

This practice also develops the process of warmth in your heart. By welcoming and opening your heart to gratitude, you open it to safety and to a supported life. And when that happens, you allow yourself to feel the warmth of your gratitude at a deep level, one which eventually transforms your very nature from one of unhappiness for what you don't have or have suffered, to one of joy for what you do have and for what you have overcome.

KEEPING A JOURNAL

Keep a gratitude diary so that it becomes a habit—a habit that has been shown to make a remarkable difference in stress. Researchers from the University of California at Davis asked a group of volunteers to write down five things they were grateful for, once a week for ten weeks. At the end of the study, the journal writers reported 28% less stress than they felt before they began the study. The people who kept gratitude diaries also ate better and exercised more. The process of writing down what you are grateful for seems to retrain the brain to be more positive and less consumed with worries. A practice of gratitude also has a positive effect on our bodies. Stress is reduced, and healthier habits—such as diet, exercise, and avoiding self-medication habits such as drinking or doing drugs—are often adopted.

To begin your own Gratitude Journal, start by writing down five things you are grateful for. Do this practice once a week. Make sure you take inventory of your relationships with your family, your partner or close friends, and your coworkers or colleagues. One Harvard University study tracked a small group of men for 80 years and found that living a healthy, happy life was more dependent on good friendships than the amount of money an individual had. So, by focusing on your relationships, and how they enrich your life, you will do wonders for your health, your happiness, and your outlook as well as how you think of those relationships.

Rather than dwelling on the ways that the people in your life fall short, disappoint or annoy you, by reflecting on the rewarding aspects of those relationships, you will treasure them—and your life—even more.

Don't stop with relationships, however. Make sure you include your job, health, children and the gifts you have in your life like your home, car, education, and any self-care and healing practices. If you're out of work, and in bad health and don't have a partner, be grateful for the skills you have acquired, the roof you do have over your head, the health you haven't yet lost, and the autonomy you enjoy in being single. Whatever it is you don't have, I promise you, there's a lot you do have, and more to gain by focusing in on that!

See if you can find other areas in your life that bring you joy, no matter how small, such as your favorite outfit, the joy of driving your car, or your loving pet who shows you so much attention and loves you unconditionally. As you contemplate these small gifts in your life, use your awareness to remind you of your thankfulness for having them in your life. This process helps us become aware of all we have and not take the gifts in our life for granted.

Keep this diary for at least one month. Then find a time and quiet place at end of month to read it back to yourself. Breathe in and out a few times and then engage your resources and reflect upon all that you have by connecting to grace and realizing that gratitude is one of the guides along the way.

ACTS OF SERVICE: YOUR THIRD GUIDE

Another way to be connected to the light within you, grace, is through acts of service. These can be helping work or other kind actions toward your partner, your family, your community, your city, your favorite cause or organization, your country, anyone or thing you care about, or just the world at large.

Through acts of service for others, you will discover a profound and powerful way to connect to that higher power or purpose. Helping others shifts our focus from our own pain to alleviating the pain of others. Service to others can be the most effective method for tapping into the spiritual process, because it transforms your relationship with others and gives meaning to your life, as you engage with this great world in new ways.

There are plenty of ways to give back. Whether you keep it small—in your family and community—or big—by contributing your time to a cause or organization, you can have a positive impact on this world. Most importantly, it isn't necessarily about being recognized for your efforts, but instead, about engaging in your spiritual practice.

As I mentioned, by having a *practice* of connecting to soul, we are changing ourselves and opening ourselves up to who we are destined to be. By using our gifts for a greater purpose than our own, we become channels of positive energy for others and the world. Being in service to others, gives us humility, and it keeps us in touch with our humanity—and transforms us into guides for others.

About eight years ago, my friend, Karen, was diagnosed with inclusion body myositis. According to the Genetic and Rare Diseases Information Center (GARD), inclusion body myositis (IBM) is a progressive and inflammatory muscle disorder characterized by muscle inflammation, weakness, and atrophy (wasting).

Karen was devastated by her diagnosis. She had two young children at home, and her husband had recently been laid off. I remember one day going to visit her, and I was shocked at what I saw. The house was full of clutter, with clothes piled on top of dressers and tables, dishes scattered everywhere and piled high in the kitchen sink, and at least ten loads of laundry strewn on the floor. The outside of the house was just as bad, with junk and clutter all over the yard. Karen's kids were feeding their cat and three dogs as well as getting their own food, because Karen could no longer stand up to cook. I was shocked that her husband wasn't doing anything to keep the home in order, but, eventually, I realized that he was seriously depressed and not doing well at all himself.

Realizing they needed help, I returned to their home three times to do the laundry, clean the house, and organize things for Karen. I got a dumpster company to come in and haul away all the junk in her yard. I then made a list of our common friends to email, and I started a fundraiser to get a housekeeper to help with daily tasks. Just being able to be of service to Karen and her family strengthened the connection to my own soul. By being able to help someone in need, my own issues became so much less important. This act brought me into my gratitude and thankfulness of my own health and life. When things were all settled and we found someone to help her, I returned home from my last trip feeling complete and whole and realizing that I'd found an avenue for me to get in touch with my soul's purpose. So, whatever it may be for you, I encourage you to check in with your availability and think about putting small or large acts of service into practice.

DAILY SERVICE PRACTICE

To start your own practice of service, try the following:
1. Make a list of all the people you know personally who need support or help. Pick at least one person to focus on for the next few months.
2. Then make a list of all the possible things you could do for them. Examples would be to bring food over if there is an illness, help for a day with household chores or repairs, visit for an afternoon over tea or coffee, or send a gift card or money to their favorite cause or foundation. There are many ways to help and support family and friends in need.

3. After you have done these acts of service, check in with yourself, and ask how it felt to be present for someone who was struggling. Did you feel joy, concern, and empathy? Or did you feel frustration, resentment, or anger? If the latter, reflect on where those feelings are coming from. Did it trigger memories of your childhood, or a time when you were forced into the service of your parents or caregivers?

4. If so, think of how you can reframe those feelings—can you tell your inner child that they no longer have to do anything they don't want to do? Can you think, instead, of all the positive results that came of your service—the ways in which you made someone feel better, improved their life, opened their heart, or alleviated their suffering—even if in just one small way?

5. Now connect this experience to your practice of gratitude, noticing how this gratitude for being able to serve another person has brought you into a deeper state of appreciation for your life.

You can also actively focus on a larger scale by participating in your neighborhood, state, or country, or by giving your time and energy toward a good cause. This can be an ongoing commitment that you believe in and support, such as a community clean-up group, a local historical society, the Rotary Club, the Boys and Girls Clubs of America, the Humane Society, or any group that can use your talents, skills, or time.

Many people have a foundation they support due to a life experience that brought them awareness of that cause. My oldest son was born with major arteries of the heart, the ventricle, and the aorta reversed. When he was only three days old, he had to have heart surgery and a blood transfusion. We were so grateful for the people and organizations that worked together to save our son's life that my husband has been donating his blood for years, and we have been supporting, with donations, Boston Children's Hospital, the provider of our son's life-saving surgery. We are not alone. Once anyone has had a life-threatening event and been gifted by the efforts of others, they discover that they do indeed have the time, money, or gifts in kind, to give to the organizations that made their own life, or that of someone they love, so much better.

SHARING YOUR STORY IN SAFE RELATIONSHIPS: YOUR FOURTH GUIDE

As you discover the gifts of your own challenging childhood and your higher purpose, it is essential to find a handful of close friends, or perhaps if you are lucky, family members, who feel safe and who are willing to be present and show up for you as you change and grow. Such people are essential to acquire in your life.

Someone who is safe, confidential, and can embody the concept of empathy is a precious gift. According to author Brené Brown, empathy is different than sympathy in that empathy is a process of feeling *with* someone rather than sympathy, feeling *for* someone. Empathy involves being vulnerable and connecting to the emotions someone is feeling, not necessarily having the same experience of that person, but following closely where they are going.

Sympathy, in contrast, sends the message that you are sad for what they are going through. Empathy is sending the message that you respect and care about their experience and pain, and can relate—either from real-life experience, or from imagining how you would feel. Empathy communicates to someone that they don't have to be alone in their suffering and that you want to be with them. It is about holding them close to you without any judgment and, in effect, saying, "You are worthy of connection, you don't have to be alone." It is not about the need to fix or make things better for them. When you want to express sympathy, you say things like "I am sorry about what you are going through." When you want to express empathy, sometimes all you need to do is just be there, saying nothing.

An important element of empathy is sharing your own story with others. By sharing your story, you communicate to others that you feel safe with them, you trust them, and that you, too, have had an experience that they can relate to.

Using this principle of empathy in your life is important, because the more you cultivate those kinds of safe, sup-portive, interdependent (not co-dependent) relationships, the more you heal. Sharing empathy gives you an opportunity, during the process of someone showing up for you, to be seen and heard and not judged, worked-on, or reacted to. It feels as if a veil gets lifted, and you are showered with acceptance and validation.

One of the many reasons for 12-Step groups, is to experience this environment of sharing with another human. When a person shares their story in a recovery group setting, their experience is received with acceptance, nonjudgment, and empathy. This is a cornerstone for those in recovery to aid in their healing. I want to emphasize to everyone that this need for safe, confidential, empathetic sharing is not just for those in recovery. It is a crucial need for all of us to feel seen, attached, and accepted.

Where do you find safe people to share your story with, to show up for, and to express your empathy toward? They are the people in your life right now who have shown up for you in the past. They can also be the people who are awaiting you in the future. So, find and cultivate a few of these connections—start with one or two.

If you already have such connections, make sure you let the people in your life know how much you appreciate them, and the gratitude you carry for their presence in your life. These relationships can make a huge difference during life's most difficult moments, when we are feeling fear, pain, shame, and depression. Sharing our feelings with a trusted individual can right some of the wrongs of our own condemning voice—the one that frequently takes over and drowns out the voice that assures us that we are loved, valued, and have place and purpose in this world. Don't let that voice be silenced.

SELF-ACKNOWLEDGEMENT: YOUR FIFTH GUIDE

As your spiritual process unfolds, you may start to recognize the many ways in which you've progressed, however small the steps or great the strides. To encourage your healthy adult Self on your journey, begin the practice of acknowledging any small progress you make daily toward your own healing. My colleague, Cara Weed, calls such acknowledgment of each gain "marking it." That means taking a moment to put words and actions, such as virtually patting yourself on the shoulder and saying, "Good job."

Acknowledging your progress can take many forms. It is not about stroking your ego or giving yourself undue fanfare. Instead, it is about uncovering the areas in your life that need growth, (especially after reading this book) and tracking that growth and healing, observing and noting it when it happens. Healing takes time so by "marking it," as you make small steps forward, you make explicit your development. You realize there is no such thing as perfection and yet, there is change happening.

This practice can be done instantly when you are present in your functional adult Self. Remember from Chapter 9, the functional adult Self has a practice of mindfulness or self-compassionate awareness. This is the gratitude part of that practice. It is this part that notices you during your day when you see those incremental changes. Examples include using your containing boundary and not yelling at someone but instead, slowing down, breathing deeply and being present for someone who needs your help, or asking for what you need and having your request denied, but not going into your reactive behavior. Instead, the functional adult Self accepts limitations and finds ways around it or learns to surrender and accept things as they are. Those are the small steps in our daily lives that lead us to big changes.

DAILY SELF-ACKNOWLEDGMENT PRACTICE

1. To begin, chart your progress in your healing journal, make a list of the areas of change that you need to focus on. I suggest using the Five Core Practices of healthy living to start with.

2. Then, whenever you find yourself acting in a more constructive manner than you might have in the past, make sure you "mark it" within yourself. Pat yourself on the back! You are on your way to healing and your journey home.

AFFIRMATIONS

Let me add a bit about using affirmations. Remember in Chapter 12 when I talked about *shame binds?* Affirmations can begin to break those negative binds you are stuck in. When you feel overcome or bound to long held feelings of carried shame, it is a perfect time to start creating your affirmations. As you reflect upon those areas that you were shamed about as a child, turn that negative self-talk into positive affirmations. It could sound like, "I have the right to experience my joy in life" or "I have to right to be respected in my relationships."

I recommend to my clients finding one or two affirmations that fit their experience from our work together and to say it daily in the morning and at night. Spiritual Self-Acknowledgment can also be fostered through the Five Core Practices.

RECAP OF THE CORE PRACTICES

Here is a quick recap of the Five Core Practices to help you chart your progress:

SELF-ESTEEM

- When you make a mistake, and you will, pull yourself up by saying, "You have inherent worth, and you are holding yourself with warm regard, despite your imperfections. You are human!"
- When you feel shame, rather than getting overwhelm-ed by it, start refuting internal shaming messages by using affirmations.
- When you feel *less-than,* remind yourself that you are reacting to events from your childhood. Tell yourself you do not need to repeat the messages you received and internalized when you were an innocent child.
- Draw on your reparenting skills to praise the child within, and practice self-empathy, rather than self-pity.

BOUNDARIES

- When you lose your protective boundary and become porous, quickly find that boundary and reflect on whether it is *true* or *not true* for you.
- When you lose your containing boundary and let out too much emotion, apologize or catch it earlier the next time.
- When you use walls in relationship to others, become aware and become more open or sharing in your

relationships. The next time you interact with the people in your life, keep an open mind, and apply patience and empathy.

- Each time you do these things, however simple, or however great, acknowledge it by speaking aloud your progress or by writing it down. Just as you'd praise a child for his or her progress, praise yourself!

BEING REAL OR AUTHENTIC

- When you lose your sense of Self and are not in touch with what is happening inside you, stop and breathe.
- Assess what you are thinking, what emotions you are feeling, where in your body they show up, and what behaviors you are exhibiting.
- Also assess if you are feeling any young historical emotional ego states from the past.
- As you do so, make corrections as needed, just as you would if you found yourself driving too close to the yellow line or turning a corner with too wide a turn—you correct your *steering*, so that you don't veer into a head-on collision. Your goal is to continue your route, safely. Pull over to collect yourself, if you need.

NEEDS AND WANTS IN RELATIONSHIP WITH OTHERS

- When you find yourself detaching from what you need, or not being able to figure it out, pause and ask yourself, "What do I need to ask for now?"
- If you can do it yourself, go ahead and do it. If you do

everything for yourself and never ask for help, try something different. Risk asking others to help—and let them help without interference or criticism.

- If you always volunteer your help and over-extend yourself, start saying, "No," occasionally and congratulate yourself for saying it.

MODERATION

- Finally, when you find yourself living out of balance and being extreme with any activity, stop and slow down to contemplate what is more moderate for you.
- Then decide to do it differently.
- Conversely, if you find yourself being too rigid, tight, and shut down, breathe and let go. Become light-hearted.
- You will discover that you feel stronger and more in control of your life—and your journey—each time you do so.

PUTTING IT TOGETHER

As you practice these steps, you will slowly, progressively, feel more whole, more alive, and more content with yourself and your life. But where do you go from here? Because we live in a finite world that is full of duality, relativism, and many value systems, we are challenged daily as we struggle between the extremes created by the world of duality. What comes out of these dualities are the historical emotional ego states that have helped us to survive, and which we learned and borrowed and made our own. However, these ego states, (discussed in depth, in Chapter 11) are borrowed identities.

We trick ourselves into thinking these borrowed identities are who we truly are. These historical emotional ego states can be restless, judgmental, disrespectful of others, mean-spirited, obsessive, defensive, and self-focused. The good news is, your functional adult Self can now step in to steer you in the right direction!

CONCLUSION

Congratulations! You have reached the conclusion of this book, which marks the start of your own journey.

As you've read through these pages, you may have realized that, like Dorothy, you've been on this journey all along. You've also held within you the capacity to find your own way home. Along the way, you've undertaken hard work, and sometimes it may feel as if you can't ever be made whole, healthy, or functional again—that the job is impossible. Yet, just as the Liberty Bell is prized for its unmistakable crack, the Leaning Tower of Pisa, for the faulty foundation causing it to lean precariously, and the Venus de Milo for her missing arms, your imperfections are your distinction. Just as these great works of art have, for centuries, survived the damage they've suffered, the broken, damaged, and flawed parts of our Selves never go away. Instead, they become integrated, always comprising a part of you that you can thank for helping you as you adapted and survived your childhood.

Having experienced childhood trauma and neglect, you may feel as if you have been made weak, but as the exercises in this book have shown you, what you may perceive as weaknesses and flaws have, in most cases, helped you to cope and to survive to this point. In other words, your imper-fections are markers of your strength, not your weakness.

In this book, I've summarized the teachings and techniques of my mentor, Pia Mellody, in a manner which I hope will help you to put her work into your own daily practice. As I've done so, I've also shown you how I've adapted Mellody's techniques into my own counseling practice, in order to heal and guide hundreds of clients from their painful pasts toward their promising futures.

As you work on your own healing journey, remember, you don't have to do it alone—nor should you. I don't know your unique story nor your challenges, so what I've presented here are just guidelines toward healing. If you are struggling with any of this material, I strongly encourage you to find a therapist who specializes in codependency or childhood trauma to help you as you recover and reparent yourself in the loving kindness you deserve.

I have a directory of professionals who have been trained in Relational and Developmental Trauma; you may peruse the list at HealingTraumaNetwork.net.

I also invite you to visit my websites at JanBergstrom.com and MountainStreamPublishingCompany.com where you will find additional resources to help you, and where I welcome you to share your own experiences.

We have all suffered in silence, but we've now learned to transform our suffering and silence into a chorus of strong voices that sing of our strength, our dreams, and our value, sharing our personal experience and strength with the wondrous world we live in.

No matter how painful the past, the future awaits you. Step into it with your head held high, because you, my dear reader, hold a wisdom inside you that is waiting to be born. You have only to bring it into the light of day, and that wisdom will take you wherever you aim to go!

ONE FINAL EXERCISE: JOURNALING YOUR LIFE EXPERIENCE AS A CHILD AND TEEN

I'd like to end this book with one final exercise, an exercise that will take you far on your healing journey. The first—most important, and most independent—step to starting out on the self-guided part of your healing journey is telling your story.

Now is the time to close this book and open another one. Take out a pen and paper, or turn on your computer, and open a document. You can use the following journaling exercise to begin to write.

For each of the Five Core Areas that we've covered in this book, I want you to write down the questions that follow. But don't overwhelm yourself. Just do one Core Area at a time. Begin by spending a few minutes to review the questions in one of the Core Areas. Then close your eyes. Allow yourself to sit back in a quiet space, your eyes closed, as you ask these questions of yourself. Some of this is *mind's eye work,* meaning that you see and observe a scene from childhood, replaying and noting with your senses the story of what happened. You may only see a few bits and pieces of the story at first, but that's okay. Just let the story come to you.

Once you get the answer to your questions, open your eyes and journal about what you discovered. Then, at another time, move onto the next Core Area, and repeat the above instructions. Once you have completed all five areas, be sure to save your journaling, so that, as you develop, heal, and gain strength, you are able to see your progress. Remember, your past will not change however, the way that you hold yourself today will!

JOURNALING QUESTIONS FOR THE FIVE CORE AREAS OF WELL BEING

1. *All children are precious and valuable.*
   How was I valued or esteemed around my attributes as a child and adolescent? Physically, mentally, emotionally, spiritually? Was I overvalued or undervalued?

2. *All children are vulnerable and need to be protected.* How was I protected during my childhood and adolescence around physical boundaries, sexual boundaries, and psychological boundaries? Was my physical being and personal property protected? Was I protected sexually? Was I protected emotionally by my parents, siblings, and others?

3. *All children are human, imperfect, and authentic.* How was I validated for my reality or sense of self throughout my childhood and adolescence? How did I

experience the world? How did I behave? How did this reality look and feel to me? How did I experience this reality in my body? Did I become what my parents wanted, or did I fight against it?

4. *All children are needy and dependent.*
How were my needs and wants met as a child and adolescent? Did I become needless and wantless and anti-dependent, or did I become too dependent on my parents in all areas? Did I get more of my wants met and less of my needs met?

5. *All children's essence is spontaneity.*
How was the essence of my being—or my spontaneity—regarded in childhood? In adolescence? Was spontaneity something that needed to be shut down and overmanaged? Or was it ignored and uncontained around others?

ACKNOWLEDGMENTS

It takes a village to bring any dream to fruition, and it took a village to give birth to this book. I began this journey, back in the summer of 2017, when I had a glimmer in my mind about bringing forward a meaningful book. I have been a therapist since 1995, and, when I learned the work of Pia Mellody back in 2002, I used her work in my private practice. I saw how transformative it was for my clients, as well as for myself. The number of hours, friends, family, clients, and colleagues that helped conceive and birth this book has astonished me.

I particularly want to acknowledge Pia Mellody for bringing this model of healing forward, in the late 1980s. She has been a mentor, colleague, and friend to me. I so appreciate her dedication to recovery and trauma. I hope that this book furthers her work, bringing it to many people's lives. I owe great appreciation and deep gratitude for all that I have learned from her, especially for her requirement that all therapists who study with her do their own work on themselves. I now use my own experience of her model in my professional practice, and I incorporate other mindfulness, attachment, and body-based methodologies for integration.

I want to offer deepest thanks to my husband, Walter Fey, for standing by me during this whole process. As difficult as it became at certain times, he always believed in me and this project.

I especially want to thank Janice Harper, my writing coach and editor. She stood by me throughout all the challenging times when we thought the book was going to be scrapped. She always had a solution and picked me up in my darkest hours.

I also want to thank my copyeditor Sarah Goodman who carefully combed through this book to make it grammatically sharp and outstanding.

I couldn't do this book without my website designer and consultant, Teresa Lauer. Her upbeat attitude and solution-oriented approach kept this whole book going. I relied on her creative ideas to produce a book that reflects my life's work and includes a personal statement of how my life has healed.

I couldn't have finished this book without my business partner at the Healing Our Core Issues Institute, Dr. Rick Butts. His consistent validation and affirmation helped me stay on the path. His ideas and clarification of the concepts in this book made it possible to put my work into new words, and to offer new experiences for teaching therapists and clients.

Finally, I want to thank my dear friends who listened and checked in with me over the past eighteen months, my dear sons who supported me the whole way, and my colleagues who cheered me on. Lastly, I will forever be thankful for my clients. They have taught me so much. I hold each of them with deep regard and respect as they travel their unique journey home.

GLOSSARY OF TERMS

Some of the terms I use in this book have unique meanings in the therapeutic context. The following terms are important to an understanding of the material. They may be unfamiliar to you, and—even if familiar—may have multiple shades of meaning. Below are my working definitions, as a point of reference, in case you find any terms confusing.

absorbed or carried feelings | Emotional states transferred to a child when a parent is irresponsible with his or her own emotional life. These emotional states become intricately woven into that individual's historical Selves and can make it difficult him or her to hold himself or herself as having inherent worth and value. Other carried states can manifest in feeling hopeless, panic and rage.

ACE Study (Adverse Childhood Experiences Study) | Conducted for the United States Center for Disease Control (CDC), by Kaiser Permanente from 1995 to 1997, with two waves of data collection, this research was one of the most significant investigations of child abuse and neglect—and their relationship to later-life health and well-being issues. Over 17,000 patients, receiving physical exams at Health Maintenance Organizations (HMOs) in Southern California, completed a confidential survey regarding their childhood experiences and current health status and behaviors.

acts of service | Helping work or other kind actions toward a person, people, community, cause, or organization, or toward anyone or anything you care about, or charitable work toward the world at large.

adaptive adolescent Self | A historical, emotional ego state of being in which we feel and act very much the way we did as an adolescent (approximately 11–18 years of age).

adaptive child Self | A historical, emotional ego state of being in which we feel and act very much the way we did as a small child (approximately 5–10 years of age).

affirmations | Positive self-talk, used to break negative binds a person may be stuck in, or to overcome long-held feelings of carried shame.

anti-dependent | What happens when a child grows up and can acknowledge their needs and wants but tries to meet their needs alone and will not accept help or guidance from others.

attachment theory | Developed by John Bowlby in the late 1960s, attachment theory claims that the ability of a child to form an emotional and physical attachment to another person depends on how that individual's parents or major caregivers attach to the child. Successful attachment, from infancy onward, gives a sense of stability and security.

attribute-based self-esteem | A sense of one's worth, based on what you *have* materially, whether physical attributes or wealth and possessions. Attributes can also include your children and their successes, your spouse or other relationships, your social status, or your family history, such as being born into a well-known wealthy family. The person with attribute-based self-esteem thinks, "I have worth because of what I have."

boundarylessness | Not having developed a healthy and functioning *protective* boundary or *containing* boundary. If you have a weak or nonexistant *protective* boundary, you may take on what another person is feeling, making it your own internal state. People who lack clear *containing* boundaries tend to share their emotions and thoughts with other people without any appropriate filtering.

centering in the body | A day-to-day practice to reconnect you directly with your personal resources; a meditative practice of re-establishing your relationship to both the ground and your body, the place where action and feeling originate. The functions of grounding and centering have been compromised during trauma, so an important part of healing is learning how to find your ground and your center again.

childhood developmental trauma | Wounding that happens from abuse and neglect due to early interactions within the family of origin. These wounds set up your template for how you engage with other people—in love and life—in your adulthood.

compassionate Self-awareness | A series of techniques (based on Jon Kabat-Zinn's work) which helps to step back and in the moment; a way of looking at yourself without judgment and observing yourself with curiosity, not contempt.

complex trauma | The traumatic childhood experiences that have a profound impact on many different areas of adult functioning; the range of psychological and somatic legacies of a wounded childhood that may or may not include Post Traumatic Stress Disorder (PTSD), sexual violence, witnessing a violent assault, losing one or both parents or siblings, becoming homeless, or being exposed to alcoholic parents, domestic violence, chronic neglect, or overly-controlling parenting that limit a child's ability to form an independent Self.

containing boundary (in speaking) | In contrast to the protective boundary, which filters information received, the containing boundary filters the information we transmit to others—what we say out loud or in writing, for example.

Core Practice #1: Loving the Self | Healthy self-esteem; an internal sense of "I am enough, and I matter;" a sense of abundance and connection to the world and to others, spiritual in nature.

Core Practice #2: Protecting the Self | Healthy external and internal boundaries, particularly in intimate relationships or partnerships.

Core Practice #3: Knowing the Self | Techniques to gain self knowledge and independent identity, which include knowing one's thoughts, emotions, body sensations and behaviors.

Core Practice #4: Taking Care of the Self | Practicing a healthy interdependence with others; learning to be aware of— and to meet—one's basic needs and one's wants in moderation; learning to ask for help when needed and to rely on one's own efforts when possible; learning to give help when truly needed but to withhold unneeded and unwanted help; and a practice of saying *no* when appropriate.

Core Practice #5: Balancing the Self | A practice to learn moderation in all things; learning to observe when we are living in extremes; and observing ways we can reset our internal thermostat for a healthy amount of spontaneity.

disempowerment | A state of feeling inferior to others, undervalued, and shamed as a result of growing up in a less-than nurturing environment.

emotional ego states | Thoughts and sensations that are reactions to historical events; parts of the Self that have frozen emotionally, such that when we see or experience something that reminds us, even subconsciously, of the past, we revert to a childhood version of who we were.

experiential therapies | Therapies that have been developed which utilize the full mind-body connection, in turn helping people to heal, not just emotionally, but physically as well.

false empowerment | A result of no-consequences parenting, or parenting that elevates a child to unrealistic heights, thus leaving them feeling grandiose or better than other people.

family systems theory (of Dr. Murray Bowen) | Psychological model positing that a family is a system, in which each member has a role to play and rules to respect. Members of the system are expected to respond to each other in certain ways, based on their roles and unspoken agreements. Within the boundaries of the system, patterns develop, as each family member's behavior is caused by, and causes, other family members to behave in predictable ways.

felt sense | All information that forms our experience, deriving from the five senses—sight, sound, smell, touch, and taste—as well as other important information derived from the body, such as position or posture, tensions and stress, movements, body temperature, and even thoughts. According to Eugene Gendlin, who introduced the term, a felt sense is, "not a mental experience but a physical one." A bodily awareness of a situation or person or event. An internal aspect that encompasses everything you feel and know about the given subject or specific event. This physical experience is the activity through which we understand how we feel in our whole body and mind.

five Core Areas of well-being | Five truths that need to be affirmed, nurtured, and practiced during a child's development as follows:

1. *All children are precious and valuable.*
2. *All children are vulnerable and need to be protected.*
3. *All children are human, imperfect, and authentic.*
4. *All children are needy and dependent.*
5. *All children's essence is spontaneity.*

5-minute check-in | A practice of pausing to see your situation in your mind's eye with curiosity, rather than judgment; that helps you center, ground, and get present with what is going on; sitting in a space of silence, asking yourself a set of questions.

functional adult Self | One's true Self or spiritual center that lives smack dab in the middle of the core practices by using compassionate self-awareness. This capital-S "Self" is an integrated, healthy, grounded version of oneself that helps the adapted childhood parts of oneself to be reparented through affirming, nurturing and setting limits to experience healing; while energetically release toxic emotions that have persisted from painful childhood experiences.

gestalt | A type of therapy developed by Fritz Perls, which uses dialogs, such as "the empty chair," to gain insight and heal an individual's wounded parts and wounded relationships. The name comes from the original meaning of *gestalt*—a whole context that comprises a bigger reality than just its component parts.

getting your story straight | Understanding your history of the events and people you experienced as you grew up; recounting the events in such a way that your child Self is not to blame and that all parties have accountability for their actions.

grace | The divine light within us, our acts of service and acknowledgment of our growth connect us to our higher purpose.

grandiosity or "one up" | Believing oneself to be better than others. Living in the extreme of grandiosity creates the "one-up" attitude and a feeling of being "above the law", as if the rules don't apply to you, but to others.

gratitude practice | A shift in awareness that changes your relationship with life—from one of rejecting the world around you and defending against it, to one of accepting the world as it is, with appreciation for all that it has given to you. This shift can be affected by a series of practical daily exercises. (See Chapter 13.)

grounded in the body | A place of focus that is not defined by formulated thoughts, but rather includes awareness of all senses and sensations. From this place, we establish our personal resources, starting with compassionate Self-awareness, or mindfulness, adding the felt sense of the body, and ending feeling strong, centered, and connected.

hero or mascot family role | A position and identity unconsciously assigned in childhood, when the child is objectified and falsely empowered by caregivers who may project unreasonably adult-level expectations, such as good decision-making, high achievement, surrogate adult companionship, and over-responsibility.

higher purpose, higher power, or divine presence | A connection or focus to help us embrace our humanity and open our hearts and minds to a larger context or greater meaning in our lives.

historical adaptive Selves | a collection of parts of oneself, formed from childhood, affected by adverse experiences and wounding traumas, formed from about 5 to 10 years of age, and again—formed differently—from ages 11 to 18. These wounded parts of ourselves need reparenting, primarily through self-talk, to integrate within the functional adult Self.

holding accountable | A process of rightful assignment of responsibility that helps the healing process by shifting the guilt, shame, and responsibility or fault away from the child who was growing up, so that the child doesn't have to keep thinking it was their fault.

idealized enmeshment | When a parent is using their child for their own purposes, by idealizing or falsely empowering the child so much that the parent essentially gives the child an adult role or position in the family. Sometimes, a child in this relationship is called a "parentified child."

interdependence with others around your needs | A balanced give-and-take between individuals that involves offering help from a place of true availability—saying *no* rather than harboring resentments and asking for help when help from others is truly needed and when help from others does not make us small or habitually dependent.

internal boundaries | The psychological boundaries that define limits in our relationships, comprised of two parts: first, the protective boundary that filters information we will allow in—to see, hear and feel; and, second, the containing boundary that keeps us from being offensive to others—filtering our own emotions, thoughts, and comments, so that we don't dump on others inappropriately.

less than, or "one-down" | Low self-esteem, feeling

diminished, and feeling inherently 'less than' other people as the result of carried shame; a beam of contempt, turned inward toward the Self.

lost child family role | In contrast to the hero child—on the opposite end of the spectrum— the lost child withdraws from the dysfunctional family by living inside themselves, and retreats to a world of fantasy and imagination. A family position unconsciously assigned in childhood, often when caregivers are overly busy or absent, relying on a child to be independent, easy going, flexible, or absorbed in hobbies and books.

marking it | Taking a moment to put words and actions to each personal gain, such as virtually patting yourself on the shoulder and saying, "Good job."

mindfulness | A self-aware state reached through meditation or Self-compassion; the ability to objectively observe what you are feeling, doing, or saying without judgment.

mind's-eye imagery | A technique that draws on images to calm and ground the body; visuals and sensory observations, from memory—pictured or described—that represent a safe and peaceful experience and place; visuals that, when vividly remembered, act as anchors to give stability in times of need.

moderation | Appropriate behavior that has some limits and that comes from a place of healthy balance; the opposite of living in extremes.

myelination of the brain | The neurological process, developing during childhood, that enables information to be processed for decision making; a process wherein a protective lipid-rich sheath (myelin) develops around nerves, which in turn helps speed up executive functioning. This process continues from birth until around age 23 or 24, allowing neurons in the brain to fire more rapidly the older the child becomes.

needless and/or wantless | The parent who neglects their child's needs, and rarely, if ever, addresses their child's wants teaches their child to be needless and wantless. The needless and wantless person is one who is not aware of their needs and desires.

negative enmeshment | A parent-child relationship characterized by a parent's yelling, screaming, shaming, and criticizing to manipulate their child into compliance with the parent's needs. This type of enmeshment can occur when the parent views the child as a reflection of their most feared qualities, and thus reacts with anger and sometimes violence to try to extinguish those qualities in the child.

neglect | A failure to attend to a child's basic needs; includes failing to provide adequate healthcare, supervision, clothing, nutrition, and housing, as well as failure to attend to the critical areas of a child's physical, emotional, social, educational, and safety needs.

other-based self-esteem | The feeling that "I matter and have worth because someone else (a romantic partner or spouse) says I do."

overly dependent | A quality resulting when, during development, a child's material and resource needs are well exceeded, but the maturing child is not taught how to create friends, foster relationships, earn money, save money, or provide for their own needs and wants. As adults they can expect others to take of these needs.

performance-based self-esteem | Identity and self-worth that relies on continued success no matter what else happens, based on the belief that "I have worth because of what I do."

physical boundaries | Clear limits on how close a person can get to you and whether or not they can touch you, or your personal property, without your consent. Children need their parents to closely monitor these physical boundaries with others, boundaries that protect children's bodies, and their physical belongings.

post-induction therapy | The premise of Post-Induction Therapy—a term coined by Pia Mellody—is that childhood trauma is the origin of developmental immaturity (formerly known as codependence). Mellody identifies Five Core Areas for healing the wounds of childhood traumas: loving the Self;

protecting ourselves through boundaries; knowing the Self; taking care of our needs and wants; and moderating or containing ourselves, especially in relationships.

protective or listening boundary (used in listening to others) | An internal clear limit that filters information and feedback received from people and the world. This boundary—or filter—allows you to hold yourself in high positive regard, even when others are giving constructive criticism, saying negative things about you, or being hurtful. And if what someone is saying is true, this boundary allows you to take it in and experience your feelings about it.

PTSD (Post-Traumatic Stress Disorder) | A psychiatric disorder that can occur after witnessing or experiencing a life-threatening or violent event. PTSD can also occur following persistent stress during a period when an individual is too young to be able to cope with that stress effectively. The symptoms of PTSD include recurring thoughts of the trauma, hyper-startling, hyper-vigilance, insomnia, nightmares, mood swings, and a number of other cognitive and neurological symptoms.

reality| The creation of our reality comes from our sensory organs as they bring information to the brain. We then form thoughts, assigning meaning to the information our brain has absorbed. These thoughts—or meanings—combine to form stories in the mind about why something was said or done and what it means about us, and about the world around us. The thoughts and stories produce emotions and physical sensations in the body, and our actions and behaviors follow. Through these actions, we create our reality, our life's narrative arc, our relationships, and our perception of the world around us.

rearranging the furniture | A metaphor used to describe the process of shifting your old childhood paradigms or concepts. In this process, the functional adult Self reiterates and affirms factual truths to the historical or adaptive Selves, such as "You were the child and they were the parents."

reparenting (our historical Selves) | Showing up for your child Self, adolescent Self, or other historical parts of yourself; paying attention and caring for that younger part, through self-talk that nurtures, affirms, and sets limits.

resources (personal) | Spaces, places, events, people, or pets that—when vividly brought to mind—bring one a feeling of calm. Resourcing, or the ability to call to mind your resources, is essential for navigating your family of origin trauma, as it engages the parasympathetic nerves, settling the body, including the prefrontal cortex—the decision-making and acting capacity of your brain. You are creating the environment in which the functional adult Self can thrive. Resources also help maintain a sense of inner integrity in the face of triggering events, sites, or memories.

rightful assignment of responsibility | Holding your parents accountable, recognizing that they are human and imperfect, *and* that they chose to have a child (or children). This process shifts responsibility or fault for childhood trauma away from the child.

scapegoat child family role | An unconscious assignment given to a child within their family of origin. The scapegoat is the one who is pointed at. He or she is blamed for all the family's problems. The child whose tantrums, meltdowns, or rebellions become the family's excuse for everything that goes wrong.

self-care | Activities, such as meditation, medical attention, hygiene, exercise, nutritious eating, cleaning one's environment, spending time outdoors or with friends—any healthy act that aims to improve our own mental, physical, material, or emotional health.

self-acknowledgment | Any technique for marking and recognizing progress and goodness in our Selves. Such monitoring may be through a healing journal or may at times be actual pat on the back.

setting limits | A limit is the line of unacceptable behaviors we impose on ourselves and on others. With children, parents set limits to what their children can and cannot do, before having consequences enforced. Most strong marriages are based on setting clear limits—no emotional or physical abuse, no betrayals, no addictions unless the addict is getting treatment, no secrets regarding finances or other serious matters, and so on.

setting the thermostat | Establishing and controlling the right degree of moderation. Pursuing balance and moderation, rather than extremes of being too tight or too loose behavior.

sexual boundaries | Protection from inappropriate touching, staring at, or sexually interacting with another person. Children and young adults interactions with others need to be supervised by a functional parent who will recognize whether anyone is crossing such boundaries with their child—and that includes relatives, family, or friends.

shame, carried | *Carried shame,* also called *absorbed shame,* is humiliation, anguish, or worthlessness that does not belong to you; it belongs to the parent or caregiver who originated it. Carried shame makes a person feel defective and *less than* others.

shame existence bind | A condition arising from being born in circumstances where a child is not wanted— typically arising when a mother never attaches to her child. Such children—and later adults—struggle with being present and taking up space. They often apologize constantly, shrink from view, or give up readily on potential talents or successes, convinced they don't deserve to be noticed.

sharing your story | Communicating to others you feel safe with, that you trust them, and that you have had an experience they can relate to. Then as you tell your story—during difficult times or during peaceful moments—you and your listener can be vulnerable, connecting to the emotions the other person is feeling, not necessarily having the same experience of that person, but following closely where they are going.

somatic body-based work | Therapeutic techniques to address the physical and emotional legacies of a traumatic childhood, such as guided meditation in which you focus on and scan all parts of your own body, articulating the sensations that arise.

soul | There are many definitions of soul, but I define it as: one's true essence; the capital-S, genuine Self—apart from ego—that fully resides in all the senses and sensations of the body and feels strongly connected to a greater purpose in being alive. Your soul is a tiny spec of the infinite.

spontaneity (controlled vs. chaotic) | All children's essence is spontaneity—or an in-the-moment self-expression of all the emotions, sensations, and creative ideas that arise out of living. If that spontaneity is shut down and tightly over-managed (controlled) or, conversely, ignored and uncontained (chaotic) by the care-giving adults, then a child's well-being and development suffers.

standing in your truth | Speaking honestly and candidly about the impact someone had on you as a child and how that shows up today; an exercise in which you use (or visualize) an empty chair to talk to your parents or anyone who has been an offender to you when you were young—not by directly confronting them—which could cause further damage—but, rather, by using a visualization to tell them any of your needs they failed to provide or any abuse you suffered from them.

3 golden rules for interacting with others | Guidelines for carrying out your needs and wants in balance with others, adopted by Pia Mellody (paraphrased as):

1. *Do what you can for yourself, and, when you can't, ask for help.*
2. *Don't say yes when you want to say no.*
3. *Don't do for others what they can do for themselves.*

walls | Overly rigid protective boundaries that can develop during child development as a coping mechanism to survive abuse and lessen the pain of criticism. Walls show up outwardly as indifference, subordination, hostility, and acting out with antisocial behaviors.

ENDORSEMENTS

"In Gifts from a Challenging Childhood, author Jan Bergstrom describes with empathy and clarity the exact emotional, intellectual and neurological ways that children's brains respond to trauma, and how the impact of that experience endures in the child's life throughout adulthood.

Bergstrom explains how our basic needs as children for love, protection, validation and expression must be met by our parents; and how, when these needs are not met in childhood, we can end up with "one-up" or "one-down" self-esteem and over-protective or under-protective boundaries as adults.

In-depth descriptions of supportive, therapeutic techniques abound in this book, from mindfulness to grounding to writing a letter to yourself.

Whether you experienced traumatic neglect or excessive control and enmeshment at the hands of your parents, this book will not only help you identify what went wrong for you, it will also provide you with validating, supportive and compassionate ways to reparent yourself."

Jonice Webb, PhD

Bestselling author of *Running On Empty: Overcome Your Childhood Emotional Neglect* and *Running On Empty No More: Transform Your Relationships.*

"Jan's book is a precious guide to untangling the complications and difficulties many of us have in our adult lives, arising from traumatic childhoods. Read it, underline it, take it with you on your personal journey. This book will bring you home."

Nick Morgan is President of Public Words, Inc, a communications consulting company, and author of *Can You Hear Me? How to Communicate with People in a Virtual World*

"The devastating consequences of childhood trauma for the individual, families, and society at large are far-reaching, and cannot be overestimated. Jan Bergstrom's new work builds beautifully on Pia Mellody's Post Induction Therapy model, offering hope and a detailed path forward for healing childhood wounds and living an authentic and empowered life."

Vicki Tidwell Palmer

Author of *Moving Beyond Betrayal: The 5-Step Boundary Solution for Partners of Sex Addicts*

"Jan Bergstrom makes available what most only find from years of therapy; how to live a life of knowing our inherent worth and a practice that returns us to compassion. Her book is a deep yet practical guide to fostering self-awareness and ultimately inherent worth. It is a game-changer for any adult or parent who wishes they had it earlier in their life."

Susan Brady

Author, *Mastering Your Inner Critic & 7 Other High Hurdles to Advancement: How the best women leaders practice self-awareness to change what really matters*

"*Ms. Bergstrom has made a significant contribution to psychotherapeutic technique in her new book. She has distilled and described in specific concrete, readable, and relatable form the work of master therapist, Pia Mellody. She has added her own creative experiential techniques which translates Mellody's groundbreaking description of the effects of trauma into workable clinical intervention. The content of this book is equally helpful to the practicing psychotherapist who works with trauma as it is to survivors of childhood neglect, abuse, and abandonment. Ms. Bergstrom clearly and effectively integrates Mellody's model of trauma with her knowledge of mindfulness/self-compassion and somatic experiencing techniques. The practices and exercises she describes and offers promote awareness, well-being and ultimately intimacy – with Self and others.*

Noted Points

She is clear, concise and very informative in her description of the impact of family dysfunction on the developing sense of Self and identity. She very specifically connects dysfunctional parental dynamics to the negative impact for future adult functioning and intimacy.

Her clinical examples well illustrate Mellody's theoretical concepts.

Her sections of "Reparenting" and "Standing in Your Own Truth" are fully compatible with other experiential trauma therapies such as Internal Family Systems (IFS). The writing is lucid and well described. They offer the client a specific road map to "unburdening" or freeing young and vulnerable inner child parts and processing trauma. Ms. Bergstrom shows the courage to describe her own path which impressed and inspired. She clearly has "walked the walk," an expert from her own experience

I enjoyed and was moved by Ms. Bergstrom's discussion of the connection between spirituality and the deep work of psychotherapy. This is often a neglected and even feared place to go in the psychotherapy world dominated by behavioral, manualized and pharmacologic treatments. It is so refreshing to hear this relationship made explicit and "outed".

Dan F. Pollets, Ph. D

Made in the USA
Las Vegas, NV
21 November 2024

12304066R00193